THE GAMES ETHIC AND IMPERIALISM

SPORT IN THE GLOBAL SOCIETY

General Editor: J.A. Mangan

The interest in sports studies around the world is growing and will continue to do so. This unique series combines aspects of the expanding study of *sport in the global society*, providing comprehensiveness and comparison under one editorial umbrella. It is particularly timely, with studies in the political, cultural, anthropological, ethnographic, social, economic, geographical and aesthetic elements of sport proliferating in institutions of higher education.

Eric Hobsbawm once called sport one of the most significant practices of the late nineteenth century. Its significance was even more marked in the late twentieth century and will continue to grow in importance into the new millennium as the world develops into a 'global village' sharing the English language, technology and sport.

Other Titles in the Series

Sport in Australasian Society
Past and Present
Edited by J.A. Mangan and John Nauright

Freeing the Female Body
Inspirational Icons
Edited by J.A. Mangan and Fan Hong

Footbinding, Feminism and Freedom
The Liberation of Women's Bodies in Modern China
Fan Hong

Superman Supreme
Fascist Body as Political Icon – Global Fascism
Edited by J.A. Mangan

Shaping the Superman
Fascist Body as Political Icon – Aryan Fascism
Edited by J.A. Mangan

Scoring for Britain
International Football and International Politics, 1900–1939
Peter J. Beck

Sporting Nationalisms
Identity, Ethnicity, Immigration and Assimilation
Edited by Mike Cronin and David Mayall

The Games Ethic and Imperialism
Aspects of the Diffusion of an Ideal
J.A. Mangan

The Race Game
Sport and Politics in South Africa
Douglas Booth

Rugby's Great Split
Class, Culture and the Origins of Rugby League Football
Tony Collins

Making the Rugby World
Race, Gender, Commerce
Edited by Timothy J.L. Chandler and John Nauright

The First Black Footballer
Arthur Wharton 1865–1930: An Absence of Memory
Phil Vasili

Cricket and England
A Cultural and Social History of the Inter-war Years
Jack Williams

France and the 1998 World Cup
The National Impact of a World Sporting Event
Edited by Hugh Dauncey and Geoff Hare

THE GAMES ETHIC AND IMPERIALISM

Aspects of the Diffusion of an Ideal

J.A. Mangan
International Research Centre for Sport, Socialisation and Society
University of Strathclyde

FRANK CASS
LONDON • PORTLAND, OR

First published in 1986 by Penguin Books Ltd, Harmondsworth, Middlesex
This edition published in 1986 in Great Britain by
FRANK CASS PUBLISHERS
Crown House, 47 Chase Side, Southgate,
London N14 5BP

and in the United States of America by
FRANK CASS
920 NE 58th Avenue, Suite 300
Portland, OR 97213-3786 USA

www.frankcass.com

Reprinted 2001, 2003

British Library Cataloguing in Publication Data

Mangan, J A (James Anthony), 1939–
The games ethic and imperialism aspects of the diffussion of an ideal – 2nd ed – (Cass series sport in the global society)
1 Imperialism – Psychological aspects 2 Games – Social aspects
3 Great Britain – Foreign relations – 19th century 4 Great Britain – Foreign relations – 20th century
325.3′2′0941

ISBN 0 7146 4399 8

Library of Congress Cataloging-in-Publication Data

Mangan, J A
The games ethic and imperialism aspects of the diffussion of an ideal / J A Mangan
p. cm. – (Cass series – sport in the global society, ISSN 1368–9789)
Originally published Harmondsworth, Middlesex, England, New York, NY, USA Viking, 1986
Continues Athleticism in the Victorian and Edwardian public school
Includes bibliographical references (p) and index
ISBN 0-7146-4399-8 (paper)
1 Public schools, Endowed (Great Britain) – History – 19th century 2 Public sports, Endowed (Great Britain) – History – 20th century 3 School sports – Great Britain – History – 19th century 4 School sports – Great Britain – History – 20th century 5 School sports – Moral and ethical aspects – Great Britain 6 Imperialism – Psychological aspects I Mangan, J A Athleticism in the Victorian and Edwardian public school II Title III Series
LA631 7 M364 1998
325′32′941–DC21 97-43854

Printed in Great Britain by
Antony Rowe Ltd, Eastbourne

For the late Eric and Phyllis Tyndale-Biscoe –
gentle and benign imperialists.
The imperial dilemmas did not pass them by!

THE SHORT CUT

Donald Hughes

In Queen Victoria's golden day,
Beneath the mild and settled rule,
The grand old game I used to play,
With decent chaps in a public school.
And I soon found out, as I played the game,
That you need not score a large amount,
But the shortest cut to the heights of fame
Is to get to know the chaps who count.

In Oxford's fields, I found it true,
For the Captain was my closest friend,
And so I acquired my Cricket Blue,
Though I always batted near the end
It is good to bowl with an action high
Or to smite the leather hard and far,
But it's better to wear the proper tie
And to keep your end up at the bar.
Leave lesser men to their golf-clubs then
Or to play with racquets and a net
For this is the game for gentlemen
Till on our race the sun shall set.
The greatest glory of our land
Whose crimson covers half the maps
Is the field where the wickets stand
And the game is played by DECENT CHAPS

CONTENTS

PREFACE

In May this year *The Daily Telegraph* published a Special Supplement on the British Empire. The newspaper invited me, most graciously, to contribute a section on sport and empire – and this was the stimulus to the re-publication of *The Games Ethic and Imperialism* within the new Cass Series *Sport in the Global Society*.

I am delighted for several reasons – among others, the fact that the world-wide response to the original volume which, produced a flood of correspondence, has ensured rewarding contacts with colleagues in Africa, Asia, the Americas, Australia and Europe and has brought intelligent, stimulating and pleasant scholars and students to my Research Centre. However, some have been frustrated in their attempts to obtain copies of the book for research and teaching. Happily this will be no longer the case.

Then I am especially pleased that Frank Cass, who has been such an innovative and encouraging publisher of academic studies of sport, will now have *The Games Ethic and Imperialism* in his lists. It is a fitting place and moment to pay tribute to Frank Cass for his visionary and bold publishing strategies and his cordial, kind and supportive professionalism and friendship. It is also appropriate to acknowledge my appreciation of his excellent colleagues past and present, who have been so rewarding and pleasant to work with – above all Norma Marson, and now Robert Easton and Jonathan Manley. This is a timely opportunity to thank them all for more than a decade of a fruitful and happy working relationship, publishing frontiers have been pushed back and academic frontiers advanced.

In the spring of last year I took the substance of *The Games Ethic* to South-East Asia to a series of lectures – new worlds of academic sports studies are opening up there and new dimensions of the role of sport as an instrument of cultural imperialism are being explored. Recent visits to

South America have shown this to be the case there also Lectures in North America, Europe and Australasia had already revealed a long-standing interest in sport and imperialism, so the future looks bright for further consideration of this fascinating and absorbing subject The *International Journal of the History of Sport* and the series *Sport in the Global Society*, both published by the enthusiastic Frank Cass, await, with his and my deep interest and strong support, the future work of academics throughout the world on the theme of sport and imperialism

J.A. Mangan
International Research Centre for Sport, Socialisation and Society
University of Strathclyde

May 1997

SERIES EDITOR'S FOREWORD

'There are fortunate men,' wrote Cecil Lewis of Edwardian England in *Sagittarius Rising*, 'to whom life is a continuous developing pattern, whose education leads them on to a career that carries them, almost in spite of themselves, to a place in the world from which, as their powers desert them, they withdraw to ease and seclusion, and whose final demise is as quiet and completing as the full stop at the end of a long and well-constructed sentence. Worthy men, good, useful men, no doubt, perhaps lucky men There are many of them. In spite of the chaos of our time you constantly find them, self-insulated from doubts and speculations, from anything which might upset the steady flow of their little stream '

The imperial variety of this now extinct 'species' is encountered in this book. His invariable characteristics were confidence, certainty and conviction The extraordinary consequences, the often moral imperatives behind them and the associated early moments of the modern 'Global Sporting Revolution' are part too of this imperial story If he did not quite manage to leave, in the words of Dr Johnson, 'a name at which the world grew pale', he certainly managed 'to point a moral or adorn a tale'

His is a remarkable tale of a strange passion, insistent persuasion and inflexible pertinacity Arguably it is this imperial moralist, not the meek, who has serendipitously 'inherited' much of the earth of the late twentieth century, even if his morality is now mocked

ACKNOWLEDGEMENTS

Thanks are due especially to colleagues for their kindness, interest and assistance. I am particularly grateful to David Brown for his unstinting and generous help with material, in addition to several fruitful and enjoyable discussions on the transportation of the games ethic across the Atlantic. I also owe much to A. H. M. Kirk-Greene of St Antony's College, Oxford, for the invigorating rigour of his arguments. I am indebted to Dean Gerald Glassford of the University of Alberta, Edmonton, for the Distinguished Visiting Professorship under the Scheme for the Advancement of Scholarship which took me to the University of Alberta in the first instance and *inter alia* allowed access to valuable research literature there. I would also like to express my thanks to Gerry Redmond, Colin Veitch and Katharine Moore of the University of Alberta for the stimulation of their company and their patient good humour when confronted with my preoccupation with imperialism. This book has benefited greatly from the all-too-short period of reflection and writing and discussion on education, history and society with Roberta Park and Sheldon Rothblatt at the University of California, Berkeley, and my most enjoyable period at the University of Maine with Bill Baker, staunch democrat and fierce anti-imperialist. I retain the most affectionate memories of our discussions.

Others, knowingly and unknowingly, have helped me on my way: Nigel Grant (University of Glasgow), John Honey (Leicester Polytechnic), Ian Jobling (University of Brisbane), John Lowerson (University of Sussex), John MacKenzie (University of Lancaster), Alan Metcalfe (University of Windsor), Terry Ranger (University of Manchester), David Rubinstein (University of Hull) and James Walvin (University of York). I have gained much from their professional friendship. I have also appreciated the interest and encouragement of Dr Shula Marks of the Institute of Commonwealth Studies, University of London.

The byways of inquiry occasionally lead to the most pleasant places and I have delightful memories of my visit to Slaley Hall, Northumberland, the hospitality of my hostess, the late Mrs Christine Priestman, and the talks with Eric and Phil Tyndale-Biscoe which brought me so close to that unorthodox imperialist and *preux chevalier*, Cecil Earle Tyndale-Biscoe. Creative energy is nothing without organizational efficiency, and my most profound thanks are once again to my wife, Doris, who has performed so many roles, inspirationalist, critic, grammarian and proof-reader, with patience, constancy and competence.

I should like to make the usual acknowledgements with gratitude to the editors of *The British Journal of Educational Administration and History*, *The International Journal of African Historical Studies*, *Emigrants and Minorities*, *History of Education* and *The British Journal of Sports History* for permission to use material in Chapters 2, 3, 4, 5 and 7 respectively. Acknowledgement is due also to Dr J. H. Baker of St Catharine's College, Cambridge, who kindly supplied the photographs of R. Davies and the St Catharine's College athletes (circa 1909), and to Oxford University Press for permission to reproduce the photograph of Montague Rendall from J. D'E. Firth, *Rendall of Winchester*. I am also indebted to David Brown, who allowed me to make full use of his personal collection of photographs of Canadian private schools, and to Eric Tyndale-Biscoe, who encouraged me to draw freely on his splendid photographs of the Church Missionary Society School, Srinagar, in his story of his father's endeavours, *Fifty Years Against the Stream* (1934).

INTRODUCTION

During the 'silly season' of the summer of 1981, correspondents to *The Times* indulged in the curious pastime of chronicling the cataloguing errors of provincial librarians, and one epistler announced with unsuppressed delight that he had recently discovered Monica Baldwin's autobiography, *I Leap Over the Wall*, relating her experiences when she emerged into the outside world after a lifetime in an enclosed convent, catalogued under 'Sports and Athletics'. I relate this unhappy tale of human fallibility in order to protect my interests. I would not like this study of cultural diffusion to be naively and erroneously catalogued under 'Games'. It is concerned with much more: with ethnocentricity, hegemony and patronage, with ideals and idealism, with educational values and aspirations, with cultural assimilation and adaptation and, most fascinating of all, with the dissemination throughout the Empire of a hugely influential moralistic ideology.

In a celebrated paper, 'They Taught the World to Play', in *Victorian Studies* of March 1959, Sir Charles Tennyson drew our attention to the part played by the Victorian products of public school and ancient university in the diffusion around the globe of British nineteenth-century ball games. He was interested in the nature of specific activities and intrigued by the astounding cultural consequences. Oddly, he expressed no great concern with the essential point and purpose of proselytization. Where youth was concerned, transmission was frequently a moral enterprise. Games of cricket on the pitches of Trinity College, Ceylon, Upper Canada College, Ontario, and Mayo College, Ajmere, and elsewhere, had a profound purpose: the inculcation of 'manliness'. As David Newsome has reminded us in his elegant study of public school manners and mores, *Godliness and Good Learning*, this concept underwent a considerable change as the nineteenth century progressed. As interpreted by the early Victorians it represented the virtues of seriousness, self-denial and rectitude: as understood by the late Victorians it denoted robustness, perseverance and stoicism.

The chosen medium for the fostering of these virtues was team games. To the late Victorian and Edwardian upper-class 'beak' and to many 'dons', to use T. C. Worsley's attractive expression, these games 'were the wheel around which moral values turned'. They were the pre-eminent instrument for the training of a boy's character. It was for this reason that the so-called 'games ethic' held pride of place in the pedagogical priorities of the period public school. And by means of this ethic the public schoolboy supposedly learnt *inter alia* the basic tools of imperial command: courage, endurance, assertion, control and self-control. However, there was a further and important dimension to the later concept of 'manliness': its relevance to both dominance *and* deference. It was widely believed, of course, that its inculcation promoted not simply initiative and self-reliance but also loyalty and obedience. It was, therefore, a useful instrument of colonial purpose. At one and the same time it helped create the confidence to lead and the compulsion to follow.

In the guise of educator, many late-Victorian and Edwardian imperial missionaries and some administrators from public school and ancient university, and sometimes from more humble institutions, clung tenaciously to these later values and with sincerity and self-confidence took the means of acquiring those precious instrumental commodities to, among other places, the lush tropical rain forests of Africa, the verdant islands of the Pacific, the parched plains of India and the windswept prairies of Canada. Whatever the aims of other missionaries from the diverse sects and organizations which attempted to spread the Christian message, their first purpose was to create a universal Tom Brown: loyal, brave, truthful, a gentleman and, if at all possible, a Christian. My concern is with this relatively small band of committed moralists and with their narrow and decent ambition.

The whole tale of this endeavour cannot be told in a single volume, and the purpose of this book is to capture merely some of the more fascinating aspects of this extraordinary, and sometimes whimsical, story of the spread of a moral imperative; to recall for modern sceptics the period certainties of propagandist, proselytizer and publicist; to place on record the central role of moral muscularity in the careers of a group of prestigious imperial proconsuls; to note a curious oddity of ideological interpretation: muscularity without the Christianity in the largest of Britain's colonial territories; to observe 'manliness' viewed as a valuable political expedient ensuring the retention of the most precious jewel in the Imperial Crown; to watch the struggle between hegemonic impulse and indigenous self-assertion waged by Canadian Loyalists on the pitches of their privileged private schools; and lastly, to follow, with more than a little admiration, in the footsteps of the more eccentric English upper-class muscular missionary and to relive his energetic and well-meaning efforts to win souls for Christ on far-flung and widespread imperial playing-fields.

As the story in its full complexity cannot be told here, it is intended that further instalments will appear in due course, in forthcoming studies of aspects of the ethic in Africa and North America. Even then, of course, completeness will not have been achieved. And it is to be hoped that, in time, others will repair omissions, reveal fresh facets, add subtlety when required and so augment my early and exploratory efforts. Consideration of the diffusion of this influential ideology is long overdue. The outcome of Waterloo would certainly have been the same without the existence of the Eton wall-game: the nature of the Empire would scarcely have been the same without the public school games ethic.

1

PUBLICISTS, PROPAGANDISTS AND PROSELYTIZERS

Ideals of Empire for Public Schoolboys

Once the Empire was established, the public schools sustained it. In the words of G. Kendall, onetime headmaster of University College School, 'The public schools . . . claim that it is they who, if they did not make the Empire (for most of them were hardly in existence when the Empire was made), at least maintained and administered it through their members.'[1] To this end they generated imperial enthusiasm. Their evangelicalism was as purposeful as Arnold's. It was Christian militancy in the guise of imperial philanthropy. Yet it was not entirely altruistic: 'In the eyes of the imperial guardian, the "white man's burden" signified moral status as well as moral duty.'[2] Headmasters of the public schools subscribed fully to the ethical imperative. They further asserted that the training they provided was the substance of success. Imperialism, they argued, was a moral endeavour and they were the repositories of effective moral education. Of course, it was scarcely as simple as this. There were at least four other more pressing motives for promotion of Empire: trade, security, emigration and prestige. Furthermore, the Empire was far from being 'one big, red lump'[3] effortlessly controlled by virtue of visible moral supremacy. The dissimilarities between Nigeria and Australia, for instance, were far greater than their similarities. In the white Dominions, muscle was frequently more valuable than morality, while in the black colonies obeisance was encouraged through the fire-power of the Hotchkiss gun. And the public schoolboy was as often ridiculed in the former as he was obeyed in the latter. Again, at the prosaic level of credentials, imperial civil and military careers required somewhat different types and training and, within the schools, classical and modern sides evolved their respective curricula and conditions in response. And where their efforts were not enough, the crammer had his part to play in the successful selection of the public schoolboy for imperial service.

The reality, then, was complicated, yet the ideal was not. The Empire, in the enthusiastic words of C. A. Vlieland, was quite simply 'the best thing that ever happened to mankind'.[4] A widespread and uncritical belief in an imperial race with a gift for government, an imperial religion of compassion and concern and an imperial educational system able to successfully inculcate the young with the necessary gubernatorial skills and the appropriate ethical attitudes, guaranteed this simple and sanguine assessment.

Public school headmasters were not backward in coming forward to assert the accuracy of such a judgement. For this elementary reason – they played the role of agents of hegemonic persuasion; they were not merely executive autocrats with an ability to impose their views: they exerted powerful moral authority. They comprised a pedagogic leadership which managed in a variety of ways – through the pulpit sermon, the playing-field exhortation, the speech-day admonition, the informal 'jaw', the classroom digression and the school magazine editorial – to suffuse every pore of the school society with their version of reality. Equally important was their ability to limit the propagation of ideas opposed to their own. Their commitment to imperial domination was assimilated by their pupils as commonsense purpose. And the extent of assimilation, while not complete,[5] was considerable. Headmasters, in short, served in the role of Gramsci's 'intellectuals', spreading and legitimatizing dominant convictions, winning over youth and 'creating unity on the contested terrain of ideology'.[6] They loudly echoed Seeley, Dilke and MacKinder. In this way, they served the needs and met the fashions of the wider world.

And they did more than merely exhort. The committee set up to administer the School Empire Tours in the late 1920s, for example, contained five headmasters among its eight members: C. Norwood (Harrow), F. Fletcher (Charterhouse), M. J. Rendall (Winchester), E. H. Stevens (Westminster) and E. Montague Jones (St Albans). Such men were the coupling mechanisms linking two interdependent spheres – school and society; they were the critical ingredients of a hegemonic paradigm – one that involved both reproduction and production of belief; they fostered a passionate adherence to the propriety of imperialism; they fashioned their own moral instruments of imperial effectiveness. To claim this is not to deny the presence of opposition and dissent, but to assert that the prevailing condition was one of support and accord.

Within the schools this support for the imperial idea came from headmasters of all persuasions and backgrounds: radicals and reactionaries, intellectuals and hearties, clerics and laymen. Adherents ranged from the obscure to the celebrated. The former included John Millington Sing,[7] Warden of St Edwards, Oxford, from 1904 to 1913, an ardent imperialist who took a strong interest in everything connected with the British Commonwealth, lectured on imperial history for the Victoria League, and acted when occasion allowed as *locum tenens* for the headmasters at Michaelhouse in Natal and St Andrew's, Grahamstown in South Africa. The latter numbered in its ranks Cyril Norwood,[8] headmaster of Harrow School from 1926 to 1934, who considered that the acquisition, maintenance and development of the Empire was the product of the English tradition of education. Fostered in the schools of the privileged, it relied largely upon games.[9] Norwood was firmly of the view that cricket had supplied a new conception of chivalry to the common stock of national ideas, but rugby football promoted the cardinal virtues appropriate to the imperialist: unselfishness, fearlessness and self-control.

Some, with a surprisingly practical outlook in view of their impractical upbringing, added mechanical instruction to muscular training in the interests of imperial efficiency. Edmond Warre,[10] headmaster of Eton from 1884 to 1905, who, with an holistic imperial view, saw the house as merely a piece of the school and the school as merely a piece of the Empire, paid for and constructed at Eton a school of practical mechanics for boys likely to go to the colonies. He did not, however, depart too far from convention; he was not a Sanderson. He was mostly unoriginal and, like many of his peers, elevated the sound body above the sound mind. This tradition was acceptable in its time: 'As long as the world seemed laid especially for the British Empire, and the Empire to be constructed like a shell round the Eton kernel,' wrote Shane Leslie, 'Eton was successful and unchallenged.'[11] It bred viceroys and rulers for the Empire as the Academy of Noble Ecclesiastics in Rome nourished cardinals and nuncios for the Roman Church. Three other famous headmasters, Hely Hutchinson Almond, Montague Rendall and J. E. C. Welldon, espoused the imperial cause as eagerly as Warre. Almost all they had in common was subscription to the imperial dream and a firm belief in its significance for the public schoolboy. Almond was a radical who challenged Scottish convention in an attempt to stimulate an excessive interest in games; Rendall was a reactionary, pursuing a medieval concept of chivalry; Welldon was a romancer infatuated with the nobility of games and the related glory of the Empire. In their different ways they will serve to illustrate the commitment of the public school system to imperialism.

Hely Hutchinson Almond became headmaster of Loretto School near Edinburgh in 1862. It was unknown: he made it famous. His methods were bizarre, his results fashionable. In the words of the man who probably knew him best,

> The foundation-stone upon which the Head built up Loretto was Physical Education . . . in his little corner of the world he set himself to teach a rational idea of the basis of health . . . It was a point of conscience, a matter of religion, to keep his body in the best possible condition . . . he always endeavoured, in the words of St Paul, to present his body as a living sacrifice. The consecration of the body was a terrible reality to him.[12]

Sensible dress, ample food and extensive exercise were the basis of life at Loretto. Almond was a visionary. His purpose in life was 'to leap the written pale of prejudice' and 'disyoke . . . necks from custom'. He preached long and often on human health, comfort, efficiency and commonsense. He called his doctrine of good habits 'Lorettonianism', and often despaired of the ignorance and indifference of the nation: 'I seem to be marching, like Sherman, through a country void of reason; and looking, like Diogenes, for a rational man.'[13] Despite his considerable non-conformity, he was a substantial conformist. The Loretto which he conceived was 'a place for the training of the governing class, in a political and social system which set that class apart and above'.[14] He had many of its pre-dispositions. He was a strong conservative with few intellectual pretensions and a natural aristocrat who preferred patronage to equality. He considered, for example, that the extension of the franchise had little bearing on the true welfare of the nation. Democracy was irrelevant to contentment. The wise leader would ensure a proper care of the physique of children, the spread of hygienic knowledge, sanitary schemes of house-building and careful training and instruction in healthy habits – the true source of general happiness.

He was unsophisticated not only in his politics, but in his religion. And both were incomplete without physical fitness. 'Loretto,' he once wrote, 'is a humble attempt to carry out, in one particular line, the Christian idea of the establishment of a Kingdom of Heaven upon earth. That kingdom must be a great many things beside being rational, but it must also be rational.'[15] His vision could not be stigmatized as simply valetudinarian. In his scheme of ethics, physical capacity was subordinated to moral quality. From health came courage, temperance and *esprit de corps* – a trinity of moral virtues which comprised his Sparto-Christian ideal. One end of this ideal was service – to God and Country. Almond's attitude was militant and his conception of life was struggle. His hero was the crusader, not the cleric. It was in this spirit, he reminded his boys, that Paul offered up his body as a living sacrifice to God:

> He no more shirked pain or disfigurement, or loss of life or limb, in fighting the battles of his King, than any of you would do if the dreams of alarmists shall some day or other be fulfilled, and you find yourselves at no holiday review, but for the first time hear shots fired in anger . . . Which of you will then rank the speed of the runner, or the strength of the gymnast, or the honours won between the wickets and the goals, . . . as the supreme end of an athletic training? You know well enough that the more strength, the more activity, the more endurance you have gained from what has been sneered at by sickly pedantry as the trivial play of young barbarians, the less you would wish to stay at home, rejoicing in your physical perfections, if once you got the chance of fighting . . .[16]

He saw his Lorettonians as wholesome and manly, carrying the banner of the cross to distant lands, and with strong arm, iron will and earnest purpose winning Christian victories among ignorant natives and coarse traders, protecting rough colonies from effeminacy and vice, and spreading 'the contagion of their vigour'.[17]

Imperial Britain was a source of pride to him. His first sermon to the school was an imperial discourse strategically located on 19 June, between the anniversaries of Waterloo and Victoria's accession. The sermon was subsequently honed to perfection and became known to the Loretto congregation as 'The Waterloo Sermon'.[18] It was published under the title 'The Divine Governance of Nations' in a book of sermons which appeared in 1899. It was an extraordinary and intemperate effort – Kingsleian not merely in its physicality but in its prejudice. Drenched in the blood of Old Testament battles, punctuated with racial invective, righteous with insular arrogance, it is an unattractive piece of chauvinism, bigotry and racism. God's divine purpose for England and the Englishman was immodestly defined: the guiding of the world's history. God's beneficent gift was proclaimed: the glorious iron crown of Duty. Almond's view, like that of many other imperialists, as we shall see later, was sacrificial:

> And as the field of 'tombless dead' passes before your eyes, will you say of those who have presented their bodies as living sacrifices in the sacred cause of driving back the foes, that a single hour of the strong joyous discipline which gave firmness to the nerves, and vigour to the limbs which now lie stiff and cold in death, has been spent in vain?[19]

Blood was the price of glory. Boys who would be men, he asserted, who meant to play a man's part in the world, should study the lives of British martyrs and heroes: Raleigh, Wellington, Livingstone, Patteson and Gordon. The blood of heroes, he announced, was the life of nations. To inscribe their names 'on the glorious roll' and further the destiny of England, he told his pupils to realize the virtues of truth, purity, courage, simplicity, hardiness and reverence; to set honesty above cleverness, manliness above refinement, character above attainments, moral and physical perfection above abundance of possessions and elaboration of surroundings. Like Percival of Clifton,[20] whose words he quoted with satisfaction, he looked for a new generation of men not characterized by literary accomplishment or varnish of culture, but disciplined and strong. In this and other sermons, he wallowed in a vocabulary of violence, strength, struggle, sacrifice, heroics and hardiness. His language comprised a conscious attempt to paint in words an image of a neo-Spartan imperial warrior, untroubled by doubt, firm in conviction, strong in mind and muscle. It was a Darwinian rhetoric.

It was said of Harrow in the 1890s that its aim was to bring up the boys as 'Christian gentlemen and patriots, and their songs and recitations were pregnant with sentiments tending to develop those qualities.'[21] Almond used the pulpit to a similar end. 'Be strong,' he exhorted his boys, in a sermon entitled 'The Duty of Strength'. 'Do not dare to neglect the Divine command to be strong.' He urged on them 'vigorous manhood, full courage and high spirit'. Where conflict and contemplation were at one with the Almighty, there could be no error: 'when men fight with their hands and pray with their hearts, faith nerves the arm and clears the judgement, and God defends the might.'[22] The imagery is that of the new crusader, strong in the Lord and the power of His might, marching confidently to the outposts of Empire in a righteous cause – the guiding of the world's destiny!

Almond's simple imperial vision was made possible by an extreme, unapologetic ethnocentricity which embraced the Continental as well as the Kaffir. He held foreigners in contempt; he never set foot outside the British Isles. He possessed a fiery patriotism, and a thin skin. Kipling's irreverence in 'The Islanders' incensed him. For a man to whom a good football player could never be a bad man, the disparaging reference to 'muddied oafs at the goals' was unforgivable heresy. The message of the poem was beyond him. The *Lorettonian* had for too long been replete with contrary verse asserting the value of games to imperial endeavour. In Almond's eyes the football fifteen was the source of the finest South African volunteers:

> Proven as boys, in our ranks we have known you,
> Proven as men, in our pride we shall own you;
> Proven in battle, when bullets are flying,
> Proven in suffering, when comrades are dying.[23]

Almond was greatly concerned by the training of the British officer: the Guardian of Empire. He deprecated the bookish nature of the work required for entry to Sandhurst, and recommended football, hunting, deer-stalking and climbing as the means of cultivating 'those qualities of brain and character most wanted in a soldier'. Certainly, he conceded magnanimously, every boy should have to do some work of the bookish kind, but 'hard' sedentary work he considered bad for the officer class. It made the chest narrower, the movements slower, the muscles less powerful and eyesight and hearing duller. Which of the two, he asked, the student and the sportsman:

> is the more likely to be sensitive and to interpret correctly faint and momentary impressions on eye and ear; to know what is indicated by the fall of a pebble, or the distant shimmer of steel, or to discern other visible or audible indications of the neighbourhood of a foe; or to march through a donga without finding out what there is about its sides – the boy who has pored over books and papers at a town crammer's, or the one who has constantly steered the ball through a football scrummage, or stalked wild-duck, or ridden straight to hounds? Which of the two is the more likely to throw off the germs of disease, to recover soon from wounds, or to endure exposure and fatigue?[24]

The don, he concluded, was a more noxious element in a regiment than even in a school.

Fitness was as necessary for the imperial civilian as it was for the imperial warrior: consequently he proposed physical tests for the Indian Civil Service. 'It should be remembered that it is not the scholar or mathematician, but the man of nerve, endurance, high courage, and animal spirits, who may avert disaster in any future mutiny.'[25] It was for these various reasons as much as anything that he upheld those 'incontrovertible' words of Herbert Spencer: 'To be a nation of healthy animals is the first condition of national prosperity.'[26] To this end his advice was constant: 'At every school in the country the elements of practical physiology should be intelligibly taught, and *applied to daily life*.'[27] On this arrangement, he maintained, 'depended the future maintenance of the physical vigour of our imperial race'.[28]

It was the Rhodes Scholarship Trust which gave another enthusiast for imperial integration under the leadership of the Motherland the opportunity to publicize his views and extend his influence. Montague J. Rendall, born in 1862, was the son of a country parson. After schooling at Harrow followed by four years at Trinity College, Cambridge, he became a master of Winchester College in 1887. He was appointed headmaster in 1911 and remained in this post for thirteen years. He was a dyed-in-the-wool traditionalist, espousing, as the twentieth century proceeded, increasingly recondite (and in reality seldom actualized) ideals of education – those 'age-long traditions' of the English public school system: 'firstly, worship, which . . . is its soul; secondly, grammar of Latin, or useless learning, or culture . . .; thirdly, the knightly manners of chivalry which shine especially in true sport; and, fourthly, public service, both in peace and war.'[29] These constituted commodities worth exporting.

Rendall was deeply affected by the tragedy of the Great War. Some five hundred Wykehamists had died. Out of their sacrifice came a 'vision of a renewed and purified Britain and Empire, springing from the example and sacrifice of the Fallen'.[30] He came to cherish a dream that the Rhodes Trust would give him a humble post as 'Schools Secretary': there would be lots to do at home and abroad. He saw the task as the most important in the Dominions. In 1924 his dream was realized. To his great delight he was invited by the Rhodes Trustees to undertake a tour of the Empire to review the method of selection of Rhodes Scholars. It was a seminal journey. Out of it came a lasting commitment to strengthening the spiritual growth of Empire not only through the exchange of students but also through an exchange of pupils and teachers.

On his return in 1926 he became Chairman of the Imperial Studies Committee of the Royal Colonial Institute and was active in the Overseas League and the League of Empire, extending further his knowledge, contacts and influence. A year later, on the recommendation of Dr Cyril Norwood, headmaster of Harrow, Leo Amery, Secretary of State for the Colonies and for Dominion Affairs, Rhodes Trustee and Chairman of the Overseas Settlement Committee, appointed him Chairman of the 'Schools Empire-Tour Committee', more accurately referred to on occasion as the 'Public Schools Empire Tours Committee'. This had developed out of a visit to England by the Young Australian League in the early twenties. A reciprocal visit to Australia was sponsored by the Church of England Council of Empire Settlement, which in 1925 set up a 'Schools Empire-Tour Committee' to make the arrangements. The original plan was to send some two hundred boys from the public schools, secondary schools and public elementary schools. Eventually, however, only forty could be collected – sons of the well-off from public schools. This set the pattern for the future.

Rendall was enthusiastic at having the opportunity of implementing his ideals. He sought to forge the links between the youth of Motherland and Empire: 'We have . . . two large bodies of boys whose childhood and boyhood have been moulded by similar inheritances, though one is more closely bound by its heritage of tradition . . . the other more free from custom and convention . . . What can we do to strengthen and perpetuate these bonds?' The answer was sensible and assured. Despite the advance in a knowledge of Empire in the schools, 'no amount of books or lectures will have half the effect of a voyage across the water. For the young, . . . seeing is believing. Personal contact is worth a ton of text-books.'[31] Between 1927 and 1939 over nineteen tours were organized and small groups of public schoolboys travelled to South Africa and Rhodesia, Canada and Newfoundland, New Zealand and Australia, India, East Africa, West Indies and British Guiana. These were tours for an élite, and while Rendall made passing mention on one occasion to this 'regrettable fact' and welcomed ideas for extending the scheme to a wider range of participants, it is doubtful if he was really over-concerned at the arrangement:

> His vision both of Empire and of education was aristocratic; he placed his confidence in an *élite* of race and of training. But the liberalism in these convictions was as strong as the imperialism. The *élite* was to be educated to the public service. The best education should be made as widely and cheaply available as possible; and the highly educated should go forth to serve the community over the largest possible field. Above all, the commercial view of life should be excluded; *noblesse oblige*.[32]

Quite simply, his concept of community was caste-ridden. A major obligation lay on the shoulders of the occidental 'Brahmin', the Anglo-Saxon, to exert a 'benevolent and firm control . . . upon the new, weaker and backward nations'. In Britain the public schoolboy was in precisely the same relationship to the elementary school pupil. He had the same obligations.

In his self-appointed messianic role, Rendall could be arrogant, tactless and clumsy. He spoke baldly to New World and imperial audiences about their shortcomings and spoke eulogistically about the inspirational qualities of 'the great English schools'. He irritated Australian 'beaks' with the contention that if they doubled the time spent on Latin, then science, mathematics, history and modern languages would gain in freshness and vigour. In South Africa he urged a headmaster in Johannesburg to replace Afrikaans with Greek. In Rhodesia, he commented upon the splendour of their Niagara Falls! His self-assurance rode criticism with calm composure. He was the Canute of the classics, certain of the validity of his crusade: 'I feel strongly that for every conceivable reason, the independent schools of the Empire need help and need it now. There is a battle being waged between narrow, shallow, materialistic education and that represented by the English public schools.'[33]

While he was warm in his praise for these schools, he was critical of their imitators overseas. He considered the best were of low quality, dismissing, for example, in his Canada review, famous schools like Upper Canada College, St Andrews, Toronto, and University School, Victoria. His prejudice showed continually in his reports. In Tasmania, he commented on a Rhodes candidate from the wrong type of background who aroused his dislike: 'He is star of the "Commerce School" with no power of leadership and no special athlete.'[34] In Rhodesia, he extracted a polite promise from the Director of Education to impress on the schools the desirability of giving added time to Latin at the expense of mathematics, which he considered overdone. His anachronistic attitude was further revealed when after an onerous set of interviews he observed to a colleague: 'We are certainly sorry to have an unbroken row of engineers for scholars; but if they have the best brains and are otherwise of the right stamp, you must give them preference. *Ceteris paribus*, you would naturally give preference to an Arts man.'[35]

It is not surprising therefore that his South African inspection, for one, occasioned criticism: 'Lots of people, who could not realize Winchester and Rendall as its personification, carped at his academic aloofness, and his "sacerdotalism" and mistook his almost monastic scholasticism for superiority and pomposity.'[36] For his part, his criticisms of South Africa were expressed with sardonic elegance:

If I were to design a medal for one of these Schoolboys the superscription might be 'Child of the Sun'; the obverse a figure of 'Independence with a Shield', or perhaps 'Venator Intrepidus', like

Pisanello's model of Alfonso the Magnanimous, where a naked boy is riding astride of a fearsome boar; but a Lion to replace the Boar, and the reverse should be just a bright Star to symbolize the Sun, *'radiatum insigne diei'*. The rest of the field would consist of several Rugby footballs and a scanty heap of books. For indeed, truth to tell, this wholesome brown boy, with khaki shirt, khaki shorts and a pair of rough shoes, who looks straight at you from rather wild eyes half-hidden in a mat of hair, is just a Child of the Sun. True, I have been thinking mainly of Rhodesia, where the fringes of life are rougher and independence has more scope; [school] terms, you will have observed, cannot be closely clipped when trains only run at intervals, and boys live in remote places . . . But, speaking roughly, the same is true of all South African boys. They are by nature Children of the Sun, Sun-worshippers, and Culture has little meaning for them. Why should parents and schoolmasters disturb this happy dream? Why worry the boys with Culture? Well, this is the plea of all children since Cain and Abel first worshipped the Sun in the morning of the world, a plea urged with childish impertinence and irresistible grace; but these Schools are not meant for Mowgli.[37]

Rendall was not ungenerous. He could bear witness to the strength and purpose of imperial schools with their 'noble chapels, fine sport and manliness'. He conceded that they kept reasonably closely to the traditions of the Motherland, but always there was a note of reservation and a disappointment barely held in check: 'culture is a plant of slow growth and is not easily inculcated (to take an example) in a squatter's son, who came to learn the elements at an Australian school as a new boy of twenty-seven. I must not be tempted to dwell longer on this theme.'[38] And, again speaking of Australian schoolboys:

The very best of them secure a tone which is as good as any school in the Empire; their worship is keen and alive: their morals are excellent, though commendation may go too far in this respect: their manners are pleasant and they are fairly forthcoming: their athletics are above reproach, or would be so, if they did not occupy the whole of the picture. But with few exceptions they regard their work at best as a powerful duty. They have not reached the stage when form-work becomes a joy: much less have they discovered the best use of leisure. Very few Australian boys read a book except under compulsion. Parents seldom encourage them to do so, and, except in the best schools, Masters are too apt to agree with parents.[39]

To the end of his long life he never appreciated that the 'irresistible' trend of the times was antithetical to his own vision:

> He regarded the Anglo-Saxon race as the rightful leaders of the world, and those who had a higher secondary boarding-school education on the English model as the élite of that élite. Liberalized and moralized as was his conception of their privilege and destiny, that of serving 'the lesser breeds without the law' by ruling them, he took that privilege and that destiny for granted.[40]

His biographer, J. D'E. Firth, has remarked judiciously on the restricted and selective nature of his journeys; on the brief references to Dutch South Africans, to an absence of mention of French Canadians, to a total absence of contact with the Australian Labour Movement, to the minimum contact with Jews or Catholics. His was 'almost a royal progress'. Similarly, in his contempt for the materialism of the United States and the Dominions, the reasons for 'the cravings of the ambitious for wealth, of the many for security, were hidden from him'.[41] He was already an anachronism before he began his tours. His ideals had already lost out to the forces of materialism, egalitarianism and modernity.[42] He was a poor messenger of unity. In reality, he could only strengthen colonial prejudices and reinforce colonial contempt for a class-dominated, antiquated Britain. This is not to say that he wholly lacked personal attractiveness. His dignity, eloquence and confidence won admirers. For these reasons it is probable that 'the main effect of his ministry . . . to the Empire lay in the personal inspiration, comfort and even conversion which he brought to individual teachers and boys.'[43] Rendall was an Arthur lacking a Round Table. His was a lonely and forlorn endeavour: to take worship, grammar, chivalry and the concept of service to the white Empire. 'The public schools of England,' he asserted, 'have clung to these four great principles . . . and England has clung to the public schools.'[44] For him that was enough.

The public school headmasters' most eloquent, persistent and opinionated spokesman on the schools and imperialism was undoubtedly the Reverend J. E. C. Welldon, headmaster of Harrow

School from 1881 to 1895. In this regard he must be considered a Hector among Trojans. He once announced: 'To consolidate the Empire, and to animate it as a whole with noble ideas, is one of the greatest needs and duties of the present day, and an empire, like an individual, lives not by bread alone but by its sentiments, its ambitions, its ideals.'[45] He did his best to live up to this statement. He was an unflagging homilist where imperial duty was concerned. At the Royal Colonial Institute's Seventh Ordinary General Meeting of the year on 14 May 1895 at the Whitehall Rooms, Hotel Metropole, for example, he read a paper on 'The Imperial Aspects of Education'. The image of Empire upheld by the Chairman, the Right Honourable Earl of Dunraven, in his opening address was, as might be expected, wholly benevolent. Disingenuously he described the role of the Institute in promulgating this image as two-fold: at a higher level to publicize the work of 'a civilizing and great peace-making influence in the world'; at a lower level to spread a knowledge of its resources so as to ensure occupations for the youth of Britain.

The Chairman's assessment of the Empire was less than modest and it served to introduce his guest-speaker in a manner which was more than generous: 'The Institute has done great work . . . and by no man has its work been more thoroughly and more ably carried out.'[46] Welldon, no stranger to flattery, accepted these accolades without demur and took as his theme the argument that education must relate to the administration of an empire. As in Augustine Rome, he argued, so in Victorian Britain: the furtherance of imperial strength, beneficence and high dignity. He quoted Virgil with approval:

> Tu regere imperio populos, Romane, memento;
> Hae tibi erunt artes; pacisque imponere morem,
> Parcere subjectis et debellam superbos.[47]

Conquest and command were the shared prerogatives. To others, he implied, could be left the accomplishments of art, science and philosophy.

Welldon drew attention to the coincidence of dates in English history which brought out in strong relief 'the connection between educational advance and imperial power': the reigns of Elizabeth and Victoria. These were chief epochs not only of Empire but of education. And the one determined the purpose of the other. Consequently, the contemporary purpose of the public schools was not classicists and mathematicians, but governors, administrators, generals, philanthropists and statesmen:

> Let me be judged, if judged at all, upon the large field of national or international affairs. If it can be said with truth of the English schools and universities that year after year, generation after generation, century after century, they send forth men not without faults, not without limitations of knowledge or culture . . . not guiltless nor immaculate perhaps in spelling, as the Duke of Wellington was not immaculate; but men of vigour, tact, courage, and integrity, men who are brave and chivalrous and true, men who in the words of the academical prayer are 'duly qualified to serve God both in Church and state', then they can afford to smile at criticisms or can listen to them without shame or self-reproach. That is the object which the educator of today may set before himself; that is the service which he can render to his country.[48]

The purpose of Victorian education defined to his satisfaction, Welldon next turned his attention to the colonizing genius of the English, which in his complacent view had enabled them not only to win, but to retain their mighty Empire, and reveal themselves superior to less-accomplished modern nations, possessors of less impressive foreign domains: the Dutch, Spanish, Portuguese and French. The foundation of superiority lay firstly in healthy, vigorous, athletic tastes: a sporting instinct had created in large part the British Empire, and in this regard Albion owed 'far more to her sports than to her studies'. He amplified this confident illustration of reductionism in the following imperious antiphon:

> Englishmen are not superior to Frenchmen or Germans in brains or industry or the science and apparatus of war; but they are superior in the health and temper which games impart . . . I do not think I am wrong in saying that the sport, the pluck, the resolution, and the strength which have within the last few weeks animated the little garrison at Chitral and the gallant force that has accomplished their deliverance are effectively acquired in the cricket-fields and football fields of the great public schools, and in the games of which they are the habitual scenes. The pluck, the energy, the perseverance, the good temper, the self-control, the discipline,

the co-operation, the esprit de corps, which merit success in cricket or football, are the very qualities which win the day in peace or war. The men who possessed these qualities, not sedate and faultless citizens, but men of will, spirit, and chivalry, are the men who conquered at Plassey and Quebec. In the history of the British Empire it is written that England has owed her sovereignty to her sports.[49]

Impressive though this quality of athletic rigour was, it was surpassed by a quality 'of which Englishmen, and especially English Public School men, stand pre-eminent –"readiness" '. Unamenable to definition in a single word, it was a hereditary gift of Englishmen fostered by their public schools. It meant courage, self-reliance, opportunism and resourcefulness. One thing it did not mean was mere intellectual facility. The worst method of choosing men for great administrative and imperial positions was by 'counting up marks obtained in a literary examination'. His own Harrovians, he added needlessly, were not remarkably clever or remarkably cultivated, but 'readiness' in difficult circumstances invariably would see them through!

At this stage in his delivery Welldon had far from exhausted his list of English qualities. A further virtue, the supreme ruling virtue of Englishmen, was 'character' – essentially unswerving honesty – fortunately so large in proportion that it overshadowed their defects: pride, intolerance, unsociability and arrogance. Add, finally, the Englishman's fear of God – Seeley's dictum won Welldon's full approval: 'If you find a state which is not also in some sense a church, you find a state which is not long for this world'[50] – and the secrets of superior imperialism are revealed: 'physical strength, promptitude, character, religion'.

Whatever the inherent talents of Englishmen, observed Welldon, nature must be reinforced by nurture. There were responsibilities incumbent upon the public schools. It was their duty to bring the magnitude and dignity of the British Empire continually before their pupils:

The boys of today are the statesmen and administrators of tomorrow. In their hands is the future of the British Empire. May they prove themselves not unworthy of their solemn charge! May they scorn the idea of tarnishing or diminishing the Empire which their forefathers won! May they augment, consolidate, and exalt it! May it be given them to cherish great ideas, to make great efforts, and to win great victories! That is my prayer.[51]

In his declaration of intent Welldon was asserting nothing out of the ordinary. Imperialism, Education and Games were an Imperial Trinity, as sacred to the upper-class Victorian educator as Liberty, Equality and Fraternity were to the Revolutionary Jacobin. He was applauded by his audience for his perception and won a tribute of special warmth from G. R. Parkin, former principal of Upper Canada College, the Eton of Canada, whose role in promoting the Imperial Trinity among the 'Canucks' will be considered later.

Although he had already been headmaster of Harrow for ten years when he addressed the Colonial Institute meeting in 1895, Welldon was still a youngish man of forty-one. He died at the age of eighty-three some time before the Second World War. Throughout his long life his facility with the pen was impressive, his energy considerable and his sincerity secure. Speeches, articles, sermons, reminiscences and even a schoolboy novel flowed from him over the years – all replete with the same doctrinaire platitudes about the value of games, the splendour of a public school education and the grandeur of the imperial dream.

The Victorian and Edwardian headmasters were eager and calculating publicists for themselves and their world, but Welldon was the pre-eminent propagandist: stamped with the hallmark of a naive rather than a calculating Goebbelism – partiality, repetitiveness, simplification and certainty. His assertions were sometimes breathtaking in their banality:

It is my earnest desire that athletic games should be kept pure of all that may lower the spirit of the game. For the lesson of fair play in sport is the lesson of honesty in business; and, as I have travelled over the world, I have been scarcely less struck than pleased by finding that foreigners, though they do not always give English merchants credit as the equals of Germans, or even of Japanese, in industry or ingenuity, or in the persistency of advertising their goods, yet acknowledge the good faith of British merchants as delivering goods which, whether they are entirely up-to-date or not, are always trustworthy alike in their material and in their manufacture[52];

in their melodramatic bathos:

How often have I seen boys going in to bat without a murmur in a bad light at the close of a long summer day's play, or playing a losing game with almost heroic determination! The boy who thinks little of himself, and much of his Eleven or his school, has not spent his Public School life in vain. It used to be told how, in the days when the ring around the field at Lord's was less scrupulously kept than it is now, a Harrow boy's nose began to bleed when he was fielding; his mother, seeing his plight, ran out from the ring to comfort or relieve him; but the captain of the Eleven bade her retire with the solemn words, 'Madam, a Harrow boy must be prepared to shed his last drop of blood for his school'[53];

and in their precious pomposity:

One remarkable instance of fighting at Harrow, if only one, I still recall. Among my pupils there was an Egyptian boy of high rank, who was admitted to the school, I think, at the instance of Lord Cromer, as it was judged on political grounds to be important that his education should take place in England rather than in France. One morning this boy appeared in school with two black eyes. I wrote to his house-master, asking him, if possible, to find out who had been fighting the Egyptian boy. After some inquiry, he sent me as the culprit, the last boy whom I should have suspected of an aggressive pugilism. I said to him, 'B—, you have been fighting. Have you any excuse to give? You know fighting is an offence against school rules. What do you mean by giving that boy two black eyes?' He hesitated a moment, then he raised his eyes and said apologetically, 'Please sir, sir, he said something bad about the British race.' The only possible reply which I could make was: 'That is enough, my boy; you may go.'[54]

Welldon achieved a curious distinction – the ability to marry academic subtlety with intellectual naivety. At King's, Cambridge, he carried off the 'glittering prizes' – winner of the Bell and Craven scholarships, senior Classic and senior Chancellor's Medallist. He became a Fellow of King's – the most highbrow of the Cambridge colleges of the time. Even at this early stage in his career, some thought him destined for the See of Canterbury. This prospect was blown away by his intransigence as Metropolitan of India. It was in the spirit of Kipling's 'Recessional' that the Empire was to be consecrated and served. He was of the belief that 'all Indians had souls and that his mission was to enlist them under the banner of

Christ whatever other faiths happened to claim their allegiance'.[55] Curzon, Viceroy, patron and friend, considered this attitude ingenuous, provocative and insensitive. He came to the reluctant conclusion that Welldon lacked the requisite skills for high ecclesiastical office: tactfulness, urbanity and sophistication.

Welldon was unmoved and unrepentant. He held fast to his view that God had endowed the British race 'with a world-wide Empire, an Empire transcending all imperial systems, not for their own aggrandisement but that they may be executants of his sovereign purpose in the world . . .'[56] In *Recollections and Reflections*, published in 1915 when, in effect, he had been shunted into an ecclesiastical siding as Dean of Manchester, he wrote yet again of imperialism and proselytism as one and the same thing:

> As the British Empire expands, not in territorial magnitude alone, but in influence and dignity; as it assumes and maintains the paramount obligation of promoting peace, justice, liberty, progress and religion among the nations of mankind, the teaching of a true imperial patriotism becomes increasingly valuable. It is a matter of public concern that the children of today, who will determine the policy of Great Britain as citizens tomorrow, should enter in a serious and lofty spirit upon their high responsibilities.[57]

Later in the book he affirmed defiantly his belief in the duty of inspiring the Empire as a whole with Christian principle, and of bringing 'the Mohammedan and pagan peoples within the Empire to the knowledge of Jesus Christ'.[58] Indeed, throughout the whole of his adult life he moved everywhere in the full consciousness of his nation's imperial greatness and responsibility. In his introduction to Pelham Warner's *How We Recovered the Ashes*, he remarked of his voyage to the Antipodes with the English team and its wives:

> We were a mixed party, but we got on well together; . . . we thought each other 'jolly good fellows'; we played our games with patience and fairness . . . We did not wholly forget that we were Englishmen and Englishwomen representative of the greatest Empire under heaven. And Sunday by Sunday we met on the quarter-deck or in the saloon for divine service as a consecration of our voyage in the sight of the Most High.[59]

The clash with Curzon and the subsequent intractability suggest that Welldon was opinionated, obstinate and naive in some things.

It also reveals a man of principle, prepared to pay the price for unpopular views, honestly held. He was no smooth, obsequious licker of Establishment boots; more a northern Methodist than southern Anglican – righteous, independent and forthright rather than adaptable, clubbable and circumspect. He was a curious spokesman for the public school quality of *esprit de corps*.

It is frequently supposed that a feature of ageing is increasing inflexibility of attitude and certainty of conviction. Welldon displayed these tendencies to the full. In his final reminiscences, *Forty Years On*, in effect a valedictory address, he could regard with equanimity the harsh criticism of the games cult which had characterized the twenties and thirties:

> If a student of contemporary school life fixes his eyes upon the qualities which affect the moral elevation of the nation's life, he may feel that the place of games is wellnigh as important as that of work. Games, or at least organized games, which alone are worthy of consideration in Public School life, are especially valuable, as evoking some high moral qualities . . .
>
> A boy who is working for a scholarship is working, not wholly, yet mainly, for himself. But a boy who is playing in a match is playing, not for himself, but for his house, or for his school. He is always ready to sacrifice himself for the success of his eleven or his fifteen. No ignorance of Public School life – at least as I have known it – can be more lamentable than that a master should speak of his boys as choosing rather to get high scores themselves, and to see the school lose the match, than to get out without scoring any runs themselves, if only the victory in the match could fall to the school. There is no need to eulogize the athletic spirit; but there is some ground for holding that masters who encourage athletic games are looking to the moral, fully as much as to the physical, value of the exercise which boys enjoy upon the playing-fields.[60]

Only once, during the Great War, did he deign to notice and rebuke the numerous critics of the system. In response to an editorial in *The Times* in June 1915 claiming that the War had put the educational system of the nation 'on trial', he retorted that if there were any institutions which had justified themselves in the nation's crisis, it was the public schools and universities whose members had sacrificed 'the pleasures and privileges of life' for country and Empire. His own pupils, he added for good measure, every day by their deaths were teaching him a higher and a better lesson than he had ever taught them.[61]

He did not entirely lose sight of Western religious tradition, the superior dignity intrinsically attached to the cultivation of the spirit over the grace of the body, but

> when the athletic games of English Youth are considered in their reference not to physical energy but to moral worth, it would seem that they possess an even higher value than intellectual studies. For learning, however excellent in itself, does not afford much necessary scope for such virtues as promptitude, resource, honour, cooperation and unselfishness; but there are the soul of English games.[62]

Such qualities produced in turn that characteristic of the British race – the power of government – the hope and honour of Empire. Public school education produced those who knew how to act and acted. His belief in the contribution of the public schools to imperial success survived W. R. Lawson, G. G. Coulton, H. B. Gray, H. G. Wells and many other critics. His vision was unsullied. For Welldon the majesty of the British Empire dwelt less in the constable's truncheon than in 'the strong hearts of her sons'. As we have seen already, he was clear about his role in the promotion of this majesty. In later life he looked back with satisfaction on a job well done in the distant past:

> When I was headmaster of a great Public School, I tried to excite in my pupils a living interest in the British Empire, its history, its magnitude, its opportunities, its responsibilities, the variety of the many races which it comprises, and the solemnity of the duties imposed upon it. I wished them to know as much as possible about it, its magnitude, its possession of the chief harbours of the world, its power of elevating subject races, its hope of welding so many widely differing constituent elements into one harmonious whole. The festivals of the Empire, like Empire Day, I tried sedulously to bring before the school. It was for the nobility of the Empire, and therefore of the citizens, who, in a democracy, all contribute to the strength of the Empire, that prayer was habitually offered not only in the Chapel, but in the Speech Room.[63]

He reflected nostalgically on his attempts to bring his boys into contact with 'leaders of imperial thought and action', recalling with particular pleasure the Harrow lectures of Lord Roberts, Lord

Wolseley and Sir Henry Stanley. And, in one instance, his efforts had a marked effect. Leo Amery, one of Welldon's pupils, and later Parliamentary Under-Secretary for the Colonies from 1919 to 1921 and then Colonial Secretary and Secretary for the Dominions from 1924 to 1929, freely acknowledged the influence on him of Welldon's imperial enthusiasm.[64]

Harrow's service to the Empire, Welldon recalled, included provision for the education of scions of native royal houses, and he remembered with special but circumspect affection

> the sons of the well-known Indian Prince, Sir Hirnam Singh; for they were not only fellow-subjects of the other boys in the school, but Christians as well. I used to tell the late Earl of Bessborough, the devoted friend of Harrow cricket, that he would live to see Harrow represented at the wicket at Lord's by two coloured princes. It would have been easy to multiply the Oriental boys, but I did not care to admit more than a certain number of them. Nevertheless, I hold that the Public Schools can, and well may, make some contribution towards inspiring the Far East with the knowledge of English Christian life by welcoming a limited number of Oriental boys to full comity with their English school-fellows.[65]

Welldon, more than any other headmaster, forged the links securely between sport and Empire. 'Sport has been a great feature of English life through all the centuries,' he wrote. 'It has been, as the very name of sportsman shows it to have been, a wholly honourable pursuit. There is no well-wisher of the British Empire who would not desire that sport should retain its lofty place in the esteem of all Britons.'[66] It was through his aspirations and actions, and those of numerous other schoolmasters in the public schools, that a unique educational ideal was disseminated throughout the British Empire – the ideal of character-training through games. As we shall see later, this was a primary purpose of upper-class education throughout the Empire. How could it be otherwise? The educational system of Dominion and Colony reflected the dominant Metropolitan system. What was good enough for young Britain was certainly good enough for young Empire – black, brown and white.

In 1899 a crowd of some two hundred Etonians and Harrovians, led by Lord Roberts of Kandahar, assembled at Victoria Station to see Welldon off when he left Harrow and England to take up the Bishopric of Calcutta with the express purpose of welding together 'still more closely "the British Empire and the Church" '.[67] It was the high point of his career. His imperial sojourn did him little good, but his dedication to the Empire never faltered throughout the subsequent years in the ecclesiastical wilderness. More than that, as one commentator has written with attractive succinctness and complete veracity: 'Welldon remained until his death an unashamed champion of the British Empire, the Church of England and those values which he saw enshrined in the public school tradition.'[68]

Almond, Rendall and Welldon symbolize a powerful movement in the Britain of the late nineteenth and early twentieth centuries. They were convinced of the desirability of games, especially team games, in the training of the young. They believed in the value of these games for the development of ethical behaviour and the formation of sound social attitudes. They were loud and forceful advocates of athleticism.[69] They held that games were at the heart of the educational process.[70] And these men were merely the more active, the more public and more visible representatives of a widespread cult. And, as equally convinced imperialists, they had a view of education that was not only national but also imperial. They saw it as their duty to give a lead to the imperial world.

And they gave it. The outcome was a unique phenomenon: in the most bizarre locations could be found those potent symbols of pedagogic imperialism – football and cricket pitches. Their rationale was not merely physiological but philosophical. Their concern was as much with an ethic as with an action and their motivation was as much moralistic as it was hedonistic. From their schools they called up a force of missionaries, teachers, soldiers and administrators to assist them in their proselytism. Here the games ethic flourished, here was enthusiastic allegiance, here were housed the embryonic diffusionists and here a seductive image of Empire was projected unremittingly.

2

CONCEPTS OF DUTY AND PROSPECTS OF ADVENTURE

Images of Empire for Public Schoolboys

In *The Harrovians*, Arnold Lunn echoed the analogous reference to Imperial Rome made by J. E. C. Welldon in his speech to the Royal Colonial Institute and had a certain Mr Handleby declare: 'The public schools aim at something higher than mere culture. They build up character and turn out the manly, clean-living men that are the rock of empire.'[1] By the end of Victoria's reign there was much truth in this philistine, but not wholly unmeritorious, assertion. The English public schoolboy ran the British Empire. He was its ruler and guardian, and not infrequently its teacher and its missionary. He was intrinsically linked, in an assortment of roles, with the New Imperialism of the late nineteenth century. Mack, Honey, Wilkinson and others give space in their works to the close relationship between the late nineteenth-century public schools and Empire.[2] All are firmly of the opinion that the schools were the training grounds of generations of committed imperialists pledged to the survival of the Empire upon which proverbially the sun never set.

Now, as every schoolboy used to know, Sir Henry Newbolt is the balladeer of nineteenth-century imperial obligation. His 'Vitaï Lampada' is the hackneyed symbol of an era now past and an ethic now defunct. Those famous verses depicting the stoical last-wicket stand on a bumping pitch in a blinding light, juxtaposed with the description of the desperate position of the British square on the blood-sodden desert sands, together with the ringing exhortation Newbolt thought appropriate to both occasions – 'Play up! and play the game' – are too well known, of course, to require quotation. Newbolt delighted in portraying the upper-class imperial warrior as young, brave and sacrificial:

> 'Qui procul hinc,' the legend's writ, –
> The frontier-grave is far away –
> 'Qui ante diem periit:
> Sed miles, sed pro patriâ'[3]

and inevitably to the fore in any action, a practice well learnt in his schooldays:

> Our game was his but yester year;
> We wished him back; we could not know
> The self-same hour we missed him here
> He led the line that broke the foe.[4]

As this stanza from 'The Schoolfellow' makes plain, he also linked, with the most naive but seductive logic, English playing-field with colonial battlefield. He gave public expression to the absolute belief that Anglo-Saxon training for conquest took place on the football pitches and the cricket squares of the English public schools. In this he merely reflected the personal convictions of scores of public schoolboys and their masters, summarized in this statement from the already much-quoted Welldon: 'If there is in the British race, as I think there is, a special aptitude for "taking up the white man's burden" . . . it may be ascribed, above all other causes, to the spirit of organized games.'

For the initiated, there was an uncomplicated relationship between courage with the leather ball and valour with the sword. The bold footballer in his 'mimic wars' demonstrated his heroic potential as a future soldier of Empire:

> A hero we may style
> The Chief in any game
> A hero in a playful war
> But a hero all the same.
>
> A hero who at football
> All boldly meets the foe
> And ever risking broken limbs
> Still fear can never know.[5]

With such credentials and training he would become a worthy guardian of England Overseas:

> Say not 'tis brutal, our noble game
> When it fans our English valour's flame
> How many a charge through the ranks of the foe
> Have been made by a warrior who years ago
> Hurried the leather from hand to hand
> And 'gainst heavy odds made sturdy stand
> 'Neath Old England's banner in every land
> Our football players to guard it, stand.[6]

The need to stand guard in jungle, desert and mountain pass played an important part in the creation of an ideal of boyhood in the schools, which was unashamedly unintellectual, brave and robust. No one personified this ideal better than 'Tom', the creation of the Harrow schoolmaster, Edward Bowen:

> Now that the matches are near,
> Struggle, and terror, and bliss,
> Which is the House of the year?
> Who is the hero of this?
> Tom!
> Tom, who with valour and skill, too,
> Spite of the wind and the hill, too,
> Takes it along sudden and strong,
> Going where Tom has a will to;
> And so let us set up a cheer,
> That Jaffa and Joppa can hear,
> And if a hurrah can waken the Shah,
> Why, then, let us waken him singing, Hurrah.

> Rules that you make, you obey;
> Courage to Honour is true;
> Who is the fairest in play,
> Best and good-temperedest, who?
> Tom!
> Tom, who is sorry and sad, too,
> When there are bruises to add to;
> Why did he crush Jack with a rush?
> Only because that he had to!

Base is the player who stops
Fight, till the fighting is o'er;
Who follows up till he drops,
Panting and limping and sore?
Tom!
Tom, who with scuffle and sprawl, too,
Knows where he carries the ball to;
Ankles and toes! look how he goes!
Through them and out of them all, too![7]

There were similar heroes in the literature of other schools – for example, Jan Rutter in E. W. Hornung's novel of Uppingham, *Father of Men*, and Reginald Owen in R. M. Freeman's novel of Loretto, *Steady and Strong*. Eventually, authors such as R. S. Warren Bell (*Green at Greyhouse*, *Greyhouse Days*, *Tales of Greyhouse*), R. A. H. Goodyear (*The Fifth Form at Beck House*, *The New Boy at Baxtergate*, *Three Austins at St Judes*), P. G. Wodehouse (*A Prefect's Uncle*, *A Tale of St Austin's*, *The Head of Kay's*) and many others, between them created scores of fictional public schools where decent, straight-backed schoolboys performed sterling athletic deeds, more often than not as part of their preparation for shouldering the imperial burden. Many of these writers, no doubt, capitalized on an image and wrote to entertain and so make a living. At the same time both in society and school the purpose of such mythologizing was unequivocal: to preach that courage, stoicism, endurance and determination were the essence of triumphant Darwinian morality.

Proselytism was frequently forceful and direct. Baden-Powell, fresh from the glories of Mafeking, wrote to the pupils of his old preparatory school, Cottesmore School, Brighton, regarding their future responsibility to the Empire:

I should like to tell you that while we are doing hard work here week after week, losing lives, and having very few pleasures, we do it because it is very pleasing, and encouraging to us to go on, when we know our efforts are being appreciated by those at home – and more especially when we know that the boys of England are watching and learning from us so that when their turn comes to do their duty for their country they will know how to do it.

And while you are yet boys is the time to learn to do your duty . . . At football you do your duty not by playing to show yourself off to the onlookers but to obey the orders of the Captain of the team and to back up so that your side win the game.

And you do your duty in carrying out the orders of your masters . . . If you can get into the way of thinking only of doing your duty while you are still boys at school it will come quite naturally to you when you grow up, to continue to do it for your Sovereign and your country, and you will never dream of trying to save your own life if your duty requires you to risk it.

And in thus doing your duty whether it be to the Captain of your team, to your masters, or to your Queen – remember that at the same time you are carrying out a higher work because you are doing your duty to God.[8]

The same proselytism, of course, could quickly become hyperbolic and vainglorious. Minchin's *Our Public Schools. Their Influence on English History*, which E. C. Mack has coolly described as 'more heavily freighted with propaganda' than any other work on the public schools written in the twentieth century, is loaded with sentiments at once grandiloquent and foolish: 'If asked what our muscular Christianity has done,' he wrote with extreme unctuousness, 'we point to the British Empire.'[9] And he went on with a snide thrust at Gallic intellectualism, the *bête noire* of the English 'blood', to argue that it would never have been built up by a nation of logicians. It was as much dependent on physical as on mental vigour. In a marvellously esoteric passage he anticipated Gramsci and his incomprehensible disciples in an absurd fashion wholly of his era: 'From the days of the Olympian games,' he exclaimed, 'there is assuredly nothing more splendidly Greek than the Eton eight in training for Henley. Such thews and sinews must give the hegemony of the world to the country that can produce such athletes.'[10] This admiration for the product went hand in hand with a touching certainty in the purpose of the machine: 'Long before the British public at large, had been fired with a faith in the British Empire, one and indivisible, that was the faith in which every English public-schoolboy was reared.'[11] He then proceeded to chant a stirring paeon to the sons of Charterhouse, Eton, Harrow, Merchant Taylors, Rugby, St

Paul's, Westminster and Winchester, who, trained to uphold the canopy of Empire, represented all that was finest in the public school system.

The blood and battle of imperial conquest fascinated Minchin. This catalogue of Rugbeian warriors was typical of his obsession:

> Out of some hundreds of brave men a few names only can be mentioned here:– Admiral the Earl of Carysfort, the only Old Rugbeian who was present at both the victories of the Nile and of Trafalgar; General Sir Willoughby Cotton, who for forty years took part in almost all the fighting that was going on from Spain to the Punjaub, from Busaco to Chuznee; Sir George Hoste, R.E., and Col. Trevor Wheler, both Waterloo heroes (to mention two only); A. H. Booth, Lieut. in the heroic 73rd, who went down in the Birkenhead on the 26th February, 1852; J. P. Basevi, who died on duty in Kashmir at an altitude of 16,000 feet, from the effects of the rarity of the atmosphere and from exposure; Sir Henry Wilmot, V.C.; H. A. Sarel, fourteen times mentioned in the despatches; General H. W. Adams, mortally wounded at Inkerman; Thomas Kettlewell of the Balaclava Charge, who served through the Crimea and Mutiny; Edward Tomkinson, J. P. Winter, and S. T. Williams, all Balaclava heroes.[12]

He had a Newboltian vision of the chapel. It was the home where the deeds of imperial heroes were recorded, the spot where an Arnold, or someone like him, informed the boys of a wider brotherhood than school or home. In Rugby chapel, he reported selectively to his readers, was to be found 'the Crimean Window, "the Good Centurion" commemorating twenty-five Rugbeians, and the Indian Window commemorating the Old Boys who . . . fell in that terrible struggle'.[13] He filled his brief histories of the schools with stories of death and daring: Hereward Crawfurd Wake of the Bengal Civil Service, the Hero of Arrah, who in the Mutiny held Puckah House against thousands of mutineers, Lieutenant Roberts who attempted to save the guns on the banks of the Tugela in the face of the Boers, Winston Churchill charging with the 21st Lancers at Omdurman and similar stalwarts, were held up for emulation. His message, like that of Newbolt, was noble negation of self:

And the boy-beauty passed from off the face . . .

And thoughts beyond their thoughts the Spirit lent,
And manly tears made mist upon their eyes,
And to them come a great presentiment of
high self-sacrifice.[14]

The Newboltian vision was shared by others. J. A. Cramb, Professor of Modern History at Queen's College, London, at the time of the Boer War, wrote lugubriously in his *Reflection on the Origins and Destiny of Imperial Britain* of youths, 'self-devoted to death' casting away their lives carelessly and contentedly, as if they were of no account. It was ordained:

See through the mists of time, Valhalla, its towers and battlements, uplift themselves, and from their places the phantoms of the mighty heroes of all ages rise to greet these English youths who enter smiling, the blood yet trickling from their wounds! Behold, Achilles turns, unbending from his deep disdain; Rustum, Timoleon, Hannibal, and those of later days who fell at Brunanburh, Senlac, and Trafalgar, turn to welcome the dead whom we have sent thither as the avant-garde of our faith, that in this cause is our destiny, in this the mandate of our fate.[15]

Poet as well as pedagogue took up the mesmeric refrain:

Ever the faith endures,
England, my England:–
Take us and break us: we are yours,
England, my own!
Life is good, and joy runs high
Between English earth and sky:
Death is death; but we shall die
To the Song on your bugles blown, England –
To the stars on your bugles blown![16]

Lady novelists also got in on the act. Maude Diver,[17] the champion of British valour in India, described the North West Frontier as 'a pitiless country, where the line of duty smites the eye at every turn'.[18] Her trilogy in honour of the men of the Frontier Force, *Captain Desmond, V.C.*, *The Great Amulet* and *Desmond's Daughter*, was a celebration of English public school virtues. Her heroes were the officers of the Raj, 'an isolated little community of

Englishmen who played as hard as they worked, and invariably "played the game" '.[19] They might expatiate nostalgically on 'Cup Day at Ascot; a July evening on the upper reaches of the Thames; a punt in a backwater [with] just enough breeze to stir the willows',[20] but they had a pre-ordained submission to a noble purpose; they were the personification of 'the myth of a stern destiny directing Anglo-Saxons to rule over lesser peoples' – stoical in the face of the foolish ingratitude of the ruled, certain of the moral and material benefits they conferred, secure in the strength of their cultural superiority, courageous in their firm suppression of the incomprehensible uprisings of the native.

Ethic and Empire became gloriously and uniquely associated, as few have appreciated better than T. C. Worsley. The highpoint of the imperialist era, he asserted in his merciless philippic, *Barbarians and Philistines*, was the period in which the public schools reached their peak. It was their Golden Age. In it they reached a perfection never to be recaptured. They had shaken down into a dazzling and exciting conformity comprising a self-conscious deification of the barbarian virtues – loyalty, courage and endurance. During this Golden Age they trained upper-class standard-bearers for service in Empire.[21] The close association between service and sacrifice was seldom questioned and frequently implicit. The *Haileyburian*, for example, recorded quite matter-of-factly of an old boy, R. T. Allen, murdered by Burmese dacoits: 'he will be chiefly remembered as having presented the Quarter-Mile Challenge Cup. He was at Balliol College, Oxford, for a year and a half; he rowed in his College eight and distinguished himself on the towing path. Eventually he went abroad, and met his death bravely.'[22]

Subscription to the games ethic was not merely the derivative source of sacrifice; it was the manifestation of the moral supremacy of white Motherland and her Dominions over black, brown and yellow 'races' and ultimately over the Kaiser's Germany. In the nerve and resolution of the man 'who plays "against the clock", either at the crease or in the field', stated Theodore Cook in his *Character and Sportsmanship*, published in 1927, lay the one instinctive factor in the English character which no foreigner would ever vanquish.[23] And this spirit was transmitted when Parsees and Mohammedans played English cricketers at Karachi and when Maoris tested the best of English footballers at Twickenham. 'By such threads,' he argued, 'are the best bonds of union woven!' The unexpressed and unexpressible constitution of the British Empire was not guarded by the sword alone! Cook was an unsubtle philathlete, yet others could be even more simplistic. Perhaps the clearest exposition of the view that sport provided the moral foundation of imperial superiority is to be found in the writings of John Astley Cooper.

In the issue of *Greater Britain* for 15 October 1892 there appeared an impressive list of marquises, lords, knights, bishops, professors, right honourables, colonels and presidents of Oxford and Cambridge sporting clubs. The list included J. E. C. Welldon in his official capacity of headmaster of Harrow School. All espoused the idea of an 'Anglo-Saxon Olympiad'. Cooper was its originator. Welldon wrote to him: 'Your proposed English-speaking festival may prove to be the Olympian Games of a larger world than the Greek.' It was predictable that Welldon should express warm sympathy for Cooper's ambition. Not only activities but also attitudes were promulgated. The 'Olympiad' was a means of promoting a moral bond between the youth of the Empire. Coubertin might have high-minded ambitions for the youth of the world; the imperialist was satisfied with a much more limited ethical conjunction. In a talk entitled 'The Imperial Significance of Games', the Reverend Dr J. R. P. Sclater, for example, declared to the Empire Club of Canada in 1929: 'in our common love of games and in our attitude to them when we play them, we have one of these uniting forces, and that of the strongest kind.'[24] Cohesion, he reminded his audience, did not come, of course, from the game itself but from the common attitudes of the British Commonwealth of Nations:

In the first place, we would rather lose a game than win it unfairly. In the second place, we would rather have respect to the spirit of the law than to its letter, in playing the game. In the third place, we would exact from ourselves and all associated with us a spirit of absolute obedience to the authorities set over us for the moment, never for a moment questioning the umpire. In the fourth place we would, so to speak, play the ball where it lies – an entirely admirable attitude to have in respect to all life's difficulties. In the fifth place we would desire to be among that company who, having started either in a race or a game, go on if we can till we drop dead. In the sixth place we would hope that that spirit would be

> developed amongst us which is not so very greatly concerned for itself, so long as the side on which we are is successful.[25]

Cooper concurred. His own position was set out in an article entitled 'Many Lands – One People' in *Greater Britain* of 15 July 1891.[26] He offered a criticism and a suggestion. Indifference in the homeland and independence in the colonies jeopardized the future of the British race. The Empire might even disintegrate. Yet there was 'a great racial network of a common literature, fine arts, academic studies and athletic exercises'. He proposed, therefore, an object lesson to the European nations and Asiatic races, that though divided by the oceans and inhabiting many lands, the Anglo-Saxons were one people: 'Why not,' he demanded, 'a Pan-Britannic contest of our social pursuits' in which 'Athletic exercises should have a place, for before we are a political, or even a commercial and military people, we are a race of keen sportsmen.'[27]

Strong support followed. William Portus Cullen offered an Australian point of view. Australia was ready and enthusiastic for athletic contests but the further suggestions of mental competitions would not be so readily received: 'it may perhaps seem a barbarous discrimination to support the proposal for a national athletic contest, to the neglect of the more intellectual features of the scheme suggested,' he argued, 'but most of our healthy instincts have been inherited from barbarians. As soon as we underrate them our civilization degenerates.'[28] A former president of the Oxford University Boating Club, appropriately named R. P. P. Rowe, also seized eagerly on the athletic component and, gliding smoothly over the other elements with the excuse that they did not come within his province, stated that although the athletic contest had been placed third in order, it was the one which had attracted the most attention.[29] He was right. It had been endorsed by nearly all the leading newspapers and periodicals. A wide range of dailies, weeklies and monthlies reacted enthusiastically. The *St James Gazette*, for one, singled out athletics for special attention:

> In the Anglo-Saxon heart is implanted a love of sport and of the fierce delight of competition, and already we are accustomed to visits of Australian cricketers and Canadian football players, while no Colonist who is stopping for a while in England would think of missing the Derby or the Boat Race. Strong is the bond of nationality, strong are the ties of

commerce; but stronger than either is the 'union of heart' which comes from devotion to the same forms of recreation.[30]

The Times also saw the opportunity as essentially athletic: 'The proposal for the periodical idea of holding a grand Imperial athletic festival may not be as ambitious as an all-embracing scheme of Imperial Federation. But it is superior in one important respect, that instead of imposing irksome burdens and fetters, it would foster a taste which the Anglo-Saxon race in all corners of the world cultivates with enthusiasm.'[31] The *Manchester Examiner* also approved of the athletic aspect of the festival: 'The proposed gathering would undoubtedly have attractions for the athletic youth of America and Australia. On the river, the running path, and the cricket field our distant cousins have already sufficiently proved that they are no degenerate descendants of the old stock.'[32] It was left to the *Bristol Mercury* to sum up a general sentiment:

> The most popular part of the scheme is, as might have been expected, the athletic section, and such is the modern rage for sports that it would not be surprising to find the suggestions some day or other put into practice. Mr Astley Cooper would have three kinds of contests – rowing, running, and cricket; and he considers that a race between the victors in the Oxford and Cambridge Boat Race and in the Yale and Harvard contest would not only draw spectators, but also strengthen the links of Saxon unity as nothing else can. His object is, in other words, to develop the sentiment of the Anglo-Saxon race through its common passion for sports.[33]

For its part, the wider Anglo-Saxon world was no less enthusiastic and no less partial. The *San Francisco Newsletter* was welcoming:

> The original proposition was for a festival at which the competitors would be restricted to representatives of portions of the British Empire, the main idea being to use the festival as a means towards the very desirable end of making a closer union and establishing a greater sympathy between the Mother Country and her numerous Colonies. This consummation would be in part effected by bringing the people of England and those of the dependencies into close touch, by their competition in the athletic games of the festival. During the discussion of the proposition, it has been suggested that the United States be also invited to send its

champions to any games that might be arranged at which the British athletes would appear. We consider the idea a very good one.[34]

The press of Australia, South Africa and Canada responded in like vein. Even the exceedingly obscure *St Helena Guardian* was inspired and trusted that its corner of the Empire would be represented and that some islander would strive for a leaf of laurel-wreath and uphold the honour of his place of nativity.[35] Only the *Saturday Review* refused to take the idea seriously, sarcastically pointing up difficulties of definition and implementation: 'The Pan-Britannic and Pan-Anglo-Saxon Festival may be dimly conceived if we can imagine the British Association, the Eisteddfod, the Indian National Congress, the Afrikaner Bund, the Marylebone Cricket Club, and the American House of Representatives taking part in a walking match across Salisbury Plain.'[36] It was a prescient opinion. For all the worldwide euphoria, Cooper's idea came to nothing in the short term for reasons of disinclination, expense, apathy and suspicion. But he had sown a seed. The 'blood bond' was consecrated in time with the creation of the Empire Games in 1930.[37]

Despite his setback Cooper did not forsake his views. In fact, he gave them fullest expression in a lecture published in *United Empire* in 1916. It was entitled 'The British Imperial Spirit of Sport and War'.[38] In it the romancer imbued with an image of imperial fraternalism, harmony and cohesion through sport became a crude propagandist for an empire under arms. He paraded the ideological clichés that simple-minded moralists delighted in: 'The spirit of sport has sustained many a healthy and productive oasis in a desert of artificialism and commercialism throughout the British Empire', and 'The underlying philosophy of all our National and Imperial games is not only to produce skill, discipline, loyalty, endurance, steadiness in attack, patience in misfortune, and other physical and mental qualities, but to encourage unselfishness, which is synonymous with good temper, a sense of humour and honour.'[39]

The war, in Cooper's view, was a 'muscular Christian' crusade. The Empire was the 'Holy Land' – not to be regained but preserved. He was elated by the fact that, at a moment when the sporting traditions of a whole people were trembling in the balance, the inbred instinct of fair play came to the fore! 'A true sportsman detests a bully and German Kultur is the antipodes of the British Imperial spirit of sport.'[40] Lion-hearted, clean-fighting heroes were chivalrously wrestling with brutish beasts who had lost their reason. It was the greatest game of all their lives – and it was a game they would win: rough out-of-door games had the edge over the gymnasium. The one produced men, the other automatons. Moreover, Tommy Atkins, he asserted, followed where Tom Brown led. Revealing a casual ignorance of the facilities of Board Schools, he quoted with approbation the curious observation of Edwin Pugh that when the war was over 'it may no longer be said that Armageddon was won exclusively on the playing-fields of the Public Schools, but in the playgrounds of the County Council Schools also'.[41] There, Pugh asserted, in a farcically sanguine assessment of resources and ethos, 'they are taught to box and swim, to play a straight bat, and to tackle their man though he be as big as a house. They are encouraged to get runs as well as marks, and cups and shields as well as scholarships. Above all, they have instilled into them, as well by example as by precept, the principles of fair play.'[42]

The remainder of the article exuded a silly, breezy jingoism in which Cooper sang loudly the praises of the imperial army involved in 'the greater game, the game which virile nations have always loved the best of all'. Flanders became an international pitch on which 'clean-limbed men and boys of British origin' played against a treacherous, hypocritical, lying, cunning and well-organized opponent. All the great and bloody 'games' of the past were reviewed, hideous in their carnage, but proving that a 'sporting, patriotic and healthy people' had survived and would survive again. He could not resist one reference to a past enterprise. The war with Germany, he concluded, had a lesson for the Briton. He would be content in the future to think imperially and confine himself to the British Empire. Cooper failed to see how the German would be tolerated in any contests in the future where square-dealing was a *sine qua non*. He was glad to see the press reviving his old idea of a Pan-Britannic games. In genial sport rested the security of the Empire, and in the spirit of sportsmanship in which imperial forces fought the war lay the future respect of ally and adversary.

Whatever we may think of its crudity, naivety, and pomposity, the evangelism of Newbolt, Baden-Powell, Cramb, Minchin, Diver, Cooper and a host of others appears to have been remarkably effective. Many of the products of the public schools were well matched to imperial and martial requirements. As James Morris has observed in *Pax Britannica*,[43] his elegant and evocative study of the Empire at its zenith, the public schoolboy of the time seemed high-spirited, self-possessed, always ready to rough it, eager for responsibility, and the rarest of his vices was cowardice. The reasons, of course, lay both outside and inside the schools.

In 1900 a group of Old Lorettonian volunteers from their Musselburgh outpost of the English public school system sailed to the early catastrophes of the Boer War. Jaunty with enthusiasm, self-confidence and 'pluck', they sang the praises of their Alma Mater in recognition of a 'Task' done well:

> We thank you for your message,
> And we'll show that we *are true*,
> For you've taught us all the lesson,
> And we'll not be false *to you*.
> Though it won't be soldier-playing
> When we hear the bugle braying,
> You'll not have to blush for the boys that you knew.
>
> We've had to change our colour
> And we may not wear *the red*
> But whether red or khaki
> We'll follow where we're led;
> Though it won't be soldier-playing
> When we hear the bugle braying,
> You'll not have to blush for the boys that you knew.
>
> If the scrums are getting roughish,
> And the hacks are getting free,
> We never fancied whining,
> And in front we'd like to be;
> The world can do without us,
> But we'll know you'll think about us
> So we send you good-bye from the Old Boys at sea.[44]

Several of the earlier quotations are drawn from the *Radleian*, *Cheltonian*, *Haileyburian*, *Eton Chronicle* and *Lorettonian*. This is not fortuitous. Indoctrination into image was, of course, employed as assiduously in the schools as in society. It is illuminating to trace the evolving attitude to imperial expansion in conjunction with an unremitting evangelism in the magazines of the English public school.[45] Examination shows official records of school life to be agents of seduction for an imperial dream of noble service and intoxicating adventure. They were, however, utilitarian as well as ideological tracts. For decades they served on the one hand as colonial travel brochure, army advertisement and farming prospectus and, on the other, as an ideological mouthpiece for 'guileless patriotism' made manifest in the act of shouldering 'the white man's burden'.

Eton, Haileybury and Cheltenham were three famous schools closely linked to imperial destinies during the autumn of Victoria's reign and it is instructive to follow the process of proselytism for the imperial idea in the pages of the *Eton Chronicle*, the *Haileyburian* and the *Cheltonian* between 1875 and 1901.[46] Together they provide a record of firm consciousness of duty, fierce chauvinism, naive romanticism and, occasionally, severe practicality. The early years of publication were years of a parochial search for purpose and identity. Eventually the mundane asserted itself over the pretentious and the vigorous football player won ascendancy over the aspiring man of letters. By the late 1870s a rather tedious formula of reports of house (and other) matches, musical evenings, visiting lecturers, together with occasional moralistic or whimsical narratives, in verse and prose, of schoolboy endeavours on the square or between the posts, was firmly established. There was little sign of the soldier, emigrant and explorer taking and filling schoolboy imaginations in these early years, but slowly there emerged an awareness of exotic places beyond playing-field, classroom and lecture hall, which exerted an ever more compelling attraction.

This early consciousness was unblushingly romantic. There was, as yet, no gubernatorial burden nor divinely ordained role, merely a fascination with strange lands, perfectly illustrated by a verse entitled 'Kafirland' in the *Haileyburian* of 1874. This celebrated the 'wild loveliness' of the Great Karroo, allegedly a landscape of pools fringed with lilies, wooded glens, bright streamlets and great plains, where clematis, jasmin and geraniums flowered in prodigality. The anonymous author expressed the gentle, Shelleyesque desire to escape to this oasis of startling beauty and spacious liberty:

> O eland and guagga and fierce snorting gnu,
> Stretch over its expanse as a limitless sea.
> Away, I am with you – Away! We are free![47]

Swiftly reality encroached on the idyll; the actualities of existence hedged round the escapist fantasies. The terrain of the North West Frontier was far removed from the mythical delights of the African veld: 'The water in many places is ghastly both in taste and smell, being full of salts. The country, too, is so remarkably hideous; there are no trees and no grass, in fact nothing but long stony hills until one reaches the Kadir plain when it becomes a howling wilderness,'[48] reported an Old Haileyburian subaltern to his Alma Mater. And reality took a grimmer form. Deaths from cholera, sunstroke, dysentery and battle in distant countries began to fill the pages of the magazines. Imperial destiny was frequently tragic:

> September 22, at Toungoo, British Burmah, of cholera, Bernard Gwyn Prance, Lieutenant 3rd Madras Native Infantry, fourth son of Courtenay C. Prance, of Evesham, and Haterley Court, Cheltenham, aged 23. (Entered College January, 1876, left December 1880.)
>
> December 18, 1884, at Trincomalie, Ceylon, after a few days' illness, caused by sunstroke, Clement Henry Brereton, Deputy Assistant Commissary General of Ordnance, second and dearly loved son of E. W. Brereton, M.A. of Cheltenham, aged 27 years.
>
> January 17th of wounds, received at the battle of Abu Klea, Lieutenant James Dunbar Guthrie, Royal Horse Artillery, aged 28.[49]

Yet the idyll never quite faded. Inglorious deaths like that of Lieutenant Arthur Clinton Baskerville Mynors of the 60th Rifles, who died of dysentery in Natal during the Zulu Campaign of 1879 without seeing action, were transformed by an act of will of the schoolboy mourners into a romantic and noble end: 'Truly a son of whom, while thus mourning his early death, Eton may speak with some tenderness and pride. His grave is on a grassy slope, amid waving palm trees, looking down towards the sea, over the lonely valley of the Tugela.'[50]

Throughout the last quarter of the nineteenth century a virtually unbroken series of imperial conflicts – the Ashanti War (1874), the Kaffir War (1877), the second and third Afghan Wars (1878 and

1879), the Zulu War (1879), the first Boer War (1881), the Sudan expedition (1884–5) and constant skirmishes on the North West Frontier of India furnished the schools with a host of soldier heroes. Their deeds were eulogized in the magazines. The *Haileyburian* sang of Lieutenants Melvill and Coghill, who fled with the colours from Isandhlwana:

> We found them with the colours of their band,
> Untarnished by the murderous Zulu band;
> And England's mighty bosom glows with pride
> To know how well her gallant striplings died.
>
> Those who would rest the calmest, sure are they
> Whom duty unto death has called away
> Whose glorious deeds through Fame's emblazoning pen
> Inspire the minds and touch the hearts of men.
>
> The fadeless star of many a gory pain
> O'er Isandula's battle gleams again;
> And still for England will her soldiers ride
> To do and die, as Melvill, Coghill died.[51]

And of another Haileybury officer killed a little later, in the Sudan, it asked what were, in effect, a series of rhetorical questions:

> Did his heart's courage fail?
> Felt he no fear?
> Did that brave spirit quail
> Knowing death near? [52]

By 1885, within a short space of ten years, there had developed in the Eton, Haileybury and Cheltenham school magazines an awareness of Empire in the boldest terms of 'glory won and duty done'. The foremost image of the public schoolboy in Empire was defined, and constant: the warrior-patriot. His purpose, as made explicit in wider society, was noble and sacrificial – to fight and die for England's greatness overseas. 'Fifty years have passed,' it was declared at the Haileybury Jubilee Commemorative Dinner in 1912, 'and Haileybury boys have lived and died for their King. And we feel as time grows, and Haileybury becomes an older school, more boys will show that they are ready to live and die for their King.' [53] Obituaries in verse and prose now told of loyal English hearts, strange lands, scorching sun, nostalgic memories of schooldays, gallant conduct and invariably a courageous death. Thus, for example, for the edification and inspiration of its readers, the *Eton Chronicle* proudly recounted the end of Lieutenant Elwes, who fell at the battle of Laing's Nek during the First Boer War after calling to a brother officer: 'Come along, Monck, *Floreat Etona*, we must be in the front rank.'[54] And, in lines reminiscent of Newbolt, the *Cheltonian*, with equal pride, described the death of Lieutenant A. T. Crawford, Royal Artillery, on the North West Frontier, during the general uprising of the Pathan tribes in 1897:

> Only five short days, and full news flashed,
> The Mullah is burning the British fort!
> Ah me! for the thousand hopes are dashed
> As a brave son's boat puts out from the port.
>
> Did he wait for a summons? What! leave his men,
> In the doing of deeds, when the foemen rise?
> He is gone – to the North-west mountain – and then
> Just one fierce fray, and he falls – and dies.
>
> And the fight groans on, till the day is done –
> Brave men, but with one brave leader less!
> His battle is over, his victory won!
> Is it peace, dear lad? And he answers – 'yes'.[55]

It is not too fanciful to assert that many public schoolboys learnt through such unadulterated hero-worship that their proper career lay, as often as not, guarding the farflung conquests of Victorian imperialism with their lives. As the *Cheltonian* asserted:

> Thy sons are noble and brave
> Ready to kill and save
> Though the rewards be grave
> For they honour thee.
> The soldier as he wounded lies,
> Lifts up his cold and glassy eyes
> Upwards to the burning skies
> While a far off voice replies
> 'Cheltonia honours thee'.[56]

Little wonder that E. C. Mack, doyen of historians of the English public school, could conclude that the public school system produced 'responsible, honourable boys, willing to give their lives unquestionably to the preservation of Empire'.[57]

And if the public schoolboy failed to live up to militaristic demands, pointed doggerel made him conscious of his shortcomings and the inferior virtues of 'unwarlike acts':

> While young the pomp and circumstance of war
> And gorgeous panoply possessed my mind
> But I was born beneath a sordid star
> And of my fond desires could nothing find;
> Then said I in my heart, I now will bind
> Myself to worldly travail and to greed
> And in the unwarlike arts I was inclined
> To seek whereon my lazy self to feed.
>
> But this was not sufficient for my need
> Till soon I chanced upon a priceless book
> Wherein I read of many a glorious deed
> Of matchless men; and then I courage took
> To follow in the footsteps of the same
> For secret labour leads to open fame.[58]

On the death of Queen Victoria in 1901 the *Eton Chronicle* published this verse, 'In Memoriam':

> Firm in her native strength, the British Oak
> Abides unmoved, nor fears the tempest's stroke;
> Her spreading boughs, her trunk's majestic girth,
> Meet emblem of an Empire wide as Earth.
> Well fitted she to symbolize aright
> Britannia's triumph and Britannia's might.[59]

It could not have been written at Victoria's accession. The transformation in awareness of 'the Realm beyond the sea', which occurred in the public schools in the last quarter of the nineteenth century, was neatly summed up by Edward Lyttelton, headmaster of Haileybury, at the school speech-day of 1900. 'In my time,' he declared, reflecting on his own Etonian schooldays in the early seventies, 'we had not the faintest notion of what was going on outside England, and did not care in the least. Nowadays we are no sooner relieved from anxiety in one portion of the globe than we get tidings just as thrilling and likely to last just as long as those we experienced elsewhere.'[60] Lyttelton was one among many who never failed, when it was deemed appropriate, to give expression to a sincere, if arrogant, altruism implicit in many imperial careers. In his 'Farewell Sermon' to his Haileyburians in 1905, for example, he urged the pupils to 'prepare for service',[61] and go where they could do the greatest good. For Haileyburians, with their historical contacts with India, this meant duty on the sub-continent. And Lyttelton left his pupils in no doubt as to the value of such work. The administration of India was, in his view, 'perhaps the greatest and most interesting of all achievements of Englishmen in the matter of political government'.[62]

This concept of imperial service was honed and rehoned by public schoolmasters and received its sharpest expression in the years before the First World War. In the Haileybury archives there is to be found an anonymous sermon preached at the opening of new classrooms in 1908 which gives a good idea of the strength of the conviction which eventually typified the schools. 'For those who have the strength,' the unknown preacher averred, 'the spirit of the school leads upwards to the crags of duty.' The going, he warned, would be hard and slippery, but with a good guide, a strong heart, heads steadied with responsibility, Haileyburians would find the summit. Tradition demanded it:

> The name you bear has its brightness from the land where from Plassey to Dargai, British men have fought against odds – and have won in Empire. Men of old Haileybury endured the solitude and deadly monotony of India; they could stand alone; they could rule provinces: and men of the new Haileybury should be strong to do like.[63]

The same fervour and certainty of belief in the nobility of the imperial enterprise is apparent in a speech delivered to the pupils of Cheltenham College by Sir Walter Lawrence,[64] the distinguished Indian civil servant, four years later. India was the tied-house of Cheltenham College, he reminded his listeners, and went on to argue that the finest work was service, and Cheltenham boys should recognize that, as citizens of a great Empire, they must serve in some capacity or other. He somewhat optimistically asserted that if the idea of imperial duty would influence and illuminate their work, if they would point the way and march along the path of loyalty, devotion and patriotism, then the mighty British Empire would never fall![65] In the same year the theme 'Haileybury and Empire' reverberated through the pages of the special Jubilee supplement to the *Haileyburian*. Diplomats, clerks, soldiers and other establishment figures saluted the contribution to Empire of the public schoolboy in general, and Haileyburians in particular. An ambassador hoped the service of the Empire would ever fire the imagination of the boys, and that the call of Island England would always find a Haileybury contingent ready; a major-general urged Haileyburians not to idle at home but to do a hand's turn for the Empire and keep in mind the glory of the imperial idea; and a bishop called for 'princely service in all lands' in the style of 'pure Christian manliness'.[66]

The previous year the magazine had performed the rare act of drawing the attention of its readers to an editorial in a national newspaper, the *Standard*, entitled 'The Unnoticed Stranger', praising both its idealism and veracity. The 'Stranger' was none other than the young ruler of Empire, at home on leave; unostentatious and unsung. The Empire, the editorial stated, was run by unpretentious and unknown schoolboys. The subalterns of the imperial corps, it continued, with a surfeit of romantic imagery, were not to be found on the tourist routes of India but in less inviting and accessible places: 'in some lonely sentry-box on the Empire's frontier, up there on the Khaiber or the Bolan, there, a clean-cheeked, smooth-haired boy will handle his half hundred wind-baked ruffians as if they were the Second Eleven and he their Captain.'[67] In such forgotten places of the earth the English public schoolboy was to be discovered, slowly bringing savage barbarism and anarchy to settled order and civilized existence. Such a career, it concluded, with the *Haileyburian*'s full approval, was 'valuable, laborious, self-sacrificing'.

The image of imperial careers in the late nineteenth-century public schools was not exclusively moralistic and sacrificial. There was also a deliberate and sustained attempt to appeal to a spirit of adventure. The magazines regularly contained thrilling tales of old boys in jungle, savannah and desert with titles which could have graced the novels of Kingston, Henty and Rider Haggard – *One Hundred Days Upon the Nile*; *Further Adventures from Kandahar*; *Through Africa to Lake Nyasa*; *With the Chitral Relief Force by a Subaltern*. Soldier heroes fought, won and lived and either returned to the school to recount their deeds, albeit modestly, and thus inspire imitation, or sent the school editor vivid descriptions of action in Zululand, Afghanistan, Sudan, Benin, Burma and many other places.[68] Explorers also returned to be fêted.[69] Links between school and Empire were also maintained through the curious expedient of the regular provision of reports of nostalgic old boy dinners in obscure and less obscure parts of the Empire. One Old Etonian writing from Calcutta, for instance, described the table there for the Fourth of June celebrations of 1880 as 'arranged with the exquisite harmonies of Eton blue'. The servants wore complementary costumes and the evening was filled with reminiscences of days past interspersed with toasts to 'Cricket' and 'The Boats' and rounded off, of course, with 'The Boating Song'.[70] Another Etonian in Ceylon supplied his old school with a list of old boy guests for the Fourth of June celebrations of 1888. It offers a fascinating glimpse of the variety of imperial occupations. Present were:

J. M. Thring, Esq.	*Planter*
Captain Morland, 5th Lancers	*A.D.C. to the Major General commanding the forces*
S. M. Burrows, Esq.	*Assistant Government Agent*
Captain Blackburn, Argyll & Sutherland Highlanders	
E. Christian, Esq.	*Firm of Messrs Murray, Robertson Ltd*
Lieutenant Sutherland, Argyll & Sutherland Highlanders	
G. Alston, Esq.	*Planter*
W. G. Selwyn, Esq.	*Private Secretary to the Governor*[71]

The *Haileyburian* for its part regaled its readers with details of Haileyburian gatherings in such places as Calcutta, Ootacamund, Kuala Lumpur, Peshawar, Quetta and Isahore, while the *Cheltonian* in turn included meetings in Darjeeling, Rangoon, Secunderabad, Negagh and Mhow.

The attempt to glamorize imperial life and to highlight its attractions can be clearly seen in this quite typical extract from 'Old Haileyburian News' in the school magazine:

Old Haileyburians in India have been well to the fore in games and sports. During the last cricket season (November to March), the Rawalpindi Eleven, one of the best in the country (this cantonment being one of the largest in India), had five O.H.s playing for it. E. G. Harrison, W. M. Watson (Duke of Wellington's Regiment), W. G. Walker (Suffolk Regiment), F. H. Montresor (Royal Sussex Regiment), A. C. Currie (Royal Artillery), the latter of whom played regularly. C. D. Bruce (Duke of Wellington's Regiment), a member of last year's eleven, would also have played had he not left the station, which he did on appointment as Aide-de-Camp to the General Officer commanding Sirhind Division at Umballa. G. W. Rawlins also played for Peshawar and C. B. Watkins for Calcutta. N. Chenery (11th Bengal Lancers), and C. W. Rawlings (12th Bengal Cavalry) are both playing for their respective regiments. At a meeting of the North Punjab Fishing Club last cold weather C. H. de I. Lacey was elected Hon. Secretary.[72]

James Morris has caught incomparably the wider evocations of the romance of imperialism that many old boys sought to transmit, rather more inadequately, to their young successors at home:

The smell of the veldt, the illicit delight of a sabre-slash in the sunshine, a drum beat out of the forested hills . . . the wheezing breath of your dear old bearer, as he lit the juniper fire in the morning, and brought the teapot steaming to your bed, the never-sated excitement of tigers, the pride of red tunic and swagger stick in the bazaars, the Colonel's lady, in your spanking tonga through the cantonment . . . The cloud of dust and jingle of accoutrement, as the dispatch rider swept in with an ultimatum for the paramount chief . . .[73]

'Strive to be ready when the call shall come,' wrote the Etonian George Drage in his book *Eton and Empire*,[74] and he continued, 'you should conquer and rule others . . . you shall do your duty.' Such exhortations had their effect; this representative page from 'Occasional Notes' in the *Cheltonian*, which provided news of old boys, offers a glimpse of how well Cheltenham boys responded:

Lieut.-Colonel W. G. Brancker, who died on May 22, became Lieutenant in the Royal Artillery 6th March, 1856, Captain 10th March 1866, Major 16th January, 1875, Lieut. Colonel 16th January, 1882. He served with the expedition to China in 1860 and was present at Sinho, Tangku, and capture of the Taku forts (Medal with Clasp). Served in the

Egyptian War of 1882, in command of a Battery of Royal Artillery (mentioned in despatches, C.B. Medal, 3rd class of the Medjidie, and Khedive's Star). Colonel Brancker entered College, August 1847, and left Midsummer, 1854.

Royal Artillery-Major and Brevet Lieut.-Colonel P. T. H. Taylor (late Bengal), Supernumerary to the Establishment, and Major J. G. Pollock (late Madras), to be colonels.

Captain C. M. Western to be Major. Lieutenant R. T. Roberts to be Captain.

Major and Brevet Lieut.-Colonels J. H. Green, Bengal Staff Corps, and A. Conolly, Bengal Staff Corps, to be colonels. Captain Laurence Litchfield Steele, of the East Yorkshire Regiment, has been appointed an extra Aide de Camp to Major Gen. Sir C. Pearson, commanding the troops in the West Indies.

Lieutenant Arthur Phayre, of the Bombay Cavalry, has been appointed Aide de Camp on the Staff of Lord Reay, Governor of Bombay.

A. H. T. Martindale to be Captain of the Bangalore Rifle Volunteers.

F. H. B. Commeline, South Lancashire Regiment, to be Wing Officer, 19th Punjab Infantry.[75]

Some years after the death of Victoria the *Haileyburian* published details of members of the Old Haileyburian Society in the Empire. They were to be found in India and Ceylon (169), South Africa and Rhodesia (43), Canada (38), Central and West Africa (19), Australia (15), Egypt (12), New Zealand (10), Burma (10), West Indies (7), Malta (7), Assam (3), and Borneo (1).[76] A more complete illustration of Haileybury's involvement in the Empire is provided by the table below:[77]

HAILEYBURY: FIVE-YEAR SAMPLE OF CAREERS, 1875–1900

	ARMY	ARMY IN EMPIRE	EMPIRE	OTHER	NO DETAILS
1875	15	8	15	40	23
1880	23	16	29	75	21
1885	27	6	24	60	22
1890	13	3	32	37	30
1895	26	9	23	49	17
1900	14	8	34	52	26

It should be remembered, of course, that those who took up army careers served for considerable periods in the Empire. In India, for example, one third of the military forces in the late nineteenth century was made up of the British Army. In 1897 there were some 212,000 officers and men in the regular army; about 72,000 were in India, 32,000 in colonial stations and the remainder at home.[78]

As Patrick Dunae has described so attractively, Victorian upper-class, younger sons flocked to the rich farmlands of Canada.[79] They also journeyed to New Zealand, Australia and South Africa in search of a good living on the land. As early as 1873 *Punch* published 'a schoolboy petition', ostensibly from a rather stupid public schoolboy with plenty of compensatory muscle, who observed that while he was not too intelligent:

> With my youth and my strength,
> I would go any length,
> To save the dear Governor's pocket;
> To Australia, New Zealand
> Or some other free land,
> If they send me, I'm off like a rocket.[80]

Emigration was constantly urged on Etonians, Haileyburians and Cheltonians of the eighties and nineties by such pioneers. And the romanticism of much of the adulation of the imperial warrior was offset up to a point by the realism of those who promoted the life of the pioneer farmer. Old boys wrote from sheep stations in Queensland, fruit farms in Victoria, ranches in Manitoba and plantations in Kenya, encouraging settlement but offering clear warnings about the rugged conditions, the need for self-reliance, the long hours and the hard work. One Old Etonian 'who went to seek his fortune in Australia' wrote, 'You will be glad to hear I like the life out here very much. Of course, it is very different from Eton life, but when one comes so far you must make up your mind to rough it.'[81] An Old Haileyburian sent a similar message to his old school from the other side of the world: 'Those who don't mind roughing it, and like an outdoor life with plenty of sport, cannot do better than come out to Canada, and go in for farming and stock raising.'[82] Frequently such advocates provided fulsome details of facilities and prospects. In 1885, for example, the *Cheltonian* contained a letter from Taranaki, New Zealand, providing information on the climate, scenery, farming conditions, social life, cost of living and investment possibilities for gentlemen farmers with capital. Many Old Cheltonians were in the area, the writer remarked by way of encouragement, and inexperience was no handicap as there were many farmers willing to educate gentlemen's sons in colonial farming.[83]

Nevertheless, while perusal of the magazines of these three famous schools reveals that in imperial affairs simple romanticism was balanced to a degree by hard-headed pragmatism, the predominant theme was duty. The *beau idéal* was the warrior and the ultimate glory, sacrificial. This verse from an elegy for General Gordon in the *Cheltonian* celebrates more than the hero of Khartoum:

> Gone from our sight, in our heart he still lingers;
> Crown of self-sacrifice – death – he has won;
> Martyr to duty, with pitiless finger,
> Beckoning onwards, our hero has gone.[84]

In urging the 'crown of self-sacrifice' on its youthful readers, the magazine of the English public school revealed itself as a vehicle for unremitting and unswerving loyalty to the concept of imperialism. The righteousness of the enterprise was never in question. Ethnocentrism, chauvinism and orthodoxy combined to ensure purposeful commitment. The magazines illustrate at one and the same time a powerful instrument of indoctrination at work and the ideological preoccupations of English late Victorian upper-class society.

The effectiveness of the indoctrination is seen in the pages that follow: public school administrator, missionary and educationist spread throughout the imperial world, more often than not imbued with a sense of moral commitment and muscular enthusiasm. They subscribed to both 'playing the game' and playing games – the administrator and soldier in the interest of inculcating obeisance, the missionary and educationist in the belief that out of manliness came morality. However, subscription to the ethic was not only a means of imperial moral armament and political control: it was frequently a source of successful selection to imperial careers themselves. Nowhere was this more apparent than in the Sudan Political Service, now to be considered.

3

MANLY CHAPS IN CONTROL

Blues and Blacks in the Sudan

I

The Sudan Political Service[1] was created in 1899. In the opinion of one, perhaps partial, observer, by the 1930s it had become 'the true successor in merit to the I.C.S.'[2] and an imperial administrative *corps d'élite*.[3] The origins of the Service lay in the British destruction of Mahdism at the end of the nineteenth century. On 2 September 1898 Kitchener defeated the forces of the Mahdi at Omdurman and the Sudan was reoccupied by British and Egyptian forces. Almost immediately 'Kitchener and his lieutenants – working under the general direction of Cromer [British Agent in Egypt], turned their attention to the establishment of the new Sudan administration.'[4] In fact this administration posed a major political problem. Egypt, now under the 'protection' of Britain, had conquered the country early in the nineteenth century and Egyptian troops under British officers had played a large part in the defeat of the Mahdists. However, Britain had no wish to return the Sudan to the corrupt and inefficient rule of the Egyptians. At the same time direct annexation would have aroused considerable resentment in Europe and yet control of the upper waters of the Nile – the life-blood of Egypt – by a foreign power could not be entertained. Resolution of the problem of control was skilfully achieved by the drafting of the Condominium Agreement of 1899. This formed the constitutional charter of the Sudan and it 'became, de jure, a separate and autonomous state distinct from and independent of

Egypt and any other country – a condominium into which were merged the rights of Great Britain and Egypt alike'.[5]

Under this agreement the chief administrator was the British Governor-General – the supreme military and civil commander. At Khartoum, the headquarters of the central government, he was attended by British military and civil advisers. Following the practice of both Egyptian and Mahdist, the country was divided into provinces, each with its British Governor. The provinces in turn were divided into districts administered by Egyptian *mamurs* monitored by British inspectors.

Initially provincial governors and inspectors were recruited from Britsh officers in the Egyptian Army.[6] However, Lord Cromer was of the opinion that this arrangement had substantial disadvantages: above all, British officers, who could be recalled by the War Office, could not ensure continuity of service; but in addition, Cromer alleged, they knew little of the language and customs of the people and consequently were too reliant on their Egyptian subordinates. Furthermore, he considered army officers inflexible martinets and therefore unsuitable administrators.[7] Cromer believed that what was required for the Sudan was a cadre of civilian administrators who would make a career of service to the country. In his view a ready supply of first-class recruits were at hand due to the happy fact that

> the system of education adopted at our Public Schools . . . is of a nature to turn out a number of young men who are admirable agents in the execution of an imperial policy. The German, the Frenchman, and others may be, and sometimes are, better educated, but any defects on the score of technical knowledge are amply compensated by the governing powers, the willingness to assume responsibility, and the versatility under strange circumstances in which the Anglo-Saxon, trained in the free atmosphere, which develops individualism, excels beyond all other nations.[8]

He set about recruiting 'active young men, endowed with good health, high character, and fair abilities' from Oxford and Cambridge, at this time largely appendages of the public school system.[9] Six 'Oxbridge' civilians were recruited in 1901 and a few more added each year. In this way the Sudan Political Service[10] was created.

From its inception it was a *corps d'élite*: conditions of service were attractive. There was extensive leave each year, retirement was possible after twenty years, pay was good, expenses were generous and service in the oppressive climatic conditions of the south counted as double. Clearly, as Martin has written, 'making every allowance for the few drawbacks which may be admitted to exist in the Sudan Government Service as in all other careers of this character, it is undoubtedly one of the finest, that without capital, interest and years of hope deferred, lie within reach of the educated and hard-working young Englishman.'[11] In consequence there was never a shortage of recruits and many applicants were rejected.[12]

The method of selection for the Service was, and was to remain, unusual and significant. There was no competitive examination – by 1900 the usual method of entry into both the Home and Indian Civil Services. Selection was by interview, first by appointed university 'dons' and then by a board of serving members. The system was, in fact, a return to the patronage system of the pre-Northcote-Trevelyan era. The successful candidate, however, while fully aware of the retrogressive nature of the system, could be well satisfied with the process: 'I would say that it went against almost all the accepted criteria – just a couple of interviews. But the men who interviewed us were sufficiently experienced and gifted judges of character to carry it off.'[13] The experience of Sir Harold MacMichael,[14] a leading member of the Service, was typical and is worth recording in full:

> The method of recruitment of civilians for the 'Political Service' was, from first to last, informal and sensible, with no competitive examination and no fixed rules beyond observance of Lord Cromer's original criterion by the Selection Board. By way of illustration I may perhaps be allowed to cite my own case. Early in 1903 I was sent a brass seal from Delhi as a memento of the Durbar.
>
> At the time I was an under-graduate at Cambridge, and I asked someone how best to discover what the inscription meant. I was advised to take it to Professor E. G. Browne, the great orientalist . . . Off I went to Pembroke and with trepidation knocked at the great man's door. Bidden to enter, I found him at his desk with a heap of papers before him. As I entered he covered them up and said 'Have you come about the Egyptian and Sudan Civil Service?' I replied that I had never heard of it and explained my object. He told me all I wanted to know . . . Finally,

> as I was leaving, I asked him what was this Egyptian and Sudan Civil Service to which he had referred as I came in. He told me that he at Cambridge, and Professor Margoliouth at Oxford, had been asked by Lord Cromer to look out for a few suitable young men to go each year to either country, that there was no competitive examination but only a Selection Board before which likely candidates would be summoned to appear in London . . . I explained that I was working for the 'Indian Civil', as well as for my tripos, with little hope of succeeding in both: might I apply also for the service which he was sponsoring while continuing to work for the rest? Professor Browne welcomed my doing so and gave me a form to fill up. I did this, was in due course summoned before the Board presided over by Sir Reginald Wingate and was one of those selected.[15]

Recruiters looked for character, an honours degree and athletic distinction. Athletic distinction was especially valued. G. R. F. Bredin has observed: 'The Selection Board which interviewed candidates for the Sudan Political Service on which I served several times, attached considerable importance to the athletic records of the individual candidates.' He considered this sensible: 'Such activity was regarded as an indication not only of physical fitness (important in a climate which was often unhealthy) but of personality, initiative and capacity for judgement and control of subordinates.'[16] In the words of the distinguished colonial historian, A. H. M. Kirk-Greene, the transparent emphasis of the service 'on the recruitment of what was believed to represent the epitome of British imperial leadership among the men-on-the-spot, modest honours graduates with a high capacity for organized games' earned the Sudan 'the sobriquet of "the Land of Blacks ruled by Blues".'[17]

It would seem that such an Oxbridge 'closed-shop' recruiting procedure strongly favoured the self-assured, hardy products which the Edwardian and later public schools – 'preparatory schools' for the ancient universities – excelled at producing. And, as this chapter will reveal, this was indeed the case. But it will reveal more. While athletic ability was undoubtedly important for selection, the frequently approved and somewhat malicious aphorism mentioned above, that the Sudan was a nation of blacks ruled by Oxbridge blues, will be seen to be something of an exaggeration but to contain more than a grain of truth. Similarly the claim that members of the Service had their roots in the English countryside and were consequently squirearchical in attitude and approach to the Sudanese people will be shown to be somewhat wide of the mark.[18] Members were mostly public school products from suburban backgrounds with public school values and habits. They came from a wide range of schools, but predominantly from those well established in image by the end of Victoria's reign. They were the 'best' types of the system rather than the exclusive products of certain schools. In the main, they exemplified the period virtues of the games-field and river. In consequence, one commentator wrote of the Sudan in the 1930s, 'everywhere one went the world of athletics was upheld'.[19]

II

As has been already stated in Chapter Two, it is generally accepted that public schoolboys ruled the British Empire,[20] but our knowledge has not yet proceeded much beyond this generalization. What schools supplied these boys? Was there a cadre of recruits from select schools similar to the military cadre from such schools as Wellington, Cheltenham and Harrow that policed the Empire? What was the effect on public school recruitment to colonial service of the growing numbers of able state-educated in the twentieth century, who certainly aroused anxiety in even the most prestigious schools?[21] We know little about such matters. The close analysis of membership of the Sudan Political Service in this chapter throws some light on these questions, and in addition supplies specific detail about imperial careers to offset vague generalization.

In part, useful tools (suitably adapted) for answering the first two questions raised above are provided in John Honey's recent study of the public school system, *Tom Brown's Universe*.[22] Honey was concerned *inter alia* with discovering which secondary schools were clearly recognized as public schools by the end of Victoria's reign. He used a novel and sophisticated process of analysis to arrive at an answer: 'the most useful criterion for the classification of schools whose members would have accepted each other as members of the "public schools community" before 1902 is a consideration of which schools interacted with one another.'[23] The ideological dominance of athleticism in the public schools of the period[24] meant that the most significant evidence of interaction was provided by games and sports competitions such as rowing, shooting, athletics, fencing and gymnastics, but competition for higher school certificates, university scholarships and army examinations also provided more marginal interaction opportunities. Honey estimated that by 1897 there were some 600 schools in Britain with pupils aged eighteen or over,[25] and drew up three tables of actual and possible public schools circa 1880–1902. The first table, comprising sixty-four major public schools, is referred to here as 'The Early Leading Schools'; the forty lesser schools of Honey's second table are referred to as 'The Early Lesser Schools'; and the sixty 'fringe' schools of Honey's third table are referred to as 'The Peripheral Schools'. Over and above the schools considered in these tables, Honey provided details of eighty-one further schools existing before 1902 and treated as public schools by mid twentieth-century commentators such as Kelsall (1958) and Banks (1954). These schools are referred to here as 'The Recent Schools'. Finally we must add a list of twenty-five schools widely recognized as public schools in the second half of the twentieth century, and referred to here as 'The More Recent Schools'.

Honey, of course, with his interaction analysis has provided a means of assessing both the absolute and relative status of the public schools between *1880 and 1902*. However, he has also provided material of value in the investigation below of the educational backgrounds of members of the Sudan Political Service recruited over the following fifty years. If his groupings are *collapsed* and adapted with the early leading and lesser schools grouped together and labelled 'Early Established Public Schools', and juxtaposed with the 'peripheral', 'recent' and 'more recent' schools similarly grouped together and labelled 'Later Public and Peripheral Schools' we have two broad categories of schools. This arrangement, as we shall shortly see, enables us to locate clear preference in the selection of members of the Sudan Political Service between 1899 and 1952.

Now that we have determined these various categories of public schools, we can allocate in Table I opposite the schools attended by

Table 1. PUBLIC SCHOOLS PROVIDING RECRUITS TO THE SUDAN POLITICAL SERVICE 1899–1952

EARLY ESTABLISHED PUBLIC SCHOOLS						LATER PUBLIC AND PERIPHERAL SCHOOLS					
Early leading schools				*Early lesser schools*		*Early peripheral schools*		*Recent schools*		*More recent schools*	
Aldenham	2	Loretto	1	Bromsgrove	2	Birkenhead School	1	Ampleforth	1	Cardiff High School	2
Bath	1	Malvern	3	Christ's Hospital	7	Exeter School	1	Bloxham	1	Gordonstoun	1
Bedford	4	Marlborough	19	Denstone	1	George Watson's	1	Downside	1	Hampton G.S.	1
Berkhamsted	3	Merchant Taylors	5	Durham	3	Hymer's College	1	Douai	1	Stowe	1
Blundells	3	Merchison	2	Giggleswick	2	Monkton Coombe	4	Glasgow Academy	2	Weymouth, St George's	1
Bradfield	2	Oundle	2	Llandovery	2	Newcastle High School, Under Lyme	1	Wellington School	1	Robert Gordon's	1
Brighton	1	Radley	4	Leeds Grammar School	2	St Bees	3				
Charterhouse	14	Reading	1	Liverpool College	1	Taunton	1				
Cheltenham	7	Repton	5	Mill Hill	2	Trent College	1				
City of London	1	Rossall	5	Monmouth	1	Wyggeston G.S.	1				
Clifton	8	Rugby	20	Perse School	1	Dean Close	1				
Cranleigh	1	Sherborne	4	Sedbergh	7						
Dover	1	Shrewsbury	9	St Peter's, York	2						
Dulwich	1	St Edward's, Oxford	3	Sutton Valence	5						
Edinburgh Academy	15	St John's, Leatherhead	2								
Eton	21	St Lawrence's, Ramsgate	2								
Felsted	1	St Paul's	3								
Fettes	1	Tonbridge	4								
Forest	1	United Services College	1								
Glenalmond	6	University College School	1								
Haileybury	12	Uppingham	3								
Harrow	7	Warwick School	1								
Highgate	1	Wellington	8								
Hurstpierpoint	1	Westminster	3								
King William's College	1	Winchester	30								
King's School, Canterbury	1										
Lancing	3										

members of the Service to their respective groupings. The preference is unmistakable.

In the later years of its existence the Service included former pupils of several 'colonial' schools: Geelong G.S. (2), Houghton College, Johannesburg (1), Saint Andrew's, Grahamstown (2), Sydney G.S. (1), the English School, Cairo (1), and Wellington College, New Zealand (1). It also included a small group of men who had attended non-public schools. These schools are listed in Table 2.

Table 2. NON-PUBLIC SCHOOLS WITH FORMER PUPILS IN THE SUDAN POLITICAL SERVICE

School		School	
Aberlour School	1	John Street School, Glasgow	1
Arlington House	1	Humberston Foundation School	1
Brighton, Hove and Sussex G.S.	1	King Edward VI G.S., Totnes	1
Canford	1	Magnus School	1
Campbeltown G.S.	1	Maidenhead	1
Dalziel School	1	New College School, Wakefield	1
Dollar Academy	1	Parkstone School	1
Duke's School	1	St Thomas of Canterbury	1
Dundee H.S.	2	St Peter's, Southborne	1
Golfe's G.S.	1	Vardean School	1
		Liverpool Institute	1

Recruits to the Sudan Political Service in the fifty-seven years of its existence numbered 393. It is now possible to classify these members in terms of their schooling as follows:

Early established public schools	Early leading schools	264
	Early lesser schools	38
Later public and peripheral schools	Peripheral schools	16
	Recent schools	8
	More recent schools	7
Non-public and colonial	Non-public schools	21
	'Colonial' schools	8

N.B. There are no details available of the schools attended by 31 members of the Service.

What is abundantly clear from these details of the members' schools is the solid preference that the Service had, throughout the whole of its existence, for boys from the public school system. This system provided 332 (91·7%) out of the 362 members whose schools are known. What is also obvious is the equally clear preference that the Service had for pupils from schools *firmly established as public schools by 1902*. These comprise 302 or over three quarters of all recruits. The main reason is not hard to find. This group of schools included those which were undoubtedly the most famous not only in the fifty years prior to Victoria's death, but in the subsequent fifty years. In this context it is interesting to note the substantial representation in the Service from the 'Great Public Schools' or Clarendon schools. Recruits from the nine famous Clarendon schools comprise 112 (33·7%) of the 332 members from the public schools, and 37·1% of members from the early established schools. In addition, three of these schools – Eton (21), Rugby (20), and Winchester (30) – provided three of the four highest individual contributions. Of the other public schools only Marlborough could match them, with 19 members of the Service.

These statistics reveal not only the firm partiality that the Service had for public schoolboys and its substantial lack of interest in the state-educated throughout the fifty-six years of imperial administration in the Sudan, but its strong preference for pupils from schools of early unequivocal status. In short, there was discrimination not only between private and state-educated but within the private system itself – the schools of early (and in many cases subsequent) pre-eminence winning most favour. A state of affairs neatly summarized by one of the few grammar schoolboys to win entry to the Service, who in the more flexible post-war years won admission by virtue of his war record: 'The Sudan Political Service had "talent" scouts in Oxford and Cambridge. The particular individual who I learnt later was the talent scout at Oxford had no regard for me . . . because I did not play games or come from one of the leading public schools.'[26]

III

If the total period of recruitment from 1899 to 1952 is divided into three separate periods:

Period I: Creation of the Service to the end of the Great War (1899–1939)
Period II: Between the wars (1919–39)
Period III: Second World War to Independence (1940–52)

and school representation is broken down accordingly, as in Table 3, further interesting findings regarding the composition of the Service emerge:

Table 3

	Schools	PERIOD I (1899–1918)	PERIOD II (1919–39)	PERIOD III (1940–52)	TOTAL
Early established public schools	Early leading schools	67	157	40	264
	Early lesser schools	8	20	10	38
Later public and other schools	Peripheral	4	10	2	16
	Recent schools	1	4	3	8
	More recent schools		2	5	7
Colonial and non-public schools	'Colonial'		4	4	8
	Non-public	1	7	13	21
	No details	10	20	1	31
		91	224	78	393

Nicolson and Hughes are of the view that the 'best' schools lost interest in colonial careers after the Great War.[27] *This is not apparent in the case of the Sudan Political Service.* As Table 3 reveals, interest only began to wane after 1945. In fact, from 1919 to 1939 recruitment from distinguished schools such as Winchester (18), Eton (11), Marlborough (10), Charterhouse (8) and Harrow (5) was substantially in excess of recruitment from less famous schools such as Durham (1), Denstone (1), Bromsgrove (1), Exeter (1) and George Watson's (1). At the same time recruitment did gradually widen during the second period to include 'colonial' and non-public schools. In consequence, the early leading schools were slightly less prominent – 157 (70·1%) as against 47 (21%) – than in the earlier period when the corresponding figures were 67 (73·6%) as against 14 (15·4%). The Selection Board was casting its net a little wider and a process of 'inclusion' now began which became more pronounced in the third period (1940–52), when representation from non-public schools rose to 13 (16·7%) from 8 (3·6%) in the period 1919 to 1939, and the representation from the early leading schools fell yet again to 40 (51·3% of the total number recruited).

The reasons for the principal absorption of pupils from less well-established or less prestigious schools are not wholly clear. Unfortunately, details of the number, background and schooling of applicants as distinct from recruits are not available. Such information would allow a much clearer picture of selection preference, long-term support from famous schools and the full extent of the increasing popularity of the Service among less famous schools. A number of points should be made, however, which might throw some light on the situation. The number of recruits increased considerably during the period 1919–39.[28] While, as we have already seen, the number from the early leading schools held up well during this period, it may well be that the relatively large expansion of the Service offered opportunities to those from other schools which would not otherwise have been available.[29] The fact that the public school system now had a standard accent and a common set of values and mannerisms would have aided assimilation and made exclusion increasingly more difficult, and perhaps even unnecessary. In addition, absorption was probably helped by the fact that occupational opportunities had greatly widened during the period between the wars,[30] which no doubt reduced the interest in the Service of some from the best schools, who by virtue of their schooling were more acceptable than others to the new employers.[31] Finally, attendance at the less distinguished schools could be (and was) offset by a respectable university career, particularly if it included athletic accomplishments. A 'blue' (and occasionally its equivalent elsewhere) could overcome the disadvantage of a humble schooling. And 'blues' from such backgrounds were not slow to take advantage of the privileges their accomplishments brought them.[32] In this context it is interesting to note throughout the whole existence of the Service, but especially in the latter stages, the relatively high number of Scottish members in contrast to those from Wales and Ireland. Of course, in part, this reflects the greater number of public schools in Scotland, as Table 4 opposite demonstrates, but at the same time it should not be overlooked that more 'non-public school' Scots gained access to the Sudan administration than any other Celtic nation. As Table 2 above reveals, of the 21 non-public schools which provided recruits to the Service, 13 were English, 7 were Scottish and 1 was Irish. Furthermore, while recruits from Scottish universities were not unknown in the Service, *not a single student* was recruited to the Sudan Political Service at any time in its existence from the English provincial universities or university colleges. This exclusion was apparently borne meekly by the Anglo-Saxon. The Irish Celt was less docile.[33] It is noticeable that, for reasons which are not wholly clear, candidates to the Service from Scottish state schools and universities were reasonably acceptable to the Selection Board and that Scots took full advantage of this imperial opportunity.[34]

IV

H. C. Jackson, an early entrant to the Service, in his evocative description of the life of a civil officer in the Sudan, wrote of his arrival with other recruits in 1907:

> . . . eight young men boarded the crowded Desert Express on its long journey from Wadi Halfa to Khartoum. We were all fresh from the Universities (five from Oxford, two from Cambridge and one from Trinity College, Dublin) . . . Although four of us were scholars and another a fourth wrangler, I think we had been chosen . . . mainly because we were athletes . . . we eight included in our number a former Rugby

Table 4. NON-ENGLISH SCHOOLS OF THE BRITISH ISLES REPRESENTED IN THE SUDAN POLITICAL SERVICE

COUNTRY	SCHOOL	CLASSIFICATION	REPRESENTATION
Ireland	Arlington House	Non-public school	1
Scotland	Edinburgh Academy	Early leading school	15
Scotland	Fettes	Early leading school	4
Scotland	Glenalmond	Early leading school	5
Scotland	Merchiston	Early leading school	3
Scotland	Loretto	Early leading school	1
Scotland	Glasgow Academy	Early lesser school	2
Scotland	George Watson's	Peripheral school	1
Scotland	Gordonstoun	More recent school	1
Scotland	Abelour School	Non-public school	1
Scotland	Robert Gordon's School	Non-public school	1
Scotland	Dalziel School	Non-public school	1
Scotland	Dundee High School	Non-public school	1
Scotland	Duke's School	Non-public school	1
Scotland	Campbeltown G.S.	Non-public school	1
Scotland	Dollar Academy	Non-public school	1
Scotland	St John School, Glasgow	Non-public school	1
Wales	Llandovery College	Early leading school	2
Wales	Cardiff High School	More recent school	2
		Total	45

football captain of Oxford and Scotland, an ex-captain of the Cambridge University cricket team, a member of the Oxford University soccer XI, a rowing trials man, a member of the Oxford and Middlesex county cricket teams, and a Somerset county Rugby footballer. It was this emphasis on physical fitness which gave rise to the aphorism that the Sudan was a country of *Blacks* and *Browns* administered by Blues.[35]

Many others who served in the Sudan have noted that success at games was frequently a pre-requisite of selection. J. P. S. Daniell, a member of the Service from 1938 to 1955, has observed, 'The general consensus of my age-group was that you had to get a "blue" . . . I did get my "blue" as a freshman at Oxford and so the way was wide open',[36] and C. B. Kendall, who was 'blueless', recalls that the inevitable question asked of his mother on his appointment was what he had got his blue for.[37] Yet while athletic success was undoubtedly an asset for aspiring Sudanese administrators the necessity of obtaining a 'blue' has been somewhat exaggerated, as Table 5 reveals.

Table 5. GAMES AND ATHLETICS REPRESENTATIVES OF OXFORD AND CAMBRIDGE IN THE SUDAN POLITICAL SERVICE 1899–1956

Period	Category	Number
PERIOD I (1899–1918)	Oxford and Cambridge representatives	24
	Oxford and Cambridge recruits	59
	All recruits	91
PERIOD II (1919–39)	Oxford and Cambridge representatives	40
	Oxford and Cambridge recruits	169
	All recruits	224
PERIOD III (1940–52)	Oxford and Cambridge representatives	7
	Oxford and Cambridge recruits	54
	All recruits	78

Note: Rifle Shooting is excluded. There were five such Oxford and Cambridge representatives in the Sudan Political Service. Undoubtedly the two world wars, with their disruptive influence on university careers, had an effect on the final total of games and athletics representatives. Furthermore, an outstanding war record replaced athletic distinction as a criterion of selection for a time after both wars.

The table shows that 71 out of the 393 recruits to the Service (281 were Oxford and Cambridge graduates) won representative honours at some form of athletic activity at the ancient universities. In short, there were many in the Service from Oxford and Cambridge who did not have 'blues'. Nevertheless an extraordinarily high percentage of 'blues' were to be found in this small imperial band. And if 'blue' is more widely interpreted to mean representative honours at any of the universities members attended, then the figure rises to 93.[38] In addition, there were internationals, trialists, county players and Olympic medallists. Furthermore, there were many in the Service who had made their appropriate school or college team without winning the coveted 'blue'. In short, there can be no doubt, as Jackson remarked, that the successful athlete was favoured. This is seen clearly from an analysis of the *school*[39] *and university careers* of those in the Service from both heavily represented schools such as Marlborough, Rugby and Winchester and less well-represented schools such as Monkton Coombe, St Bees and Sutton Valence.

Table 6

	FORMER PUPILS IN SERVICE	SCHOOL ATHLETE	UNIVERSITY ATHLETE
Marlborough	19	9	9
Rugby	20	14	3
Winchester	30	16	6
Monkton Coombe	4	4	2
St Bees	3	3	1
Sutton Valence	5	4	0

Note: School or university athlete means simply representation at any physical activity considered worthy of mention in a school register or in the Sudan Political Service.

Towards the end of the nineteenth century the *Uppingham School Magazine* included these possibly sardonic lines of doggerel:

> And none shall serve his country, clean or dirty,
> Who can't show a mile covered in four-thirty.[40]

The imperial emphasis on athletic prowess, illustrated so clearly in both this Uppingham jingle and Table 6, will not surprise readers of the earlier chapters of this book. As they will now readily appreciate, and indeed as is now widely known, the schools wholeheartedly subscribed to the view that games were the potent means of developing leadership qualities of courage, decisiveness and self-confidence.[41] Sir Harold MacMichael in his introduction to *The Sudan Political Service* made much of the value of athletic accomplishments to the Service, not merely as an indication of the physical fitness necessary to an occupation so physically demanding, but precisely because in the selection of candidates such qualities of leadership counted above all else:

> It may be wondered why this record contains references (by no means complete) to athletic distinctions in the University or international field.

The reason is that we were proud of them and did not regard them as altogether irrelevant . . . in selecting candidates regard was paid less to intellectual brilliance than to qualities of leadership and physical stamina – in fact to Lord Cromer's desiderata . . . The majority of candidates who were selected for interview had taken second or third class 'honours' and from among these the final choice usually fell upon those who had achieved distinction in the athletic world.[42]

It was a view held with equal force by others recruited to the Service. R. J. S. Thomson has argued:

My schooling was an excellent preparation for my career in the Sudan Political Service. From an early age one was taught to be self-reliant and to accept responsibility. The virtues of self-discipline and physical fitness, both essential elements in public school training, were to prove of estimable value as also was the exercising which one gains from being a house and subsequently a school monitor.[43]

And J. P. S. Daniell has written in similar vein:

At school we learnt not to think of yourself as a little tin god just because you were in the XI. In the Sudan everyone was a hero outside it, but we were all really just ourselves, tested by the climate, plagued by insects and disease, but from our physical training we had learnt to look after ourselves in body and soul and to be loyal to, and proud of, something more important than ourselves whether it was your House or your Team or your School.[44]

The consequences of a public school education can be seen from this statement from another member of the S.P.S.:

It is characteristic of the British official wherever his duties may take him . . . to make the best of the situation in which he finds himself for the time being. He speedily settles down in his strange surroundings, . . . and forthwith he sets about forming a tennis, squash-racket, or a fives court. To 'keep fit' is his main concern, and this can only be done by regular and violent exercise, even in a sweltering climate like that of Central Africa. Many of the provincial officials, young men who have immense districts the size of principalities to look after, find it difficult to fit in much recreation with the performance of their multifarious duties; but they prefer to sacrifice a portion of their customary sleeping-hours rather than forgo their quantum of physical exercise. They cannot afford to become flabby or 'run down'; to avoid qualifying for the sick-list any sacrifice will be made, and almost any inconvenience will be endured.[45]

While physical fitness, toughness and stamina were valuable qualities in an occupation in which 'the young District Officer spent much of his time trekking usually on foot, and working long hours in a demanding and debilitating climate',[46] it is also important to recognize that the administration of the 'backward peoples' of the Sudan was frequently a game of political bluff requiring superb self-assurance on the part of the handful of administrators involved – never more than 125 on the ground in an area 150 times bigger than Yorkshire.[47] The hero-worship that accompanied an extrovert school 'blood' (athletic hero) was a highly effective means of creating this self-assurance. This fact goes a long way to explain the frequent appearance of 'bloods' and 'blues' in the Sudan Political Service. As Sir James Robertson has observed, 'athletic prominence at school and university gave us the self-confidence to cope with loneliness and being on our own in charge of large areas of population.'[48] Similarly, the French observer, Odette Keun, on a tour of the Sudan in the 1930s, was greatly impressed by the self-discipline, authority and efficiency of the district officers in their isolated circumstances. Comparing them to 'an order of Samurai', she concluded that the possible explanation of their success lay in the nature of their education:

They are all drawn from the British Universities. They are all appointed when very young. The Commissioners of the Sudan who examine them personally in England make a point of knowing their athletic record, and their physique is taken into consideration. Many of these civil servants were rowing Blues in their time, or well-known cricketers and football players.[49]

It must not be thought that the Service was staffed largely by robust 'hearties'. The reality was infinitely more subtle.[50] The academic credentials of many members of the Service were highly respectable, as demonstrated overleaf in Table 7:[51]

Table 7. CLASS AND SUBJECT OF DEGREE-HOLDERS IN THE SUDAN POLITICAL SERVICE, 1899–1952

FIRST-CLASS HONOURS

	Classics	History	Law	Pol/Econ.	Eng. Lit.	Geog.	Mod. Lang.	Anthrop.	Maths	Nat. Sci.	Mech. Sci.	Chemistry	Agric.
Oxford	3	2	3		1	1	1		2				1
Cambridge	5	1	1					1	2	1			
Trinity College Dublin	1		1						1				
St Andrews	1												
Glasgow							2						
Edinburgh													
Aberdeen													
London													
Wales		1											
Totals:	10	4	5	0	1	1	3	1	5	1	0	0	1
Total	32 firsts												

SECOND-CLASS HONOURS

	Classics	History	Law	Pol/Econ.	Eng. Lit.	Geog.	Mod. Lang.	Anthrop.	Maths	Nat. Sci.	Mech. Sci.	Chemistry	Agric.
Oxford	28	22	6	5	3	3	2			3	3	2	
Cambridge	6	18	5		1	4	6	4		3	3		1
Trinity College Dublin				1									
St Andrews				1									
Glasgow													
Edinburgh				1					1				
Aberdeen							1						
London		1		1						1			
Wales													
Totals:	34	42	11	9	4	7	9	4	1	7	6	2	1
Total	140 seconds												

THIRD-CLASS HONOURS

	Classics	History	Law	Pol/Econ.	Eng. Lit.	Geog.	Mod. Lang.	Anthrop.	Maths	Nat. Sci.	Mech. Sci.	Chemistry	Agric.
Oxford	22	22	3	9		1	3		1			1	
Cambridge	1	8	3		1	3	2	1	4	5	1		
Trinity College Dublin													
St Andrews													
Glasgow													
Edinburgh													
Aberdeen													
London													
Wales													
Totals:	23	30	6	9	1	4	5	1	5	5	1	1	0
Total	93 thirds												

OTHERS

	Others	
Oxford	Classics IV:	2
Cambridge	Law IV:	1
	P.P.E. IV:	1
Trinity College Dublin	Moral Sci. II:	1
	Econ. II:	1
St Andrews	Medicine II:	1
Glasgow	Theology III:	1
	Orient. Lang. III:	1
Edinburgh	History IV:	1
Aberdeen	Edinburgh: Vet. (no class)	1
London	T.C.D.: Medicine (no class)	1
Total	5 fourths	

Note: Under Class of Degree, a Cambridge 'Pass' degree has been equated with the Oxford 'Fourth'. Under Subject, a commonly understood terminology has been used rather than any specialized vocabulary. For example, at Oxford, Law is called Jurisprudence, Classics are known as Lit. Hum. or Greats, and Politics is subsumed under P.P.E. (Philosophy, Politics, and Economics), also known as Modern Greats. Anthropology is not offered as a first degree at **Oxford**. Engineering has been grouped under Mechanical Science.

It is interesting that in the period 1946 to 1952 the qualifications of recruits from Oxford and Cambridge fell. Both 'firsts' and 'blues' were less in evidence and it is possible that concern over the future of the Service resulted in highly qualified students seeking more secure careers[52] and in this way the door was opened a little to admit the less athletically distinguished, the slightly less well academically qualified and the members of the less famous universities.

This latter tendency to draw slightly more heavily on Irish, Welsh, Scottish and Dominion universities scarcely hides the fact that Oxford and Cambridge were the favoured recruiting grounds. As noted already, not a single provincial university or university college in England supplied a member of the Service.[53] Clearly, in the view of Cromer and the subsequent selection boards, the cream of English youth were to be found in 'Oxbridge' colleges. The complacency underpinning this view has been described somewhat picturesquely in angling terms as follows: 'other sources . . . may well have matured better fish, but the pools did not have to be fished when so few fish were needed to fill a small creel each season . . . selection was basically through trusted searchers at Oxford and Cambridge where "most suitable" fish could be found with minimum of fuss and maximum assurance of success. There was no need to cast the net wider . . .'[54] However, as we have already seen, it seems that recruiters were prepared to admit that some suitable 'fish' were resident at St Andrews, Edinburgh, Glasgow and elsewhere. Those universities, other than Oxford and Cambridge, from which applicants were accepted, are as follows:

Table 8

PERIOD I (1899–1918)	PERIOD II (1919–39)	PERIOD III (1940–52)
Trinity, Dublin (2)	St Andrews (2)	St Andrews (2)
Edinburgh (1)	Edinburgh (3)	Edinburgh (3)
Dublin University (1)	Glasgow (2)	Glasgow (1)
	Melbourne (1)	Aberdeen (1)
	London (1)	Trinity, Dublin (1)
		London (2)
		University College, Wales (2)
		Victoria, N.Z. (1)

Those from Irish, Scottish, Welsh and Dominion universities who 'gate-crashed' the Service were few in number, often extremely well qualified, both academically and athletically, and perhaps more to the point, the majority (17 out of 24) came from public schools!

V

A former member of the Service has summed up the relationship between a public school education and a career in the Sudan in these words: '. . . the really important thing about a public school background is that you virtually couldn't get into the S.P.S. without it . . . I can't think of any of my S.P.S. colleagues who didn't have one.'[55] This chapter has revealed the general accuracy of his impression. And the privileged nature of the Service is further underlined by the fact that for most of its existence many recruits came from the leading public schools even at a time when attempts to recruit boys from these schools to other branches of imperial service were increasingly more difficult. Public school domination of the Service was ensured by the method of selection and while there can be no guarantee that selection by competitive examination would have greatly widened the range of schools and changed the nature of membership, there can be little doubt that selection by interview meant elimination of those from 'the wrong background, school and university' and ensured a strong public school presence. Those of lesser 'caste' were mostly excluded. Of course, it can be argued that since recruitment from the public schools and Oxford and Cambridge produced, according to many accounts,[56] a most able administration there was little point in changing a winning team. In any case, prior to the Second World War equality of opportunity was scarcely the shibboleth of the times. Consequently, without fear of contradiction, it can be asserted that membership of the Sudan Political Service for the whole of its existence was largely a prerogative of the public schools. The challenge from the state-educated, although it was evident after the Second World War, was never strong. The Service was, in the words of the correspondent quoted earlier, 'an old boy net'. He added firmly, 'and it worked'. After successful residence at Oxford or Cambridge the major criterion for selection would seem to have been robust self-assurance, and the philathletes of the public school system had this quality in abundance.

As in the case of Nicolson and Hughes's colonial governors,[57] there is no evidence that the Sudan Political Service and its governors were carefully selected members of 'a British governing, upper or ruling class' or representatives of a capitalist clique. The neo-Marxist theories of Hilferding, Luxembourg and others to the effect that imperialism was the product of industrial and financial interests appear to have little relevance to the Sudan. Nor, for that matter, is Schumpeter's concept of imperialism as a social atavism[58] any more germane. The members of the Sudan Political Service hardly represented a military aristocracy or the belligerent vanguard of a warrior race.[59] If anything, as we have seen in Chapter Two, they were more closely associated with Langer's[60] view of the imperialist who, in a heady climate of chauvinistic enthusiasm, was driven by the same powerful psychological forces as motivates the nationalist to the utmost exertion and even the supreme sacrifice.[61] In such a climate, as Thornton aptly remarks, when nationalism was everywhere rampant, imperialism was 'only an extension of its field of operation'.[62] The truth of the matter was that the Service was mostly staffed by sons of upper-middle-class families with few close connections with great commercial, industrial or political dynasties. Rather than naively embrace the seductive dogmas of political theorists, it is simpler and more accurate to recognize that the Sudan Political Service was a form of occupational self-patronage largely enjoyed by Oxford and Cambridge graduates with a public school and upper-middle-class background.

Three observations should be made firmly, however, which will serve as correctives to bland assertions of early writers on imperial careers: members of the Sudan Political Service were not drawn predominantly from South-East England,[63] nor was membership wholly conceded by the industrialists in the Midlands and North to the British professional classes,[64] nor did they come virtually exclusively from the landed gentry or its collateral branches.[65]

The Service did not – in fact could not – restrict itself to a small coterie of influential families from Mackenzie's ruling counties of the 'South Eastern heart-land' of England.[66] It was forced to recruit widely rather than narrowly from the upper middle classes and the public schools. In order to get 'the right type', members of the Service in its half-century of recruitment came from some ninety eventual public schools (and elsewhere) and from all parts of Britain as well as the Dominions. And it is simply not possible, in the specific context of the Sudan Political Service, to wholly agree with the assertion of Hughes and Nicolson that colonial government was a role conceded to cadet branches of the leadership subsection (professional classes made up of vicars, officers, doctors, etc.) by the nineteenth-century industrial movement centred on the English Midlands and the North. With regards to concession, it is as well to recall that many nineteenth-century and twentieth-century industrialists were strong supporters of the public school system and that, on occasion, they aspired to imperial careers for their sons to better their own image.[67] These sons might have been outnumbered but they were to be found in the Service.

To lay seductive myths about squirearchical imperial Englishmen in the Sudan it is more important still, however, to disagree with Robert Collins in his twin assertions about the nature of the membership of the Service and the origins of its ethos: far too much is made of both the country gentry associations and the allegedly corresponding 'squirearchical' traditions of the Service. In his rather fanciful view: 'Born and reared in the atmosphere of the country gentry, if not actually a member of that class, they [members of the Sudan Political Service] were imbued from birth with a sense of the duties, responsibilities and privileges of the gentry.'[68] He himself is imbued with a somewhat romantic vision of noble, white squires and an appreciative black peasantry. As one former member of the Service has remarked: 'Collins has perhaps something of an obsession with "the English rural squirearchy". I think he has got this wrong (perhaps deceived by the manner and accent of most of the Service) . . . the strong sense of service comes from the Public School, Oxbridge background of all but a few.'[69] And another is of the opinion that Collins has it the wrong way round and 'may almost have missed the point in that the task of the Sudan Political Service was itself a rural squirearchy. I won't go so far as to say that the post of District Commissioner demanded this attitude, but it certainly helped if one adopted it.'[70] While in the early days of the Service there was some truth in the claim that members came from English country homes and had their roots in the English countryside, Collins is given to exaggeration in the matter. He writes with a settled notion, an injudicious brevity and casual vagueness: 'Almost to a man the members of the S.P.S. came from country families, or from families of members of the imperial civil service or professional classes who had their roots and traditions in the English countryside'; and, more extravagantly still: 'None came from either the working classes or even the managerial groups which inhabited the large industrial centres of England or from the growing suburbs with their cadres of business or professional people.'[71]

There is a surrealist indistinctness about this analysis. It overlooks the 'colonials' born and bred thousands of miles from the 'coloured counties', the grammar schoolboys from Brighton, Humberside, Newark and Lewisham, far removed from the acres of the landed gentry; but more to the point, what of those members of the Service from Scottish schools without any roots in the rural shires of England?[72] Scots joined the Service from the urban, industrial communities of Clydebank, Dundee and Motherwell, from the professional cadres of the Edinburgh suburbs and, in at least one instance, from Bridgeton, a working-class area of Glasgow. The forty-one men from Scottish schools who joined the Sudan Political Service included the sons of city businessmen, doctors and lawyers, urban clerics and small-town drapers as well as the sons of a shipbuilder, an industrial mill-owner, a steelworker, a bank agent and a teacher. Most came from the industrial and commercial central belt of Scotland. Furthermore, association with urban centres and professional suburbs was by no means restricted to Scots members of the Service. An analysis of the social backgrounds of the last hundred men to join the Sudan administration reveals that they included the son of a civil servant, a red-brick university registrar, a teacher, an estate agent, a journalist, a university lecturer, an architect, a stockbroker, a draper, a prison governor, a chartered accountant, a wine merchant, a bank manager and a trawlerman, as well as the sons of urban and suburban engineers, businessmen, doctors and solicitors, together with two army sergeants! Most of these later entrants had their homes in city or town. And the working-class representation should not be overlooked. Several members of the Service came from this background.[73] It appears that there was an inclination in the late twenties and after to add a sprinkling of working-class men, provided, of course, that they had Sudan 'credentials' – university experience and games ability – so as 'to allay the "Tatler Group" image of the Service'.[74]

How wide of the mark Collins is on occasion in his incautious generalizations is well illustrated by brief biographical details of an Englishman and Scotsman respectively. A. K. Markland, who joined the Sudan Political Service in 1946, was the son of an electrical engineer who had been educated at Manchester Grammar School (his father in turn was a butcher in Bolton). After experience as a power station engineer in Glasgow, Markland's father became a manager with the British Thomson Houston Company based at Rugby in the industrial Midlands. Markland himself became a day boy at Rugby School after winning a scholarship place from a local secondary school. From Rugby he went to Queen's College, Oxford, as an exhibitioner. He took a degree in engineering but, more to the point, represented the university at cricket, hockey and squash and so gained the right credentials and the right patina for recruitment to the Sudan Political Service.[75]

James McCargow, who joined the Sudan Political Service in 1943, was the son of a Glasgow steelworker who had worked in a foundry in the east end of the city. In 1924 the company collapsed, McCargow's father became unemployed and subsequently worked only intermittently. Throughout the years of his childhood in central Glasgow, McCargow, in his own words, was 'a working-class boy from a working-class family'.[76]

An analysis of two interesting sets of entrants in 1939 and 1942 respectively and from Sutton Valence School underlines the need for the investigator to pick and scratch in patches in order to reveal the whole mosaic and not to leap to early conclusions about the pattern by merely uncovering a corner. In 1939, of the six entrants to the Service, only one was an Englishman – the son of a preparatory school master from a business family in Bedford. All the others were Scots – one the son of a crofter, one the son of an army officer, two the sons of Glasgow businessmen and one the son of a member of the Indian Civil Service who has written of his childhood with Collins's observations fresh in his mind: 'Although my father was in the I.C.S., I was, in fact, brought up by my aunt and uncle who had a small family business and lived in the village of Dunlop in Ayrshire . . . All my near relatives on my mother's side were in business – and it was in this environment that I grew up.'[77] The seven entrants to the Service in 1942 included a Welshman and three Scots as well as three Englishmen. As was quite typical of recruits in the thirties, forties and fifties, they came from a wide range of backgrounds; their fathers included a steelworker, a jute-broker, a civil engineer, a university registrar and a minister from Dundee as well as an army officer and a vicar. An analysis of the occupations of the fathers from the intake to the Service from Sutton Valence School,[78] a minor English public school, *over a period of thirty-nine years* in Table 9 reveals a typical spread of twentieth-century commercial, industrial and professional careers.

Table 9. RECRUITS TO THE SUDAN POLITICAL SERVICE FROM SUTTON VALENCE SCHOOL

MEMBER OF THE SERVICE	SERVED	FATHER'S OCCUPATION
M. S. Wheatley (Sir)	1907–1928	Chartered accountant
I. H. Watts	1938–1946	Schoolmaster
R. A. Geake	1945–1951	Bank officer
J. P. Tripp	1946–1954	General merchant
H. Colville-Stewart	1946–1955	Author and journalist

Finally, it is instructive to consider the occupations of the fathers of the Civil Secretaries of the Sudan (the highest office in the Sudan Political Service) between 1926 and 1954.[79]

CIVIL SECRETARY	PERIOD	FATHER'S OCCUPATION
Sir Harold MacMichael	1926–1934	English parson
Sir Angus Gillan	1934–1939	Scottish minister
Sir Douglas Newbold	1939–1945	Businessman
Sir James Robertson	1945–1953	Jute factory owner
A. C. Beaton*	1953–1954	Railway inspector

* Acting Civil Secretary.

Of course, even in instances where members came from the shires, reality blurs the sharpness of romantic visions of English rural life and its influence on the Sudan administrator. It should be remembered that squirearchical practices were not always those of nobility and altruism. The 'unacceptable face' of the British nineteenth-century landed system is vividly recorded by various commentators.[80] Moreover, its benevolence, where it existed, should not be overestimated. As F. L. M. Thompson has remarked, 'over rural England as a whole village paternalism has always been a patchy affair.'[81] And, of course, by 1905 when the *first* civil recruits to the Service were appointed, this 'village paternalism' had been considerably reduced by the erosion of political and administrative power and by straitened circumstances.[82]

If, as one member of the Sudan Political Service has correctly written of the supposed squirearchical composition of the Service, it comprises a 'very loose generalization',[83] Collins's propensity to equate experience in rectory, vicarage and manse with the assimilation of benevolent squirearchical attitudes eventually transmitted to the Sudan is equally insecure. It is a curious and interesting fact that over a third of the members of the Service were the sons of clergymen, but these men were not invariably wealthy 'squarsons' or even younger sons of landed families; nor, in fact, did they necessarily spend their professional lives in pleasant rural livings where they developed squirearchical instincts through proximity to the gentry. They ministered to their flocks in Sevenoaks and Huddersfield as well as Ross-on-Wye and Steeple. They were schoolteachers, prebendaries, and even urban deans.[84] They served God in, among other places, a Durham pit village, a Yorkshire spa town, a Lancashire industrial port and a Cheshire residential suburb. The majority held only small livings[85] and their sons frequently won scholarships both to public school and university, where their muscular Christianity won them credentials for successful selection to the Service.

And caution, in conclusion, must be exercised even where clerical fathers held rural livings! The father of D. C. Carden, a member of the Service from 1942 to 1954, spent twenty-five years in the Indian Ecclesiastical Establishment; he then returned to England to a peaceful Hampshire vicarage. Carden has observed:

In my case the ethos of service did not come from land-owning forebears or knowing the squires in the Hampshire countryside in which I spent my holidays from the age of twelve to twenty. It derived first from a family connection with the Church (not only was my father a vicar, but my mother was the daughter of one), second from my parents having spent twenty-five years in the service of the Government of India . . . and third from my schools, both private and public.[86]

Insistence that the members of the Service in their attitude to their gubernatorial tasks adhered to the squirearchical traditions of the English village and even the village cricket pitch is less valuable as an observation that a realization that many members had assimilated the strong message of 'duty' preached so forcefully in public school chapels. In the late nineteenth and early twentieth centuries public school pulpits resounded with earnest declamations of the obligation of 'service'. Cyril Norwood's exhortation to his Marlborough pupils is wholly typical:

What is the justification of the games we play so much here save this ideal of service? . . . Team games are played in order that you may learn to serve your side, to combine and avoid selfishness; in proportion as games lead to purely individual glorification they cease to be of value . . . You are not learning to win Olympic championships on the Marlborough playing fields. You are learning to serve . . .[87]

And at the time headmasters and others frequently saw 'service' in the immediate context of the Empire.[88]

In a sermon preached at Ardingly in 1883 the Reverend Harry Meynell, with not a little complacency, declared:

Much of that nobleness of mind which stamps a true English gentleman comes from the training he has received in a public school, where large numbers are boarded together and educated by scholarly men, graduates of the universities in Holy Orders. For it does seem best that a boy should leave home and enter the little world of a public school. It is there he learns manliness . . . In the Chapel he learns the Faith, in the playground he learns self-control, endurance, forbearance [and] his duty . . .[89]

It is now a commonplace to observe that the public school system had remarkable success in moulding the sons of squires and others of the upper middle classes into stoical, Victorian young gentlemen imbued with its conformist core of ethics. And in this context we should perhaps pay some attention to the oriental aphorism that men resemble their times more than their fathers. Unsurprisingly, therefore, many surviving public school members of the Sudan Political Service have no sympathy with the view regarding the influence of the English squirearchy on the 'service ethos' of the Sudan administration. An Old Rugbeian member of the Service has commented bluntly: 'It came from two sources: the discipline, self-reliance and team-work of the first administrators following the re-occupation, the majority of them ex-soldiers with their army training and traditions. The second source was . . . the traditions and training of the public school.'[90] A Scottish view of the origins of the 'service ethos' is provided by a former pupil of Glasgow Academy who served in the Sudan Political Service for sixteen years: 'In my case the "service ethos" had been implanted at school . . . we were "privileged" to be at G. A. and it was our duty when we had established ourselves in our chosen careers to "serve the community". In my case it had nothing to do with England or squirearchy. These were the traditions of the school pre-war.'[91] Pithily, an Old Marlburian member of the Service has summarized a widespread view among former members: 'Precious few of the Sudan Political Service came from the landed gentry, but virtually all came from public schools. We were the product of the Arnold ethos, not the Squirearchy.'[92] Others have written, even more forcefully, in the same vein.[93] Some former members have attempted to relate 'public school traditions and training' more specifically to their duties in the Sudan. One has written, for example:

> The sense of independence, responsibility and fair play which their boarding schools instilled into their senior boys stood them in good stead when, as District Officers in isolated stations, often under primitive and unhealthy conditions and far removed from supporting or controlling authority, they were required to maintain high standards of conduct and industry as the representatives of their Government.[94]

And another has argued:

> The ability to sift evidence, give a decision and stick by it must often have gone back to a house prefect's often painful experience – one can't

honestly call it training. Above all, the ability to live on close terms with people you don't like – learnt in the cattle market conditions of a public school but practised in the more exacting situation of a small station with no outlets – stood many of us in good stead and avoided many nervous breakdowns.[95]

In short, it is the influence of the public school system rather than the squirearchy which appears to have been much in evidence in the Sudan administration.

The fact that so many recruits came from rectory, vicarage and manse certainly adds yet a further dimension to the 'service' impulse of the Sudan administration. There was, in the attitude of some, more than a trace of Kipling's decent if self-congratulatory shouldering of the 'white man's burden' – filling the mouth of famine and bidding the sickness cease. This commitment is well expressed by J. P. S. Daniell, who joined the Service in 1938 and who has written of:

a strong concern to help those less privileged than ourselves by offering our lives in their service with such skills and standards as could be deployed in a variety of fields: the maintenance of law and order, the dissemination of moral ethics, the spread of higher education, the establishment of sound commercial bases in production and trade, the importance of public health, agriculture and animal husbandry, journalistic honesty, child welfare.[96]

Of course, simple adherence to a fashionable imperialist impulse, assimilation of a public school ethic, Christian missionary zeal – these scarcely exhaust the motives of recruits. The lure of exotic places, the appeal of long vacations, membership of an occupational élite all played their honest part in attracting applicants. As one former member has commented, 'What was its attraction as a career? Lots of things played a part – so in no particular order . . . rightly or wrongly the Sudan Political Service had a very high reputation . . . and it is always a temptation to get a job in an outstanding regiment or university or anything else [and] like most young people I wanted responsibility, travel, independence and an outdoor life.'[97] And another has commented perceptively: 'I think the proper context of the "almost to a man, etc." is that we shared a love of the open air and the wide open spaces. That prospect was a main factor in applying to join the Service whatever one's background.'[98]

In short, not only fashion, upbringing and education had a hand in determining the composition and character of the Service but also 'similarities of temperament, character, physique and achievement. Virtually all achieved distinction at school and university in games and in terms of leadership rather than in terms of academic honours, were physically and mentally robust with an inclination towards outdoor adventure rather than indoor study.'[99]

In the last analysis the Service favoured its own kind – those with the values, habits and inclinations of the earliest civil recruits admired by Cromer. It constituted an élite *within* an élite and it reflected in its composition, attitudes and ethos the games-inclined upper middle class of late Victorian and Edwardian Britain, not the 'huntin', shootin', fishin' ' gentry of late Georgian and early Victorian England. This games-inclined social class possessed considerable confidence in its self-generated values. Consequently it expected orthodoxy and suspected deviance, yet it threw up occasional mutants, who combined morality with muscularity, but not in the combination typical of the period muscular Christian. One such mutant was the creator of modern Nigeria – Sir Frederick Lugard, who will now provide a further facet of the role of the games ethic in empirical ideology.

4

'GENTLEMEN GALORE'

Athleticism and Atheism in Tropical Africa

Sir Frederick Lugard (1858–1945) is a neglected educationist of some interest. He was one of the great imperial proconsuls.[1] He believed strongly in the civilizing role of British Imperialism. Within this civilizing process the English public school system and its games ethic held pride of place. Lugard's certainty in the moral inferiority of the native races of the Empire stimulated in him an intense interest in education as a means of moral improvement. It was his view that the public school was a proven instrument of effective moral training and he urged its creation in tropical Africa. This chapter, then, is a record of one's man desire to take the ideals and structure of English upper-class education to the African continent in the alleged interests of its indigenous peoples and as such it is an example of attempted ideological diffusion from possibly the best of motives but certainly the narrowest of perspectives.

In the role of self-appointed moralist, idealistically if incongruously,[2] Lugard transported the ethic of the Victorian public school from the temperate meadows of England to the equatorial rain-forests of West Africa. He was a zealous agent of diffusion and, despite assertions regarding his originality,[3] in his zeal solidly reflected his schooling, his class and his era. It is Lugard the ideologist not Lugard the administrator who receives attention here. Lugard was one of a band of imperial diffusionists who loyally attempted to take the values of the English upper-class system of education to 'less favoured' peoples with an ethnocentric certainty in the soundness of their offering. In his own words:

> As Roman imperialism laid the foundation of modern civilization and led the wild barbarians of these islands [Britain] along the path of progress, so in Africa today we are repaying the debt, and bringing to the dark places of the earth – the abode of barbarism and cruelty – the torch of culture and progress . . . we hold these countries because it is the genius of our race to colonize, to trade and to govern.[4]

We will meet more of these diffusionists in later chapters. They represent an energetic effort, as yet largely unrecorded, to spread Victorian upper-class educational ideals throughout the Empire; ideals encapsulated in the now evocative expressions popular with Almond, Rendall, Welldon and legions of schoolmasters: service, fair play and *esprit de corps*. The public school system of the nineteenth and early twentieth centuries, as we have seen, considered their inculcation both its responsibility and its right.[5]

Lugard was educated at Rossall, a windswept outpost of the English public school system, set oddly in proletarian Fleetwood on the Lancashire coast. His time at the school (1871–7) largely coincided with the last years of the Reverend Richard Henniker, an inadequate schoolmaster, who apparently failed in most things and who certainly failed in the most basic skill required of a public school headmaster – to maintain and if possible increase the numbers of pupils in the school. The historian of Rossall School dismisses the regime of Henniker in one, brutal sentence: 'Between 1865 and 1875 the work and discipline and reputation of Rossall had rapidly degenerated.'[6] Lugard was similarly peremptory in his dismissal of the man: 'I cannot think of anyone less fitted to be a master or headmaster.' Such disillusion led unsurprisingly to an abrupt rejection of the worth of his own schooling. 'I left Rossall almost completely uneducated and have deplored the waste of those years all my life';[7] yet paradoxically he was to preach the value of a public school education to tropical Africa with conviction and persistence. Resolution of this paradox is not easy. It may lie in fading memory, perhaps in a knowledge of better schools, or even in later years in an uncritical acceptance of the confident assertions of numerous headmasters concerning the merits of a public school education. Perhaps the answer to the paradox lies in part in the transformation of Rossall achieved by Henniker's successor, H. A. James,[8] Lugard's headmaster from 1875 to 1877. James brought from Marlborough those Cottonian features which had provided the college with an unassailable public school image: games, a house system, athletic assistant masters: the potent instruments of character-training so favoured by Lugard in Africa.[9] And yet again the paradox may be partially resolved by a narrow interpretation of Lugard's use of the term 'uneducated' to mean a lack of training in matters of immediate practical value to a career or occupation. For in any analysis of his educational policies for the African it must be recognized that Lugard was both idealist *and* pragmatist. His policies for tropical Africa are characterized by a determination to provide vocational training as well as the inculcation of moral soundness, a resolution which may have owed something to his adolescent experience of Henniker's shortcomings and James's obsession with classics.[10]

Lugard's idealism and pragmatism in educational matters were first apparent in his successful attempt when Governor of Hong Kong to provide the colony with a university. This early effort at educational innovation deserves attention, for his arguments on this occasion were a rehearsal of his later more fulsome Nigerian apologetics.[11] Lugard accepted the governorship of Hong Kong in 1907 after years of adventuring, exploring and soldiering in India, Burma, Uganda, Bechuanaland and West Africa. He was forty-nine. He remained there until 1912 and it was his last year in the colony which saw the establishment of the university. It was very much his brainchild – 'a chosen, personal task'. This task arose out of the fact that on his arrival at the colony he discovered that education was one of his many responsibilities. As he struggled to find the revenue to increase educational standards among the Chinese population, he became fascinated by the subject.[12] The concern of the influential and wealthy Chinese at the time was higher education. It provided the chance of access to the technology which had ensured the supremacy of the Occident over the Orient, and to those high-status civil service posts traditionally so highly esteemed in Chinese society. The issue of a university had been raised by the local press some time before Lugard's arrival. He fanned the flames of enthusiasm with an early statement that a university in Hong Kong could become the Oxford and Cambridge of the Far East! This vision excited the interest of a wealthy Indian resident, Mr H. N. Mody, who immediately offered $150,000 towards construction and $30,000 for an endowment! The enterprise was thus conceived but its birth was to be lengthy and painful.

Lugard hoped to find a ready supply of students both from Hong Kong and from those Chinese who took advantage of scholarships to the United States (made possible by her Boxer indemnity).[13] He argued that it was less alienating to study at home rather than as servile guests of a patronizing foreign power. This anxiety over cultural alienation characterized much of Lugard's writing on colonial affairs over the years. He had a sensitive awareness of the destructive force of Western technological ideas and practices on other cultures, the ideological vacuum which they frequently created and the materialism which more often than not filled it. As a result he became obsessed with creating colonial educational systems in which moral values took precedence over material ones, throughout the whole of his administrative career putting his weight forcefully behind 'teaching the value of truthfulness, courage, love of fair play and justice, self-control, reverence and respect for seniors and those placed in authority, good manners and what is meant by "playing the game".'[14] This obsession dictated both the nature and structure of his university. It was to be entirely residential, the British staff were to be chosen for their 'moral' as well as their academic distinction and it was to be provided with playing-fields through which morality was to be diffused.[15]

It must be frankly recognized that Lugard's preoccupation with the pre-eminence of a non-materialistic education of course illustrated class prejudice as much as colonial altruism. In keeping with his public schools peers, Lugard was scornful of 'money-grabbing traders',[16] myopically associating these men not with the wealth that created public school privilege and life-style but with a vulgar, demeaning materialism. As Tawney wrote with elegance and insight of the public schoolboys of the period: 'Das Gentleman Ideal has them by the throat; they frisk politely into obsolescence on the playing fields of Eton.'[17] Lugard was wholly typical. At Rossall, during a bad academic patch, his response to his father's earnest endeavours to find him a career in the sugar trade was blunt. His honour was offended. He replied curtly that he preferred the Indian Civil Service, 'a thoroughly gentlemanly occupation and look on it how I may I can't bring myself to think that an Assistant in a Sugar Factory is such. Of course, "a gentleman is a gentleman wherever he is" but still the Lugards have been in the Army and the Church – good servants of God, the Queen . . . few if any have been tradesmen.'[18] It was not merely snobbery, nor simply a powerful romantic bias in the education of the ruling classes, as Corelli Barnett suggests,[19] which brought about this state of mind in public schoolboys; it was also a strongly realistic appreciation of the relative attractiveness of life in office and factory and life in the army and the Church! And before we leave the matter of materialistic and non-materialistic values in education, it should be further observed that Lugard's enthusiasm for moral education was also in fact an enthusiasm for *indoctrination in fealty*, a point which will be developed more fully in due course.

This is not the place to include a detailed description of the steps by which Hong Kong University was created, nor to outline the many obstacles Lugard overcame. This is fully dealt with elsewhere.[20] However, one element of Lugard's scheme touched on above requires re-emphasis in the context of this chapter – his determination to elevate character-training above technological expertise. As he declared, 'the University sets before it as its foremost ambition the training of the character of its students and the inculcation of a high moral standard.'[21] This is a familiar assertion to students of Victorian upper-class schooling.[22] Equally familiar is Lugard's associated assertion that 'field sports, for which playgrounds are provided, will, under the guidance of British masters, bear their share in the moulding of character'.[23] 'Field sports', in fact, were the keystone in the arch of the ideological edifice which he constructed for the natives of the Empire.[24] He was very much a product of his age.

As already suggested, hand in hand with Lugard the ideologue travelled Lugard the utilitarian. While character was the foremost aim of his university (and his later Nigerian schools), occupational usefulness was never far behind: 'For those who succeed,' he wrote of his university, 'China offers unlimited scope, and a larger field for employment than is possible in India and Egypt. From the clerk and the comprador to the officers of State in Peking and in the provinces there is an immense demand for educated Chinese, which not one, but twenty Universities, could not supply.'[25]

Hong Kong University was the product of Lugard's noted

persistence, determination and energy. After many difficulties the foundation stone was laid on 16 March 1910. There were to be medical and engineering faculties, an arts section, libraries, hostel accommodation – and playing-fields. And in his speech for the occasion Lugard made much of the high moral character of the British staff.

While Lugard was watching over the birth of his university the British Government was considering the amalgamation of the Southern and Northern Protectorates of Nigeria, the former established in its final form in 1906 and the latter created out of Niger Territories of the Royal Niger Company in 1900. Lugard's reputation as a brilliant administrator possessed with Linnaean powers of order, together with his earlier unequalled record of endeavour in West Africa on behalf of government and trader, convinced the Colonial Office that this was the one man to initiate unification of these two disparate territories.[26] For his part, as *The Dictionary of National Biography* records, 'Lugard felt it would set the seal on his own work for Nigeria . . . and undertook the task.'[27]

In September 1912, therefore, he became Governor of the two protectorates, and in January 1914, arrangements for amalgamation complete, he became Governor-General of 'the largest and most populous unit in the British colonial Empire'.

In the midst of difficulties of many kinds and responsibility for a vast range of administrative functions he made time to concern himself with the education of the new Nigeria. In his view, 'of the many problems which Amalgamation presented there was none more comparable in importance and urgency'.[28] Indeed, by now he had come to the conclusion, as Perham records, that the education question was 'the most important both at Home and in our Colonies'.[29] Throughout his colonial service he held to this position. And on his retirement from the Governor-Generalship of Nigeria in 1919 he remarked sadly, 'There are many tasks which I greatly regret I shall not be able to see come to fruition . . . First among these is education.'[30]

The fullest account of Lugard's educational ambitions for Nigeria and, indeed, the whole of tropical Africa, are to be found in the two chapters on education in his famous work *The Dual Mandate in British Tropical Africa*, first published in 1923. In Chapter 21, entitled simply 'Education', the full force of the conditioning of his early years is unashamedly revealed. Lugard opened the chapter with what is in effect a definition of education as training for service: 'the object which education in Africa must have in view must be to fit the ordinary individual to fill a useful part in his environment and to ensure that the exceptional individual shall use his ability for the advancement of the community and not to its detriment.'[31] Such pronouncements were, of course, standard ingredients of headmasters' sermons in public school chapels – the accepted location for appealing for steadfast devotion to duty, the submergence of self in the community and the adoption of uncritical allegiance.[32] And in his autocratic pursuit of a similar educational orthodoxy for the new Nigeria, Lugard had much in common with those nineteenth-century educational despots.

Much of the remainder of the chapter was devoted to the means by which those objectives were to be achieved; but first Lugard devoted space to his acute concern about the dangers of cultural confusion facing the young African through exposure to Western education, to the inadequacies and frustrations produced by a literary rather than a technical education, and to the prospect of unrest and sedition produced by training the intellect 'to the neglect of moral discipline and standards of duty'. As we have already seen, Lugard was haunted by the incubus of an exclusively intellectual education producing disaffected agitators and he selected for his readers' edification various West African colonies as examples of purveyors of a pernicious and unsuitable education for young native men, who, in consequence, lacked integrity, loyalty and self-control, and who were characterized by 'discontent, suspicion of others and bitterness masquerading as racial patriotism'.[33] Since mission schools educated most natives,[34] then logically, in Lugard's view, the education they provided had proved unsatisfactory. He was especially critical of the alleged lack of self-discipline in the mission schools, a lack which, in his opinion, had occurred because these institutions 'had not been animated by the traditions governing our English public schools'.[35] It is necessary to consider briefly Lugard's own philosophical development. In his childhood he had been a model of Victorian godliness. He had lived up to the spiritual admonitions of his parents. Both were devout Christians. His father, a clergyman 'of markedly evangelical stamp',[36] was for many years a chaplain in the Madras establishment of the East India Company. In adulthood, however, Lugard abandoned Christianity and became 'a hopeless atheist'.[37] This affected his stance on educational issues. In Hong Kong 'he followed the official policy of granting limited support to Christian missionary institutions', while believing 'that Britain could offer in secular form those qualities of character which religion had done so much to develop'.[38] He advocated a new morality derived from, but having dispensed with, Christianity. It seemed to owe something to the moral code of the public school system: 'Educated British gentlemen,' he wrote, 'may be trusted to have a high standard of morals.'[39] By the time he administered Nigeria, he had adopted the secular views of a body called the Moral Education League. In his *Amalgamation Report* of 1919, its views were incorporated into his educational policy for Nigeria:

> I conceive that if a short period daily be devoted to placing before children, in an attractive way, the social and other incentives to gentlemanly conduct, the success which rewards self-control and industry, with similar lessons by the aid of illustration and anecdotal biography, it would form a valuable adjunct to the inculcation of the same ideals of right living, as enforced by religious precept and practice.[40]

Both Colonial Office and Missionary Society opposed him. His ambition came to nothing. Nevertheless it remains as a fascinating historical oddity – a belief in part in the ethical value of public school muscularity without the Christianity. In short, he proposed an atheistic athleticism. It embraced stoical rather than Kingsleian moral precepts, and it was probably closer to the reality in the public schools than some would have us believe.[41] It is worth a close examination as an imperial aberration.

Lugard remained convinced of missionary shortcomings to the end of his life. As late as 1937 he was to observe that 'Education was first left to the missions whose teaching must necessarily be a disintegrating influence . . . it did nothing to inculcate civic duties.'[42] However, he was of the opinion that *both* governments and missions were to blame for this state of affairs: governments because their grants were dependent on purely intellectual tests and missions because they concentrated too little on discipline and too much on producing examinees and evangelists.

Having analysed the nature of the problem to his own satisfaction, Lugard next turned to a consideration of possible solutions: firstly, mission societies should take council with colonial administrators, and, it was inferred, be guided by them; secondly, colonial governments should exercise control over all unaided schools; thirdly, governments should seek to establish a code of practice which would embody those principles which would give effect to *sound educational ideals*. Lugard quoted as a good example his own Nigerian Ordinance in 1916. The first principle read: 'the primary object of all schools should be the formation of character and habits of discipline, rather than the mere acquisition of book-learning or technical skill and . . . grant-in-aid should be paid in part based on success in this direction.'[43]

The main objectives of education for the African youth now defined in terms wholly indistinguishable from those for the Anglo-Saxon public schoolboy, Lugard next considered the instruments to be employed in order to effect these objectives. These included:

1. residential schools
2. an adequate British staff
3. the delegation of responsibility for discipline to school monitors
4. encouragement of games
5. grants to aided schools to be partly dependent on tone and discipline.

Several of these ideas were markedly similar to those of Curzon when, as Viceroy of India in 1904, in a move to improve their tone, he introduced reforms into the Chiefs Colleges – the Etons of India.[44] This is scarcely surprising, of course, as both Lugard and Curzon were products of an educational system which had total confidence in itself and its value in the self-appointed task of inserting a moral backbone into the native races of the British Empire.

And on the matter of the insertion of a moral backbone Lugard had much to say.[45] As his Ordinance reveals, it was dependent, in the first instance, on boarding schools closely modelled on the lines of the English upper-class school down to such specifics as 'school houses, dormitories, class and living rooms, playgrounds and the rules respecting school boundaries, roll-calls, "exeats", meals, and hygiene'. Clearly, despite his own unfortunate experiences, as he remarked elsewhere, he had always been a warm advocate of the English public school system![46] In such an environment, Lugard affirmed, a boy 'learns to be less self-centred, take pride in the corporate body of which he is a member – the school, house and the games team, and to understand the meaning of "playing the game" of loyalty and of co-operation in a common ambition and a united effort'.[47] In the training of a boy's character none of the above features were optional, but Lugard made much of the necessity of games: cricket,[48] football and athletics brought staff and pupil in close touch and were especially effective in the creation of moral fibre. Consequently, it was 'in the play-fields and recreation hours more especially that the public-school spirit can be evolved'.[49] Lugard never shifted from this position and continued to make this point consistently in memoranda, speeches, articles and lectures. For the rest of his life he wished sincerely 'to share [with the Africans] the English values in which he had so much confidence, and which he himself had been given through his training as a gentleman at home and at his public school'.[50]

In an attractive expression Perham has observed that Lugard had a streak of liberalism in the authoritarian marble of his nature.[51] This is undoubtedly true. In his later years, in particular, he had a clear vision of imperial responsibilities which was far-sighted and decent: 'to encourage the African to be proud of his own race, to feel it has its own contribution to make in world progress and that contact with Western civilization should not mean servile imitation, but an opportunity of selecting all that can assist the growth of what is best in his institutions and equally in his culture.'[52] It remains true, however, that Lugard was of an ethnocentric disposition. On one occasion, for example, he wrote:

> Among the primitive tribes ethical standards must be created – among few are they a vital and potent force. If, for instance, in his village home the African boy perceives that self-indulgence and lack of self-control excite no reprobation; that thrift, ambition, and initiative are conceptions as foreign to his associates as an alien tongue, for which his language has

no appropriate terms; if justice, fair-play, truthfulness, and mutual obligation have no influence in guiding the actions of those around him – then these conceptions must be created and built up. I do not for a moment mean to infer that there is a complete lack of such qualities among Africans who have not been brought into contact with the higher standards, for I profoundly believe that these conceptions are all innate in humanity, and are exhibited in a greater or less degree, even in the primitive savage, but they are generally undeveloped, and are not enforced by the public opinion of the community, and lack the sanction of local custom;[53]

and on another:

The English public schoolboy has from infancy been habituated to the standards which 2,000 years of Christian ethics have created in the society in which he lives. In his home-life, in the books he reads, among the people with whom he mixes, he has learnt to discriminate between what is honourable and what is dishonourable. He is well aware when he transgresses the unwritten code. Among primitive people this ethical code has to a large extent to be created by the force of example, and hence the necessity, at least in the early stages, of a strong British staff of the right type, who in the daily social intercourse and in the play-fields will impress on the boys what the school expects of its members: self-respect devoid of vanity, truthfulness, courage, good manners, self-control and honesty – because these qualities are the necessary essentials which make a gentleman.[54]

Such passages demonstrate Lugard's orthodoxy. He reflected a general upper-class attitude to the 'blacks' and 'browns' of the Empire. His sure superiority, his restricted vision and his complacent assumptions were wholly Victorian. Robert Huttenback has written: 'Britons in the mid nineteenth century were developing a sense of racial uniqueness.'[55] They began, in fact, to believe 'in an Anglo-Saxon genius for the government of inferior peoples'.

To Victorian eyes this inferiority was in part the product of immaturity, in part the product of inadequacy, and in part the product of degeneracy. In the first instance, many Victorians embraced with enthusiasm the 'Myth of the African as Child'. It provided an attractive excuse for intervention and control in Africa. As Charles Lyons has observed, 'as it was the moral right and obligation of adults to discipline, guide and protect children, so the more "mature" races had a similar right and obligation to "child races".'[56] Explorers, traders, administrators and missionaries wrote of the childishness of the African native sometimes approvingly and sometimes (often where sex was concerned) disapprovingly.[57] Lugard's own experiences ensured his strong support for this crude Victorian racial generalization. He claimed that the typical African was 'a happy, thriftless, excitable person, lacking self-discipline and foresight, naturally courageous and naturally courteous and polite, full of personal vanity, with little sense of veracity'. He concluded, 'the virtues and defects of this race-type are those of attractive children.'[58] Natives had a novel fascination, he admitted, 'for we are dealing with the child-races of the world.'

The outcome of an adherence to the 'child-race' theory was the Schoolmaster Syndrome. As Heussler has remarked of imperial Africa, 'the Briton was an underpaid schoolmaster in an overpopulated school. He lived in the house and took a full part in its life, without ever crossing the line. He knew the boys well and liked them and he sympathized with their problems. His discipline was unyielding and fair, and it was as constant as sun and rain.'[59] Such a role came easily to the ex-public schoolboy administrators of Briton's black colonies, as we have already seen in the case of the Sudan Political Service.

Where natives were not seen as egotistical but lovable children, they were criticized as indolent and uncooperative adults. Such criticism resulted, as Syed Hussein Alatas has shown, in *The Myth of the Lazy Native*: 'The ideology of colonial capitalism evaluated people according to their utility in their production system and profit level. If a community did not engage in activities directly connected with the colonial capitalist venture, the community was spoken of in negative terms', and the image of the lazy native became 'a major justification for territorial conquest, since the degraded image of the native was basic to colonial ideology'.[60]

The colonial ideologist stressed the incapacity and unwillingness of the 'backward' native to exploit the natural wealth of his country:

It will probably be made clear, and that at no distant date, that the last thing our civilization is likely to permanently tolerate is the wasting of the resources of the richest regions of the earth through the lack of the elementary qualities of social efficiency in the races possessing them. The right of those races to remain in possession will be recognized; but it will be no part of the future conditions of such recognition that they shall be allowed to prevent the utilization of the immense natural resources which they have in charge.[61]

And when judged in these terms, the native 'justifiably' forfeited his independence. It was conveniently overlooked, of course, that in any European exploitation of resources the natives were invariably given the lowest, most onerous menial tasks of an alien wage economy, and that their living and working conditions were often brutal, unnatural and regimented. Not surprisingly, they preferred their indigenous way of life!

There is another even less attractive aspect to Victorian imperial arrogance. It is illuminating to consider the views of Frederick William Farrar, distinguished novelist, theologian and educationist, who was first a master of Marlborough and then at Harrow. In his paper 'Aptitudes of Races', read to the Ethnological Society in 1867 when he was an assistant master at Harrow School and a year before he published his famous radical educational work, *Essays in Liberal Education*, Farrar divided mankind into three broad groups – the Semitic and Aryan breeds who had to their credit all the great achievements of mankind, the semi-civilized 'browns' and 'yellows', and 'the irreclaimable savage', comprising mostly the black peoples of the earth. The views on race of this gentle, bookish, sensitive author of sentimental schoolboy stories represent crassly insensitive, ethnocentric nonsense:

Let us take one specimen of the 100,000,000 of Africa, and that not the most degraded types, Hottentots, or Bosjesmen, or even Amakoso Kaffirs, but a much higher race, the pure-blooded negro. With keen senses, and singularly powerful physique, yet, mainly owing to his salient animality, and the crimes of cruelty, laziness, and superstition which, if we may accept the accounts of hosts of successive travellers, mark his native condition, he is not untameable like the Indian, but so mentally apathetic as to bow his shoulder to the yoke of race after race of Asiatics and Europeans. Ever since civilization has existed, he has been conterminous to, and even in contact with it from an unknown period. Yet this natural imitativeness has given him no proficiency even in the mechanical arts. He did not learn architecture, writing, or organization from the Egyptians; the brilliant Phoenician could not teach him so simple a lesson as the taming of his native elephant; neither Dutch, nor French, nor Spaniards, nor Americans, nor Anglo-Saxons have weaned him, on his native continent, from his cannibalism, his rain-doctors, his medicine-men, his mumbo-jumbo, his gris-gris and ju-jus . . . The grand qualities which secure the continuous advance of mankind, the generalizing power of pure reason, the love of perfectibility, the desire to know the unknown, and, last and greatest, the ability to observe new phenomena and new relations, – these mental faculties seem to be deficient in all the dark races . . . What hope is there for their progress? As they were probably the earliest to appear on the earth's surface, 'covering the soil since an epoch which must be determined by geology rather than by history', so will the vast majority of them in all probability be the first to disappear by a decay, from which not even the sweet influences of Christianity, at least as we have taught it, have hitherto been able to rescue more than a small and insignificant number.[62]

It was Farrar's considered view that the savage might have learnt glorious lessons, but he had learnt only what was vicious and degrading. Consequently he was doomed to perish because 'darkness, sloth and brutal ignorance cannot coexist with the advance of knowledge, industry and light'. To those of Farrar's righteous persuasion it was just as well: the black savage represented 'the most hideous features of moral and intellectual degradation'.[63]

Buttressed by mythology, insensitivity and stupidity, by the end of Victoria's reign this belief in an Anglo-Saxon superiority was firmly established. In 1900 J. A. Cramb, whom we met in Chapter Two, argued with simple-minded patriotism:

There is a widespread belief in men's minds that every race must have its period of world-dominion. History does not ratify such a belief . . . The genius for empire in a race is like the genius for art in an individual, innate but not innate in all. One has it, another has it not. It is a gift from the great God himself, as Polybius knew, as Tacitus, Dante, Machiavelli knew – as every man who studies history knows.[64]

This genius for government, product of genetic superiority, demonstrated innate moral superiority to the initiated. Two quotations, from a soldier and a bishop respectively, catch this arrogant certainty to perfection. Sir Francis Younghusband, Commander of the British Expedition to Tibet of 1903, stated in *The Heart of a Continent*:

> No European can mix with non-Christian races without feeling his moral superiority over them. He feels, from the first contact with them, that whatever may be their relative positions from an intellectual point of view, he is ~~stronger~~ morally than they are. And facts show that this feeling is a true one. It is not because we are any cleverer than the natives of India, because we have more brains or bigger heads than they have, that we rule India; but because we are stronger morally than they are. Our superiority over them is not due to mere sharpness of intellect, but to the higher moral nature to which we have attained in the development of the human race;[65]

and the prolific J. E. C. Welldon, one-time Bishop of Calcutta and recognizable by now as an imperialist of some fervour, at about the same time observed in *Recollections and Reflections*: 'The high character of Anglo Indians in India is probably the asset of the highest value to the stability of the British Empire. The Oriental man respects superiority; it respects moral superiority most of all, and it yields instinctive obedience to a Power which is recognized as morally superior.'[66]

As we have seen, Lugard shared these convictions. In this respect he was wholly conventional in his prejudices and shibboleths. Hence, in Nigeria he displayed the typical upper-class Englishman's ethnocentricity shot through with reforming administrative certainty. One outstanding example is his recommendation, described above, that government grants should be allocated in part for tone, discipline, manners and character. This was the practice in his own Nigerian schools. 30 per cent of marks determining the amount of the grant were awarded for tone, discipline, organization and moral instruction, 20 per cent for the adequacy and efficiency of teaching staff, 40 per cent on results of periodical examinations and general progress, and 10 per cent for buildings, equipment and sanitation.

Lugard was keen to promote tone, discipline, manners and character not only through personal example and contact on the games field but by moral instruction in the classroom. As we have seen earlier, this moral instruction at an elementary level involved the skilful use of illustration and anecdote to demonstrate the success attending honesty, self-control and industry; but at a more sophisticated level it involved instruction in 'the true meaning of patriotism' and the duties and privileges of citizenship![67] In a rather curious and intimidating expression he remarked that this imperial patriotism should be *enforced* by the stories and dialogues selected for school reader and textbooks; clearly on the same lines of imperial Indian textbooks which contained a chapter entitled 'Angrezi Raj Ki Barkaten' – Blessings of the English Raj, which celebrated the virtues of imperial rule including the elimination of disease, the introduction of law and order, and the building of schools, roads, bridges and canals.[68] It was Lugard's view that:

> A cursory acquaintance with the evolution of democracy under Cromwell may do more harm than good, by inducing 'the boy patriot to deplore the woes, and discuss the regeneration of his country, instead of attending to his lessons', and encouraging him to believe that he can accomplish in a decade what England has taken some centuries to achieve. History, said Sir H. Hadow, in his presidential address to the Teachers' Guild in January 1921, 'ought to be taught from the point of view of showing what England has been in the past, what England has done for liberty and civilization, for invention, for industry, and for the spiritual, moral, and material welfare of mankind.'[69]

Here we get to the heart of the matter. It is abundantly clear from his writings that, for Lugard, native education was substantially *an exercise in sensible subservience*.[70] It was to develop respect, obedience and loyalty as much as anything else. Implicit in the attempt to develop such qualities was the British imperialist's certainty of purpose, self-confidence and readily assumed right to dictate ends and means. In Lugard's opinion education as the inculcation of obeisance was quite proper. He possessed a personally satisfying rationale for domination:

> In the political sphere the British ideal is that there should be equal opportunity for every man, irrespective of colour or creed. Where this principle has been disregarded the motive is, I think, to be sought rather in the desire of the White race to maintain its dominant position than in any crude prejudice against Colour. Nor is this an unworthy motive, for the White race represents – e.g. in South Africa – a civilization and an

advanced system of government which fears lest it should be submerged were the subject races, which are predominant in numbers, to gain absolute political equality.[71]

In short, for Lugard the issue was simple. Educational aims, valued so highly at other times and in other contexts, such as the development of an inquiring mind, independence of thought and the questioning of established orthodoxies, were unacceptable in an environment of primitive backwardness.

The perceptive will be well aware that Lugard's colonial policy had obvious parallels to that of the public school system. Both sought to create habits of respectfulness, obedience and loyalty. Individuality was suspect, non-conformity was discouraged, *esprit de corps* was exalted.[72] It is understandable that Lugard was irritated by insecure, resentful, and sometimes pretentious native youths who appeared to him both ill-educated, unappreciative and tiresome; but it would not be unfair or incorrect to see in his administrative emphasis deliberate policies for submission and conformity in order that, as he saw it, he should bring carefully selected benefits of his own society as speedily as possible to the African continent.

Lugard was a natural autocrat, who resented blunt criticism by the southern, educated Negro and delighted in the courteous 'subservience' of northern feudal Muslim chiefs. In consequence, for the Negro population of Lagos:

Every major proposal and every major act of the new Governor added confirmation of his autocratic tendencies, his negrophobia, and his desire to reduce the people to submissive slavery – the amalgamation proposals first, with their destruction of the judicial system, the inauguration of provincial courts, the reduction of the embryo Parliament to the status of a municipal board, the attempt to impose water-rate in Lagos, and then direct taxation, the abolition of Egba independence, the quarrel over the position of the Oba of Lagos, the proposal to enforce Government inspection of private schools, a proposed censorship of the press, a mounting total of disturbances, repressed with increasing severity. These were the chief incidents in the remaining years of Lugard's administration, and each was a proof to the educated élite of Lugard's despotic tendencies.[73]

However, there was more to his autocracy than mere inclination. Lugard was representative of a widespread colonial belief in the need for the firm government of the inferior native races. Christine Bolt has discerned in his dislike of missionary education not simply disappointment with its moral effectiveness but

> the very familiar prejudice – frequently advanced about the effects of missionary work . . . – that Christianity might produce dangerous notions of democracy, of human equality, among those who should rightly be kept in a position of inferiority; this might be avoided, without embarrassment to the conscience, and with the blessing of modern science, through the implementation of separate labour codes and legal and educational facilities for colonized peoples. Here disguised is the white passion for strong government over 'savages'.[74]

There is clear evidence from Lugard's own pen of just such an attitude. In his *Dual Mandate*, the outcome of long personal reflection, he paid lipservice to liberal political values emerging in the twentieth century, but could not really endorse them with confidence even in a limited context:

> While . . . the educated native has not proved himself able to govern communities of which he is in no way representative, it is, on the other hand, most desirable that natives who have the necessary qualifications of character and education should be afforded every opportunity of participating in the government of the community to which they belong, whether as civil servants or as unofficial members of municipal boards and councils, even if at first their standards of attainment fall below those of the British staff, for it is only by the exercise of actual responsibility that efficiency can eventually be attained, and that a tradition of public service can be created . . . I am, however, reluctantly compelled to admit that, so far as my own experience goes, it is extremely difficult at present to find educated African youths who are by character and temperament suited to posts in which they may rise to positions of high administrative responsibility.[75]

With regard to his educational policy for Nigeria, the main elements of his educational reforms – wider government power, extended government control, more government schools and grants to mission schools on government terms – can be clearly seen to be deliberate instruments for the realization of moral, social and political conformity. Yet while Lugard was a rigid conformist in some things, it was a feature of his own educational non-conformity that for him European benefits included not merely moral imperatives but also practical skills. Many of Lugard's ambitions for the Nigerian were extremely pragmatic. He saw education in simple functional terms at an occupational as well as an ideological level. At the occupational level, in Lugard's view, Africa required: agricultural and craft training to both preserve and improve native culture; technical training to make effective use of Western technology; and literary training for clerical and administrative posts. As he saw it, each type of training demanded its own system of schools. In consequence these should be of three kinds: village schools 'adapted to the requirements of peasantry'; apprentice schools for training surveyors, artisans and mechanics; and schools to train the more promising boys from village schools as teachers, as clerks for the native courts and as interpreters. It was the latter which were to be 'public boarding schools'. Admirable though Lugard's pragmatism was, it too was suffused with ethnocentric assumptions.[76] It is perhaps instructive that Lugard never concerned himself with long-term planning for institutions of higher education.[77] Was it that with the British in political, professional and scholastic authority a satisfying and satisfactory moral climate was assured? Or was it, as Nduka suggests, that 'Lugard himself thought little of an African engineer holding a technical degree, since he considered his head to be "full of formulae" whose meaning he could not appreciate'?[78]

Lugard regretted that in his *Dual Mandate* there was insufficient space for a detailed consideration of curriculum, standards and evaluation; however, he made some general and sensible points about the foolishness of teaching Latin and Greek, the irrelevance of learning the geography and history of Britain (as distinct from the British Empire) and the wisdom of a good knowledge of English and the three R's. But, as might be expected, his final thoughts on education in his *opus magnum* were firmly focused yet again on the necessity of placing character-formation before the training of intellect in order that 'the traditions that give to English public schoolboys that discipline and training which have fitted them for the work of the Empire might be passed on to their African peers'.[79] He took up the same refrain in much of his later writing. 'Public school education' for Africa was frequently in his thoughts.

Lugard's actual influence on the educational development of Nigeria cannot be said to have been impressive. His own efforts were certainly restricted both by early opposition to his policies and by the Great War, which left him short of officers and finance. Little was achieved in his time and subsequently colonial Nigeria failed to develop a network of schools with the games facilities and character-training ethos of the English model.[80] This was hardly surprising in view of government penury. Furthermore, the truth of the matter was that Lugard's moralistic aims, noble, perhaps, according to his lights, were hopelessly unrealistic in the conditions of a culturally bewildered society:

> In giving moral instruction, Western education often ran counter to the example given by other agents and agencies which were popularizing the Western way of life among the natives. It was, for instance, unrealistic to expect the public school code of honour to take root in the social confusion resulting from colonialism. More often than not, the attempt to introduce this code of honour led to no more than the adoption of the outward trapping of the English gentleman.[81]

However, from a historical perspective Lugard's educational influence is less important than his educational *intentions*. These clearly owed much to those features of the English upper-class educational system of which he himself was such a perfect example. He wished, in Nduka's acidic phrase, 'to produce gentlemen galore'.[82] Perham has remarked of Lugard's *Political Memorandum* (a guide he wrote for his colonial junior administrators) that it reflected his ambitions rather than his accomplishments.[83] This chapter is a brief record of Lugard's personal desire to implant the ideals of English upper-class schooling in the minds of Nigerian youth. As such it demonstrates ambition rather than achievement. It is a study of attempted ideological diffusion which embraced ethnocentricity, autocracy and idealism. The ethnocentricity and autocracy certainly lend themselves readily to modern obloquy; the idealism, while perhaps less certain of outright condemnation,[84] clearly contained elements of impracticality and incongruity.

Even more incongruous, in the light of missionary effort in Africa and the sustained attempts of the upper-class missionary to create Tom Brown in Africa – Christian, courageous and compassionate[85] – is his curious combination of atheism and athleticism. In moral training, muscularity was more than acceptable: Christianity was not. In adopting this position he was interestingly idiosyncratic: a curious mixture of the conventional and the unconventional: in his time an imperial oddity. It is time now to meet diffusionists of more Kingsleian orthodoxy.

5

ETON IN INDIA

The Careful Creation of Oriental 'Englishmen'

One important consequence of the Mutiny of 1857 for Imperial India was the reassessment of British policy towards the Indian States. Annexation of territory, formerly popular in the interests of the salutary dispersal of sober British rule, was now abandoned. The Marquis of Dalhousie's[1] unfortunate annexation of Oudh, a major cause of the Mutiny, was vivid in the memory. There was, in addition, a new awareness of 'the value of the princes' cooperation, and the hold which they still had upon their subjects'.[2] On the one hand, dispossessed royalty, such as the Rani of Jhansi, Begam Hazrat Mahal, Queen Regent of Oudh, and the notorious Nana Sahib, had proved ferocious leaders of the Indian peasant in the struggle against imperialism. On the other, sovereigns like Sindhia of Gwalior, Halkar at Indore and the Nawab of Bhopal had remained steadfastly loyal to the British and thereby made the task of reconquest easier. The lesson seemed clear. In the interests of continued dominion traditional rulers had to be wooed, rather than spurned. There was a further imperative: the need to resist external aggression. A Russian invasion of the sub-continent seemed a real possibility at this time.[3] Loyal Indian States would be useful buffers in such an event.

Symbolic of the change in attitude towards the States was the issue of special 'sanads' of adoption to the major princes by Dalhousie's successor, Lord Canning, Governor-General from 1856 to 1862. On the express condition of loyalty to the Crown, these sanctioned once more the traditional right to adopt an heir. Dalhousie had forbidden adoption in those States dependent on the

East India Company. These had then lapsed to the British, which gave rise to understandable resentment, suspicion and insecurity among the indigenous rulers and their subjects. Canning's action meant, in effect, that the India of 1858 became petrified and the result was a 'conglomeration of seven hundred States covering two-fifths of the peninsula, and varying in size from Haidarabad . . . larger in size than Great Britain, to some tiny Orissan State of a few hundred acres'.[4] In his action, also, was to be found the origin of the policy of 'indirect rule' which spread with the imperial flag and saved men, money and effort. Significantly, its chief apologist in later years, Sir Alfred Lyall, was at this time an influential Indian civil servant. The third edition of his *Rise of the British Dominion in India*, first published in 1893, contains the clearest statement of imperial purpose:

> . . . the true frontier of the British dominion in Asia . . . does not by any means tally with the outer edge of the immense territory over which we exercise administrative jurisdiction . . . The true frontier includes not only this territory, but also large regions over which the English crown has established protectorates of different kinds and grades, varying according to circumstances and specific conditions . . . whatever may be the particular class to which the protectorate belongs, however faint may be the shadow of authority that we chose to throw over the land, its object is to affirm the right of excluding a rural influence and the right of exclusion carries with it the duty of defence. The outer limits of the country we are prepared to defend must be called our frontier.[5]

Interestingly, for reasons that will become clear shortly, Lyall laid the foundation stone of Mayo College, Ajmere, in 1878.[6]

It was too much, however, to expect stern, ethnocentric moralists like Sir John Lawrence, who became Viceroy[7] in 1864, to abandon a long-held belief in the need to raise the standards of rulers and people. And it was certainly too dangerous to allow the States complete independence from British Rule. The British, while interfering as little as possible and demonstrating their goodwill by such gestures as the re-introduction of the principle of adoption, retained their control. A British Resident was appointed to the principal States as an adviser. The government kept to itself the absolute right to control administration when, in its judgement, cases of gross misrule occurred, to maintain ministers in office, to regulate succession and to depose unsatisfactory rulers. The principle of intervention was eventually given written expression in 1875 in the judgement on the case of Baroda, where the British arrested and deposed the tyrannical ruler, Malkar Rao Gaekwar: 'If gross misgovernment be permitted, if substantial justice be not done . . . if life and property be not protected, or if the general welfare of the country and people be persistently neglected, the British Government will assuredly intervene.'[8] The Indian States were neither feudatories, protectorates, nor allies, and to explain their curious status a new word – paramountcy – was employed. The combination of imperial seduction and coercion worked. The Indian royal families remained staunch supporters of British rule until Independence; for, as one Indian commentator has written, 'as long as they danced to the imperial tune, they enjoyed security without struggle.'[9]

During the Mutiny it was not only royalty who had influence. On the outbreak of hostilities in 1857 the tenant farmers at Oudh followed their former landlords with enthusiasm on to the battlefields of Upper India against the imperial forces.[10] The British concluded that the peasantry preferred life under their frequently oppressive local squirearchy, which had been dispossessed by the Benthamite liberals of the East India Company in the years before 1857, to freedom to own their own land.[11] In the changes which followed the Mutiny, therefore, the aristocracy was not overlooked. The government set about re-establishing the land-owning class, so laboriously disestablished in the pre-Mutiny years. Zamindars in Bengal, sirdars in the Punjab, talukdars in Oudh and mulquzars in the Central Provinces, now found themselves in favour. They were appeased, courted and ultimately given a part in local administration.[12]

There was paradox in all this. In the 'orientalization'[13] of British rule in the years after 1857, imperial values were to remain distinctly superior, and were diffused with total conviction. Expedience might dictate political compromise but observation demanded moral indoctrination. By the process of unceasing reiteration, the British had convinced themselves by now of their civilizing role.[14] The idea of a messianic mission had become detached from the multiplicity of motives which had brought them to India and had been elevated to the level of an exclusive rationale.

The imperialists were sure of their own moral strength; firm in the conviction of oriental moral infirmity; certain of the gifts of character they had to bestow. To the confident and uncomprehending European eye, Indian culture in its many guises often appeared degenerate, lascivious, revolting and cruel.

The ultimate contribution of the benevolent imperial despot, therefore, was to bring the indigenous peoples of India to moral maturity: 'It was a message carved in granite, hewn out of the rock of doom.'[15] Curiously, one tangible symbol of both political expedience and moral conviction was the creation of a system of 'public schools' for royalty and nobility. The ideological purpose behind this step was quite unambiguous. By means of this system the British hoped to win over some, at least, of the traditionally influential minority and so succour a band of political evangelists sympathetic to the gubernatorial standards of the imperial race.[16]

The establishment of public schools was equally an attempt at 'indirect rule'. This aspiration is well described by Captain F. K. M. Walter, the agent of the Bharatpur Agency, in his annual report of 1869–70:

> I think we ought in future, without fear of consequences on the score of prejudice or misinterpretation of our intentions, to insist upon the youth [of Indian royalty] being brought up as a gentleman should be. But to carry this into effect we must first establish an Eton in India . . . If we desire to raise the chiefs of India to the standard which they must attain in order to keep pace with the ever advancing spirit of the age, if we wish to make clear to them that our only object is to perpetuate their dynasties and to make them worthy feudatories of the crown of England, we must place within their reach, greater facilities for bestowing on their sons a better education that they can possibly now attain. Then and not till then can we hope to see the native princes of India occupying the position they ought to hold as the promoters of peace, prosperity and progress among their own peoples and hearty supporters of British authority.[17]

Later Lord Curzon spelt out the requirements of the Indian States in more detail: 'Young Chiefs . . . to learn the English language, and become sufficiently familiar with English customs, literature, science, modes of thought, standards of truth and honour, and . . . with manly English sports and games . . .'[18] These alumni, Curzon added, while not forgetting their own heritage, would proudly acquire in their own public schools the attractive physical, moral and executive accomplishments of the English gentleman to the lasting benefit of their subjects. He summed up the general objective as follows:

> It has become apparent that neither private tuition, nor the practices and institutions of Native States or territories, succeed altogether in giving the sons of Chiefs and nobles, that all-round education, particularly in relation to character, that is admittedly the product of the English public school system. To many of the Indian nobility, the discovery has come slowly; to some perhaps it has not come at all. Nevertheless, of the general existence and steady growth of this feeling among the upper classes of Indian society, there can be no doubt, and it was partly to meet this demand, where it has existed, partly to anticipate it where it had yet not found expression, that Government has interested itself in the foundation of a small number of colleges, directly designed to provide a superior type of education for the sons of the princely and aristocratic families of India.[19]

In conjunction with the political practicalities there was a strong hegemonic impulse; paternalistic and patronizing. It was well caught in the pages of the history of the Rajkumar College at Rajkot, in which it was announced that the school owed its existence to the fact that the Political Agent at Kathiawar, Major R. H. Keatinge,[20] on behalf of the British imperialists, had had in mind 'founding a College on the lines of an English public school due to a "kindly desire to raise subjugated nations to like privileges with themselves" '.[21]

It was a theme taken up again and again by viceroys in the remaining decades of the century. Prize Days at Mayo College, eventually the most famous of the schools, saw them regularly preaching the necessity of 'English habits of thought and action'.[22]

In time, two grades of public school emerged, the one for the leading and the other for the lesser chiefs and nobles. Five major 'Chiefs Colleges', as the first-grade schools were known, were eventually established: Rajkumar College (1870), Rajkot, for Kathiawar and later all the Bombay Presidency; Mayo College (1872), Ajmere, for Rajputana; Rajkumar College (1872) at Nowgong for Bundelkhand;[23] Daly College (1876), Indore, for

Central India; and Aitchison College (1886) at Lahore for the Punjab.[24]

By virtue of their pre-eminence the first-grade were the cynosure of government attention. Consequently their development is more fully documented than the lesser institutions, which included such schools as the Talukdari School at Sadra in Gujarat and the schools for Girasias at Wadhwan and Gondal, all in the Bombay Presidency; a school for the descendants and relatives of the Nawab of Murshidabad in Bengal; Colvin School, Lucknow, in the United Provinces; Rajkumar College in Raipur[25] in the Central Provinces; and Nizam College in Hyderabad. The Chiefs Colleges also served as models for the less august schools and concentration in the following pages on the four colleges at Rajkot, Ajmere, Indore and Lahore[26] will provide insight into the early evolution of the Indian public school.

All four colleges were subject to the general control of the Indian government and each was governed by a council or committee, responsible for general administration and made up of distinguished British and Indian members. For example, Mayo College Council comprised:

President: His Excellency, the Viceroy
Vice-President: The Hon'ble Agent to the Governor-General of Rajputana
Members: The Commissioner of Ajmere
Seventeen Chiefs of Rajputana
The political officers to the several States
Secretary: The Principal of the College.[27]

As regards the day-to-day organization of the schools, in the early years Mayo and Aitchison Colleges divided internal control between a military officer (the principal at Mayo, the governor at Aitchison) and a European headmaster. In both schools the officer held overall responsibility for administration while the headmaster was responsible for the teaching. At Rajkot and Daly Colleges, on the other hand, the European headmaster (the principal) was the sole official in charge during the whole period of British administration of India.

While the colleges were certainly founded on the initiative of the British,[28] they were financed initially by large contributions to endowment funds by the native chiefs themselves as well as by less considerable government support. And, as numbers increased, the Indian royalty and nobility gave generously to provide extra classrooms, houses and sports facilities. By 1903 the financial arrangements of the colleges were as described in Table 1 (below).

Table 1. FINANCE[29]

MAYO COLLEGE		AITCHISON COLLEGE	
	R		R
Interest	25,488	Fees (Nat. States)	36,629
Govt. contribution	12,000	Govt. grant	9,000
Nat. states	4,728	Interest	8,256
Other receipts	5,610	Other receipts	5,862
TOTAL	47,826	TOTAL	59,747

RAJKOT COLLEGE		DALY COLLEGE	
Fees and misc. receipts	44,000	Fees	13,941
Interest	9,000	Interest	850
Govt. grant in aid*	5,000	Rent†	2,520
TOTAL	58,000	TOTAL	17,311

* Grant in aid varied between R3,000 and R5,000
† Paid by principal, students and Holkar House
Note: in 1903 the exchange rate for the rupee against £1 sterling was 15 rupees.

As may be seen clearly from Table 1, fees made up the bulk of annual revenue in all the colleges except Mayo, where the munificence of the Chiefs' endowment fund made this unnecessary. The fees were paid by the individual State or the estate of the family and were generally determined by the political officer according to means. The cost of educating individual pupils was by no means standardized as in the public schools of England, and could vary considerably. V. A. Stow in his *A Short History of Mayo College 1869–1942* tells of the Maharaja of Kotah, who in the early days of the college arrived with 200 followers, for whom a special village was built, and of the Maharaja of Alwar, who had a stable of over twenty polo ponies and four carriage horses! There were also substantial differences in educational costs between the four colleges:

MAYO COLLEGE	AITCHISON COLLEGE
R4,300 (Ruling chief) R2,940 (Wealth Thakur) R 780 (ordinary boy with horse)	R1,250 ave. (Muslims) R1,300 ave. (Hindus)
RAJKOT COLLEGE	**DALY COLLEGE**
from R5,000 to 2,200 (no details)	R2,250[30]

The salaries of the staff at the various schools reflected both the relative wealth of the institutions and interesting differences in the assessment of professional worth as Table 2 below clearly demonstrates:

Table 2[31]

MAYO COLLEGE		AITCHISON COLLEGE	
	R		R
Principal*	1,250	Governor*	400
Headmaster*	500	Principal*	500–50–1000
9 assistant masters	50–150	Vice-principal*	400
3 drill instructors	27 (ave)	4 assistant masters	50–100
		Science master	70
		Drawing master	75
		3 oriental teachers	30–60
		Gymnastic instructor	25
		2 boarding house musahibs	40
		Assistant musahib and riding master	35
		Assistant musahib	25
Total annual cost of staff and establishment	41,500	Total, etc.	33,000

RAJKOT COLLEGE		DALY COLLEGE	
	R		R
Principal*	1116	Principal	750–50–1000
Chief assistant master	250	Superintendent	180
8 assistant masters	50–100	4 assistant masters	30–100
Cricket coach	75	Riding master	35
Gym teacher	50	Drill instructor	10
Riding master	15		
Total etc.	35,424	Total etc.	24,000

* European staff

Note: (i) Most of the Indian masters had low educational qualifications; a few, however, were graduates of Indian universities.
(ii) For the value of the rupee against £1 sterling see Table 1 above.

In the internal organization of the schools, the British clung faithfully to the familiar educational blueprint which served their own upper classes so well. For example, throughout the late nineteenth century the Mayo timetable, set out below, was virtually indistinguishable from its British counterpart.

MAYO COLLEGE TIMETABLE[32]

6.15 a.m.	First morning bell
7.00 a.m.	Roll-call (taken by monitors)
7.00 a.m.–7.30 a.m.	Morning P.T.
7.30 a.m.–8.30 a.m.	Prayers and preparation
8.30 a.m.–10.00 a.m.	Breakfast
10.00 a.m.–1.00 p.m.	Classes
1.00 p.m.–2.00 p.m.	Recess (free time)
2.00 p.m.–4.00 p.m.	Classes
4.00 p.m.–6.00 p.m.	Recreation
6.00 p.m.–7.30 p.m.	Prayers and evening meal
7.30 p.m.–8.30 p.m.	Preparation

(Wednesdays and Saturdays were half holidays)

Then there were boarding houses, housemasters and tutors. In the early years, however, the shortage of European staff ensured that the house system was not quite as in England. Houses were supervised not by English housemasters but by musahibs or motamids, native staff who were rarely teaching staff. They were responsible for such matters as tidiness and general behaviour. There were ten houses at Mayo, organized on a territorial basis. At Rajkot there were two houses, wings of the main building, and the boys simply took rooms as they became available. The arrangements at Daly were similar and Rajputs, Kalthis and Muslims were mixed together in four houses. At Aitchison, on the other hand, the three houses were for Muslims, Hindus and Scholars respectively. As at Eton, private tutors were a feature of the schools. Their role, influence and numbers, however, varied from college to college. They served as instruments of British rule. In all cases they had to be approved by the government, and were frequently selected by political officers. Occasionally, when the pupil's status merited it, they were Englishmen.

The character of the academic work in the schools was similar to that of the state high school, and in several respects not unlike their English model. Details of a typical week's work is set out below:

Table 3[33]

Subject	MAYO 1st class	MAYO 2nd, 3rd classes	AITCHISON 1st, 2nd classes	RAJKOT 1st, 2nd, 3rd classes	DALY 1st, 2nd, 3rd classes
English	9	15	9	9	6
Vernacular Language	—	—	—	6	4
Class Lang.	4½	4½	2½	—	—
Maths	10½	4½	7	5	8
History	—	4½	3	5	6
Geography		4½	3	5	2
Science	9	4½	2½	4	—
Drawing	—	—	1½	—	—
TOTAL (in hours)	33	33	25	29	26

English was a vital element in the curriculum in all the colleges, as Table 3 illustrates. Differences of ability, motivation and facility with English meant that the pupils completed their studies at varying speeds. At Mayo it took about eight years to complete the curriculum and pupils remained from about the age of ten to eighteen. At Rajkot six or seven years were sufficient to complete the course and pupils arrived at eleven and remained until their late teens. Aitchison pupils spent between eight and ten years at their studies, arriving at eleven and often remaining until they were in their early twenties. At Daly ten years was the usual period in residence: pupils arrived at between eleven and seventeen and remained until their mid-twenties.

Academic standards in the schools left much to be desired.[34] This was the result of professional complacency on the part of the staff and idleness on the part of both masters and pupils. Much of the curriculum was of dubious relevance to the education of Indian princes, the English teaching was not as thorough as it might have been, and general studies suffered from a want of definition of aim. There were further reasons for the poor intellectual standard. These were described bluntly by a Mr E. Giles, education inspector of the Bombay Northern Division, in a report on Mayo College. He found a tendency to idleness and indifference due to the lack of necessity to learn, pupils' prolonged absences from the college (they were dilatory about returning at the end of vacations) and antagonism towards the school in the boys' homes.[35]

He was not unduly dispirited, however, by this state of affairs. He reminded his readers that, in estimating the value of the institution as a whole, attention ought to be directed 'not so much to what pupils learn as to what they are'. And he was greatly impressed by their admirable training in discipline, truth, manliness and uprightness, which sent out the boys 'honest and straightforward gentlemen, who may become worthy rulers of their own people, and the loyal and enlightened subjects of the Empire'.[36] In short, Giles's sense of proportion was due to the fact that, while a certain casualness represented the schools' approach to intellectual matters, there was one area in which thoroughness was most evident – character-training for leadership. In this connection, as in the English public school, the games field was the instrument of achievement.[37] Offended by the frequently vicious idleness of the native ruler, the British wished above all to develop physical and moral robustness in the allegedly effete sons of chief and noble.[38] *The Report of the Commission on Indian Education* of 1883, for example, stated that it was not, of course, desired to make the young chiefs great scholars, but to encourage in them a healthy tone and manly habits.[39] Morality, as every English schoolboy of the period was aware, grew out of muscular effort! Thus it was written of the Rajkumar College at Rajkot that 'the promoters and founders of this institution deliberately selected the English Public School system as its model and sought to reproduce its most salient features here.' This meant closely following the lines of an English public school on athletic matters to which the English sensibly attached a great deal of importance.[40] One devoted old boy wrote admiringly of his college, 'The moral value of properly organized games is strongly upheld by the [European] teacher of all grades.'[41] And it is true that the ideal of manliness was patiently pursued in all the schools by generations of public schoolmasters imported from England for the purpose.[42]

In an Indian setting, these men built up the facilities, encouraged the mannerisms, enacted the rituals and created the symbols of the English public school. No one is a more apt archetype than Chester Macnaghten (1843–96), the now forgotten 'pioneer of the public school education of the feudatory chiefs'.[43] Macnaghten came from a family with a long history of service in India.[44] After an English education he returned to the sub-continent in 1867 and became, initially, tutor to the son of the Maharaja of Darbhanga, and then, in 1870, principal (headmaster) of Rajkumar College in Kathiawar, the first of the Chiefs schools. It may fairly be said that he took to heart the words of Sir James Peile[45] pronounced at the opening ceremony: 'We shall discipline their bodies in the manliness and hardihood of the English public schoolboy.' Macnaghten attached 'the utmost value to games as a training in character'.[46] In his view, they developed 'energy, promptitude, judgement, watchfulness, courage, generous emulation, appreciation of the merits of others and the highest standards of truthfulness and duty'.[47] In short, he taught his boys the value of manly exercise because it was conducive to manliness – an explicit moral condition. He liked to read his Indian princes the passage from *Tom Brown's Schooldays* in which the Captain of the Eleven (Tom Brown himself) kept his team steady and faced his work bravely in a match crisis. On one occasion Macnaghten followed the reading of the extract with the exhortation: 'In hours so spent you will learn lessons such as no school instruction can give – the lessons of self-reliance, calmness and courage, and of many other excellent qualities, which will better fit you to discharge the duties and face the difficulties, which the future must bring.'[48] And on another occasion he wrote during the vacation to one pupil 'for whom he feared': 'Be temperate and pure and do not be idle . . . Take plenty of outdoor exercise – riding, running, walking, cricket, lawn tennis, shooting . . . and begin the day with that.'[49] Macnaghten was a typical late-Victorian public school headmaster, homilist and athlete. He gave the standard addresses on duty, courage, zeal and *esprit de corps* and clung to the common belief of the time that moral and physical improvement were more remarkable than the mental; because, though scholarship was important, behaviour was far more so. In implementing his games system, he appears to have possessed the pragmatism of G. E. L. Cotton of Marlborough, together with the idealism of Hely Hutchinson Almond of Loretto. As *The Times* reported, 'He [Macnaghten] introduced education on the lines of the English public school model for the sons of chiefs who did not want it, and who clung tenaciously to their old traditions.'[50] His pupils were fractious and unenthusiastic; they viewed each other with the open hostility of traditional enemies. The anonymous author of 'A Run through Kathiawar' in *Blackwood's Magazine* of October 1876 furnished exotic details of sentries guarding the cricket pitch and wild-looking gentlemen sleeping close to their princes for fear of attack from traditional enemies.

Macnaghten himself once recalled of the early days of the school: 'They were wild times . . . and I remember how every evening two bands of armed men marched into our court, and took up their station in front of the rooms inhabited by their young student masters.'[51] Like Cotton, therefore, he used games as an expedient to create order out of disorder. Eventually he established an amiable and enthusiastic climate in which 'boylike simplicity' ultimately prevailed and, in a spirit of comradeship, the school 'played cricket and rounders and football together'. To achieve this state of affairs, like Almond, he inspired both by example and precept: he constructed playing-fields, gave their upkeep his constant attention, joined in all the boys' games and, as we have seen above, lectured them constantly on the moral value of exercise.

Cricket, of course, was the pre-eminent instrument of moral training. Macnaghten, as the extract from *Tom Brown's Schooldays* he chose to read to his students illustrates, believed strongly in 'the moral advantages of cricket'. And so did his peers elsewhere on the Indian sub-continent. During the same period, for the same reasons, 'cricket played a very important part in the life of the Mayo College . . . In fact, cricket . . . formed half the existence of the Mayo College boy. It was apparently often played every day of the week including Sundays.'[52] Cricket was clearly a prophylaxis as beneficial to morals as the better-known apple was to bodies!

Macnaghten, in fact, was no eccentric zealot. He was followed at Rajkot, for example, by C. W. Waddington, who was quite in the Macnaghten mould, 'sportsman, scholar and gentleman'.[53] His predilections are evident from a speech celebrating his virtues recorded in the impressive history of the early years of the school. After making the required, brief obeisances to Waddington's concern for academic standards, the speaker, a local ruler, thrust to the heart of the matter: 'Not neglecting the progress of the Kumars in their studies, Mr Waddington was unremitting in his exertions to bring the Cricket of the College up to the mark from the time when he was placed in sole charge of the Institution, and his labours were crowned with well merited success.' All this was in pursuit of moral excellence, as the same speaker made clear:

> . . . it is often in the playground that the schoolmaster's greatest triumphs are won . . . It is on the cricket ground that a master gets to know the boy as he is out of school, becomes acquainted with his character and has perhaps the most favourable opportunities of moulding that character as he desires. Mr Waddington, himself an expert at all games and sports, has from the first recognized their educational value.[54]

Waddington's successor at Rajkot was J. C. Mayne,[55] another enthusiastic and able sportsman, who joined his Kumars in all their games and sports. Mayne wrote for the college the obligatory, moralistic song of the period – so typical that it slips smoothly over the edge of banality.

> Here many a happy year we spent.
> Here many friendships made;
> And school-boy friends are life-long friends
> Through sunshine and through shade.

We owe her these – and more beside
That none can e'er repay –
The lesson we have daily learnt
In classroom and at play.

Headmasters such as Macnaghten, Waddington and Mayne were loyally supported by their assistant masters. An outstanding (and tragic) example was Francis John Portman,[56] who excelled in running, tennis, cricket and racquets. Conscientious to a fault, he quite literally ran himself to death racing with the Kumars before breakfast during their training for the school sports – an ill-advised activity for a European in the Indian climate. The English public school fraternity saw only nobility in his devotion to duty: 'Young India needs training in the spirit of chivalrous manhood, and that is exactly what her sons have learnt from contact with Francis Portman.'[57]

The eventual success of Macnaghten and his proselytizing successors in smoothly translating an educational ethic from England to India may be estimated from complementary sources. The first is a photograph of the Mayo College Cricket Eleven of 1906,[58] who gaze out upon the world in their elegant striped blazers and immaculate white flannels with the calm self-confidence that membership of a public school eleven brought, in those halcyon times, to boys who were physically talented as well as wealthy and well born. The second is this assessment of Mayo College at the same period by a local inspector of schools:

> On the whole, the instruction given throughout the classes appeared to be careful and thorough . . . In the games there was every indication of keenness and proficiency, and I do not think that the most captious critic would have any fault to find with the general arrangements for recreation and physical instruction, which are in my opinion admirable. The boarding houses appear to be excellently managed, and the whole college, with its large numbers, approaches more nearly to the model of a good English public school than any institution I have seen in India. I have only to add that, throughout the college, the manners and bearing of the boys are excellent. They appear to be gentlemen in every sense of the word.[59]

At about the same time Ian Malcolm, a visiting journalist from England, found, to his delight, at the school 'three cricket and football elevens, each with a capital ground' and wrote magnanimously: 'it would be difficult to have a prettier cricket field than the match ground, with its views of trees and distant mountains.'[60] The facilities, he further discovered, included a racquet court, lawn tennis courts, a running track and a gymnasium. A quintet of energetic English games masters ensured there was not a loafer in the place! Malcolm concluded complacently, '. . . in the matter of public schools, India is following closely in the footsteps of England.'[61] Clearly, the earlier request of Captain Walter had been fully met, namely, that the Indian public schools should be staffed by 'thoroughly educated English gentlemen, not mere book worms but men fond of field sports and out of doors exercises'.[62]

The arrogance of the British inception was enormous. Ancient Indian educational practices and long-established hedonism ensured that the relatively Spartan, games-oriented public life was viewed by many upper-class Indians as a most unpalatable alien oddity. Both Hindu and Muslim possessed their own educational systems long before the arrival of the British. Schools of learning were dutifully supported by rulers, nobles, the wealthy and the religious. These were to be found in mosques, temples, in the open air and in the homes of the rich. Pupils entered at the age of twelve and continued to study for a period of up to twelve years. The teaching was predominantly oral and the discipline exceedingly harsh.[63] While Hindu schools concentrated on the teaching of literature, law and logic, the Muslim schools, for their part, taught forms of correspondence, legal processes and Persian and Arabic.[64]

It is not clear, however, how many of the leading chiefs and nobles took advantage of the indigenous education prior to and during the British occupation of India. Some were privately educated. Sir Syad Khan, the famous Muslim educational reformer, came from an ancient family of Oudh and was educated at home. However, he was one of the first to recognize the inadequacies of the old Muslim educational practices for modern society, and in 1875 established the College at Aligarh for the Muslim aristocracy. One old boy claimed its main purpose was to inculcate loyalty to British values. It was certainly run on the lines of an English public school. How closely it resembled this institution may be seen from Wilfred Scawen Blunt, who, in his report of a visit in 1883, enthused over both the public school image and the facilities created for its implementation. He was more than satisfied to find the boys playing cricket under the benevolent tyranny[65] of the headmaster: 'We went over the College, which is certainly a wonderful work. It is on a large scale, but without pretence, and no money has been wasted on ornament. The boys were out playing cricket, which they did as well as an average lot of English schoolboys, and seemed to take full interest in the game. Among them was the new Principal of the College, Mr Beek.'[66] Parents and pupils were pleased with the innovation. It was reported by the same old boy mentioned earlier that the Muslim exhorted the Englishman: 'Leave us our God; in all else make us English.'[67] Regardless of the strong enthusiasm of the convert, several authorities have expressed a poor opinion of the attitude to education of the offspring of the more powerful princes and aristocrats. One British observer wrote of the Indian princeling: 'From his boyhood everything about him combines to thrust education into the background. The influence of the zenana [that part of the house in India reserved for the women] is generally opposed to any enlightenment. Early marriage with its hindrances and distractions . . . in some case hereditary instinct leads him to regard education as scarcely better than a disgrace.'[68] An even harsher critic of the local prince was the Anglophile Indian, Narullah Khan, an old boy of Mayo College and a Cambridge graduate. He wrote caustically of the education of royalty before the coming of the Raj: 'a great deal may be said but not of a pleasing nature.'[69] It was, he explained, in the hands of hereditary servants, called durbaries, neither educated nor enlightened, who supplied only flattery. Others were of a similar opinion. Major R. H. Keatinge considered a prince's education comprised exclusively of 'ruinous habits' from contact with slaves, opium-eaters, drunkards and fawning, self-interested, native tutors.[70] In consequence, it has been argued that despite British efforts to set up schools for their benefit 'the cadets of the aristocratic and opulent Indian families were frequently brought up to lead idle lives.'[71] Certainly, while some indigenous leaders proved enthusiastic supporters of the Chiefs Colleges,[72] many were indifferent or antipathetic towards them. It was noted frankly in the *Fifth Quinquennial Review*: 'On the whole the Colleges have not been cordially supported by the distinguished class for whose benefits they are maintained.'[73] By the turn of the century, after some twenty years in existence, the schools could only muster between 180 and 190 pupils between them.[74] At Mayo College, which drew on a possible clientele of eighteen ruling chiefs and 300 aristocratic families, the situation was hardly reassuring:[75]

Places available	Numbers at school	Highest number at one time
150	50	80

The college roll from 1875 to 1895[76] reveals how unsatisfactory the response had been down the years:

1875–6	1876–7	1877–8	1878–9	1879–80	1880–81	1881–2	1882–3	1883–4	1884–5
23	31	39	37	32	45	62	62	68	74
1885–6	1886–7	1887–8	1888–9	1889–90	1890–91	1891–2	1892–3	1893–4	1894–5
80	76	71	70	79	73	68	63	57	68

Both the low numbers and the status of entrants produced disappointment. In 1897, for example, it was noted with acute regret: 'As regards rank and numbers, the chief drawbacks are that no heir or ruling chief from the three first class States of Udaipur, Jodhpur or Jaipur has attended the College, nor has any prince or thakut been entered from the States of Bundi or Dungaput.'[77] By 1902 the Viceroy, Lord Curzon, was complaining that only twelve out of thirty-two ruling chiefs of Kathiawar had been educated at Rajkot.[78] It was no better elsewhere. Most chiefs of the Punjab failed to send their sons to Aichison College, and Daly College never received the sons of the larger central States such as Gwailior, Bhopar and Dewa: a state of affairs which earned the families concerned a public rebuke from the Viceroy.

Self-respect as well as self-indulgence no doubt played its part in the widespread rejection of English upper-class education. In her study of Bengal in *Education and Social Change: Three Studies on Nineteenth-Century India*, for example, Vina Majumdar points out that the richer classes clung to their own culture and were far from keen to give their children an English education. Only when the large size of the family or declining returns from the land reduced their wealth, so that the sons had to earn a living, were they sent to schools run on English lines. The crude ethnocentricism of the education – drill, gymnastics and cricket would scarcely have impressed the traditional Hindu and Muslim – must have had its effect; but there were other important reasons for lack of support. By the turn of the century complaints about standards in the colleges circulated widely. His Highness the Gaekwar of Baroda, for example, criticized the standards of the schools in *East and West* in January 1902. His criticisms were reproduced in the *Voice of India* and synopsized in the *Kathiawar Times*. Curzon was, therefore, under no illusion about the chiefs' dissatisfaction with the high cost and general irrelevance of the education provided there. He shared much of this dissatisfaction himself and felt compelled to act. He called a conference at Calcutta the same year to discuss the reform of the constitution and curriculum of the Chiefs Colleges. It lasted four days and was attended by the principal political officers, representatives of the native chiefs and the heads of existing colleges. There was a further conference at Ajmere in 1904. Reformation of the colleges followed. It included more European staff attracted by greatly increased salaries, the introduction of political economy, political science, elementary law and revenue into the curriculum, a leaving examination and a diploma, the introduction of regular inspections, the abolition of dual command at Mayo and Aitchison, the abolition of the system of private tutors and the allocation of boarding houses to European housemasters.

Curzon's aims were several – to improve academic standards, to make the curriculum more relevant to the needs of future Indian rulers and, at the same time, to make the colleges even more like the English public school and thus raise their tone. It appears that his efforts were remarkably successful. One of Curzon's actions in 1903 was to reduce Daly College to the status of a feeder college for Ajmere, yet his reforms improved things so much that in 1905, at the request of the local chiefs, who provided the land and much of the money, Daly was enlarged and raised once more to the level of a major college.[79] Again on the introduction of Curzon's reforms, Mayo College immediately increased its intake. By 1912 numbers at the colleges had risen to a total of 413.[80] A large building programme was mounted and there was a considerable expansion of facilities. In 1921 a fifth college, Raipur, was admitted to the ranks of Chiefs College. In 1928 Aitchison College announced that it had been in full working existence for forty-one years, had amassed many public school traditions and now considered itself sufficiently established to aspire to a proper register of its old alumni.[81] Shortly afterwards Mayo College claimed to be 'widely supported by Ruling Chiefs . . . The attendance of Ruling Princes and Old Boys at the recent prize gathering was, except for the jubilee celebrations, a record and is a happy augury for the future.'[82] It is clear from statistics and statements such as those above that the system of public schools in India was now established. Against the odds the British had persisted. They had planted in tropical soil a foreign seed, which slowly grew into a sturdy miniature of a much larger English plant.[83]

The Indian public school was created out of a hotch-potch of Victorian motives – imperial calculation, ethnocentric self-confidence and well-meaning benevolence. It is interesting to reflect on the possible course of events had the British courted the urban professional, industrialist and entrepreneur, the backbone of the nationalist movement, as sedulously as it attempted to win over the royalty and aristocracy, and established a larger system of public schools embracing academic, merchant, landlord and prince. Even in its more socially restricted form, however, the early Indian public school system provides a fascinating illustration of the cultural diffusion of an educational ethic arising out of imperial conquest. And, in only gently modified form, it has survived the imperialist.[84] As it happens, this is also true of a markedly different part of the Empire – the white Dominion of Canada to which we now turn to see how the white colonial took to the ideals and activities of the upper-class educational system of the Motherland.

6

DISCIPLINE IN THE DOMINION

The 'Canuck' and the Cult of Manliness

'The Loyalists in Canada,' it has been suggested, 'have had an influence out of all proportion to their numbers. They were after all the Chosen and they soon occupied positions of leadership and power . . . thousands of their descendants proudly call themselves Loyalists to this day . . . Once a Loyalist, always a Loyalist.'[1] Arthur Lower, whose preoccupation with the nature of Canadian identity lasted a lifetime, took a jaundiced view of English Canada's lengthy homage to the Crown, seeing it as a kind of 'filial piety' which had produced merely onlookers at the great plays staged in London and left the 'Canuck' – 'parochial, imitative, provincial, uncreative'.[2]

Our concern is also with filiation, piety and identity. These elements had much to do with the process of moral, educational and recreational diffusion whereby the English public school games and their allegedly ethical attributes found their way to such diverse Canadian provinces as Ontario, Manitoba and British Columbia. Yet the concern is also with adaptation and replacement, and with sport as a symbolic and actual manifestation of both association and separation. In such complicated circumstances the games of the Canadian 'public schools' served contradictory purposes. They were certainly intended to make a contribution, however insignificant and tangential, to Sir John MacDonald's ambition of imparting 'solidity and substance to a flimsy political entity and to make [Canada] an auxiliary Kingdom within the Empire',[3] but at another level they were equally representative, however unrecognized and unappreciated, of Henry Bourassa's concern with a concept of nationality which espoused autonomy and rejected assimilation. The influence of the 'public schools' was far from exclusive. The French-Canadians, as well as other ethnic groups of Continental origin, not to mention the indigenous tribes, had their games and related ethics. The concern for manliness extended far beyond the Anglo-Saxon private school but, as we shall see, it became firmly established within it, and mores and machinery were borrowed from Britain. It is, of course, this British connection which concerns us here.

There is nothing remarkable in the pioneers of a new country engaging nostalgically in what has been referred to scathingly, in a Canadian context, as 'submergence in past values and activities'.[4] Certainly this was as much to maintain an emotional 'umbilical cord' as anything else, but it was frequently more. Mott's remark regarding the nineteenth-century Manitobans was widely applicable: '[They] played and promoted manly games, not only because they were certain these activities revealed and nurtured many desirable qualities, but for another reason . . . the sense of duty they felt to establish and maintain British culture in their new, still only semi-civilized part of the world.' He continued, 'The pioneers identified with a Canada that was an integral part of the British Empire and could not be imagined as separate from it. Their empire was at that time reaching the apex of its power and influence, and from their point of view represented man's highest achievement in the development of governmental and social order. Therefore those things that were "British" simply had to be transplanted in Manitoban soil.'[5] Implicit in this assertion is the familiar Anglo-Saxon certainty of belief in the value of 'manly games' for imperial supremacy. Mott later makes it explicit: 'in large part through games . . . Britain had gained the physical and moral strength to acquire and govern their vast Empire.'[6]

Imperial reproduction of those features of civilization located on English playing-fields was not restricted to the Protestants of the prairie provinces. It was a widespread phenomenon which, it is sometimes suggested in naive subscription to the over-abundant rhetoric of religious writers, more often than not represented in large measure an evangelical pursuit of the virtues of Kingsleian Christianity. In reality, it represented this and a great deal more besides: 'sentimental attachment to an old English institution, patriotic emotions, the yearning to keep Canada within the British Empire, the desire to create a leadership class imbued with the ideals of Christian service, the search for an alternative form of education to the state system'[7] as well as more Darwinian motives. The uncomplicated liturgy of religious enthusiasm as exemplified by the founders of Bishop Ridley College, whose aim 'was to produce Christian gentlemen for "the Christian character is the highest type of character; the true Christian is the true gentleman" ',[8] should not be swallowed whole. Christian conviction represented convention as much as commitment. Ironically, the ideal of the Christian chevalier was not easily compatible with the ethos of individualistic competitiveness of nineteenth-century entrepreneurial society or, for that matter, with the ruthless political struggles of the period: 'such a figure might be out of place amid the harsh bargaining of the board room or the crude atmosphere of backroom politics.'[9] Yet to square the concepts of Christian gentleman and Darwinian entrepreneur is not all that difficult. Some progress can be made by reflection on this image of John Bull which has strong Canadian associations: 'the English, for their part, have been Puritan rather than Christian, . . . they have admitted the terms virtue, manliness, strength, steadfastness, efficiency, but they have had too strong a sense of "right and wrong" to have given them much insight into the essential Christian ideal of charity and love.'[10]

Further progress to a resolution of the conundrum can be achieved if there is a sustained attempt to separate rhetoric and reality, image and substance, precept and practice in Canada as well as in England. In the cultivation of both chivalric altruism and capitalistic egotism, the Canadian 'public schools' did not depart too markedly from British precedent as might well be believed if too much attention is paid to Purdy's bewilderment at an apparent discontinuity between educational ideals and public morality.[11]

In nineteenth-century Ontario the founders of all the leading boys' boarding schools save one 'were drawn from the ranks of Anglican clerics and businessmen'.[12] This fact highlights an essential feature of early Canadian education. It was heavily religious. Seventeenth-century Recollects and Jesuits built schools in an attempt to convert Quebec to Catholicism, while subsequently the Society for the Preservation of the Gospel built schools in New Brunswick, Nova Scotia and Newfoundland in an attempt to nourish Protestant souls. The remainder of the colony, however, was neglected and the majority of English-speaking, Protestant colonialists left to their own devices.[13] The resulting Denominationalism led eventually to rival schools in the hands of Methodists, Baptists, Anglicans and 'Romanists'. After the American Revolution, Empire Loyalists from the United States also played their substantial part in the development of Canadian education; a fact that brings us back full circle to 'the Chosen'.

Their allegiance to Britain, touched upon above, was blatantly self-interested:

> In the state, privilege was more invidious than in the church, for it had no moral basis to rest on. It was because of this that the little group of individuals who managed to keep the good things to themselves, the so-called 'Family Compact', were so sensitive on the question of allegiance. The only warrant for their conduct was the King's will: they, therefore, were unremitting in their attempts to maintain themselves as the sole channels of royal grace and in efforts to make it appear that those who challenged their authority challenged the throne.[14]

Their involvement in Canadian education was similarly motivated. They brought the English public school system to Canada and encouraged and fostered its development in their own interests. Their support for a state system of education was muted. They proved reluctant 'to vote money for the tentative beginnings of public education in Canada'.[15] By the late nineteenth century this privileged élite was forced to share its traditional prerogatives with 'less tightly knit clusters of different élites' from the growing ranks of middle-class merchants and manufacturers.[16] What they all had in common were their Anglo-Saxon origins, associations and affections. The Anglican faith, of course, has traditionally represented the faith of the Anglo-Saxon wealthy élite in both Britain and its Empire, and the Episcopalian schools modelled on the English 'public' school had been long favoured by the upper echelons of Canadian society.[17] As late as the 1980s 'the percentage of teachers familiar with the English public schools either as pupils or staff was still in some schools as high as twenty per cent,'[18] and a recent international survey of private schools concluded that those of English-speaking Canada approximate more closely to the English original than any other.[19]

The location of these schools, of course, followed the process of settlement and ensuing prosperity. While the fortunes of the private school system ebbed and flowed and numbers rose and fell with circumstance, the present pattern reflects this historical process. Thus Ontario has some twenty private schools, British Columbia ten, Nova Scotia three and Alberta two.[20] For the most part the schools faithfully and gradually reproduced the orthodox features of the lauded English public school – a house system, prefects, team games and fervent ideological subscription to the games ethic. An editorial from the *Montreal Gazette* in 1861 demonstrates particularly well the mid-century Canadian belief in the desirability of theoretical and practical borrowing from the mother country:

> Sports that would not interfere with the hours of study, should constitute an essential part of education in every school and college in Canada, sports that would 'mould the characters as well as the forms of our youth', that would brighten and quicken the intellectual faculties, giving energy to every action of mind as well as body; these should be as much a part of education as the teaching of the classics, or any branch of studies.[21]

The significance of imperial 'sports' to these essentially Loyalist institutions can be best seen in one symbolic fact: in society as a whole, as indigenous values and enthusiasms manifested themselves and cricket declined in popularity, the game remained an essential component of Canadian 'public school' education.

In this assertive and confident departure from social fashion the role of the headmaster, and to a lesser extent that of assistant master, was critical. They were powerful agents, first of change and then conservation: 'Headmasters and masters . . . right across the country . . . were more often than not the driving force behind the athleticism movement; they initiated, nurtured, monitored and guided it.'[22] How is this uniformity of purpose to be explained? As in the case of Cochrane's *Railroad Leaders*,[23] the period Christian leaders were characterized by preconceived ideas about appropriate professional attitudes and actions. The pervasive bias was muscular and owed much to English precedent. Ascription to the bias was the test of legitimacy, popularity and success. There was, of course, divergence from the ideal but, in general, variability was limited by strong social prescription and 'men likely to favour wide departure from conventional ways' were excluded from appointment. In short, behaviour was less individual than normative. Only the compliant found favour, rather like the dog in the Russian proverb who was allowed to join the pack because he did not bark but merely wagged his tail. And the corporate vision shaping action was remarkably similar to that of Mellot in Kingsley's *Yeast*. Like him, these men frequently saw everything in its ideal – 'not as it is, but as it ought to be, and will be when all the vices of this pitiful civilized world are exploded'.[24] They were Platonists who saw, or claimed to see, virtue in the efforts of athletes. Such efforts epitomized in their myopic eyes late-Victorian Christian manliness!

The English concept of manliness changed dramatically in connotation during the Victorian period.[25] To the early Victorians it meant the successful transition from Christian immaturity to maturity demonstrated by earnestness, selflessness and integrity: to the late Victorians it represented neo-Spartan virility as exemplified by stoicism, hardiness and endurance – the pre-eminent virtues of the late-Victorian English public school. Extrinsic and intrinsic discipline was exemplified both literally and metaphorically by 'the stiff upper lip'. Headmasters of the Canadian 'public schools' admired the same virtues, enunciated the same pieties and adopted the same means of realization as their English counterparts. They would have agreed without difficulty with the Reverend N. Burwash, chancellor of Victoria University, when in 1904 he spoke warmly of 'Imperialism in Education' and urged adoption of an English ideal of 'Moral Manhood',[26] and would have found little to disagree with in the admonitory words of J. O. Miller, the first headmaster of Bishop Ridley College, Ontario, to his pupils: 'Self-control is the basis of all Character, and the root of all the virtues. Without it, man is like a ship that has lost its rudder, and tosses helpless upon the waves.'[27]

Carl Berger's fascinating study of Canadian imperialism as nationalism,[28] with its concentration on 'the intellectual contents of Canadian imperialism' and the associated contention that the imperialists were in fact nationalists, has been considered recently 'at a working level'. In 'Empire Day in the Schools of Ontario: The Training of Young Imperialists',[29] by means of a series of powerful and convincing period quotations from the last decade of the nineteenth century, Robert Stamp has demonstrated the force of feeling for an imperial connotation of Canadian national identity expressed through the symbolical medium of Empire Day. As he shows in the influential arguments of men like Ontario Minister of Education, George Ross,[30] love of country was subsumed within love of Empire: 'Empire Day suggests that larger British sentiment which . . . now prevails throughout the empire, and to which Canada has for many years contributed not a little. The proudest sentiment which the old Roman could express was "Civis Romanus sum". The greatest sentiment, as well as the most stirring which we could put into the minds and hearts of our children . . . is "Civis Britannicus sum",' and, he added significantly, 'to give the sentiment its fullest force we should broaden it so as to include the whole British Empire.'[31] Through energetic advocacy and professional influence Ross harnessed public feeling to civic celebration. Later ministers such as Robert Pyre, Henry Cody and G. Howson Ferguson perpetrated Ross's early passion with diligence. It was not difficult. They were caught up in a general euphoria. Stamp again:

> the success of Empire Day was due even more to its compatibility with the concepts of loyalty and patriotism prevalent in early twentieth-century English-speaking Ontario. These years witnessed the climax of the movement to use the schools for patriotic purposes. Children in Ontario and other provinces received a daily dose of flag saluting, allegiance pledging, and patriotic singing and poetry reading. To a certain extent this was a manifestation of English-Canadian nationalism.[32]

Conjunction of imperial association and public school ethics was achieved by Governor-General Earl Grey in 1909 in a speech to Toronto school cadets: 'I want you boys to remember what Empire Day means. Empire Day is the festival on which every British subject should reverently remember that the British Empire stands out before the whole world as the fearless champion of freedom, fair play and equal rights; that its watchwords are responsibility, duty, sympathy and self-sacrifice.'[33]

Careful promotion of the enmeshed qualities of imperial loyalty and social morality among the young through the schools was typical of three other prominent 'Georges' of the day – George Grant, principal of Queen's University; George Denison, a Toronto magistrate; and George Parkin, headmaster of Upper Canada College from 1895 to 1902.[34] Parkin was the consummate synthesist – blending imperialism, education and Christianity in a rich, evangelical mixture. His adult life was spent propagating the interrelated concepts of imperial unity, élitist education and Christian morality. He became (in a splendid and deservedly much-quoted expression) 'the prince of imperialists and their first missionary'.[35] His imperial mission is to be understood not in terms of individuals or even countries, but rather in terms of race.[36] He did not make a virtue of conceptual clarity, however. Unhappily his concept of race was a muddled one, 'exhibiting a confused anthropological mixture of monogenist, Christian polygenist, and evolutionist racial theory'.[37] The superior 'race' was variously described as 'Anglo-Saxon', 'British', 'English', 'English-speaking', 'white', 'northern', or 'Teutonic'. This loose collection of synonyms 'defined the white people of the United Kingdom and the Dominions (and in some contexts the United States as well) who had acquired over the generations certain common racial instincts based on a shared history, commercial energy, climate, parliamentary traditions, religion, and culture, a group which for all important purposes were one in emotions, traditions and ideals.' As Parkin saw it, the unification of the Anglo-Saxon race was not an end in itself but a means to an end: 'Through the Empire he felt that he could best provide his own brand of Christian ethics and public morality.'[38] In other words, the Empire was a route to the realization of his Christian idealism which viewed man 'as an embodiment of spirit and ideals, not as a creature of blind instincts and base deviations',[39] and the rationale for the maintenance of Empire was a moral responsibility for the elevation of the weaker races of the world. Towards the end of the nineteenth century this 'idealist creed' was fashionable among 'a dazzling array of statesmen, whites, civil servants, educators and churchmen',[40] including Alfred Milner, J. C. Smuts, R. C. Morant and R. G. Collingwood: 'with its concentration on citizenship and patriotism, with its exhortation of Christian and moral responsibility towards society's weaker members, idealism also actuated the new imperialism – or at least that aspect of it which viewed the Empire less as an economic and strategic concern and more as an agent of the white man's burden and as an embodiment of lofty national ideas.'[41] The English Canadians were caught up in the nobility of this enterprise: 'they, too, pictured themselves as part of a ruling race, whose mission it was to carry "British and Christian" civilization (in the late nineteenth century the two words were equated) to the ends of the earth.'[42] Parkin was their Moses.

Yet Parkin's real mission was education: 'he was a teacher long before he became an imperialist.'[43] The ethical imperatives of his idealism found practical expression in his educational work, first as principal of Upper Canada College and then as secretary-organizer of the Rhodes Scholarship scheme. In both endeavours character rather than commercialism was the essence of education. Manliness rather than Mammon was the true end of the training of youth. Upper Canada College 'with its emphasis on producing Christian gentlemen of "character", with its inculcation of the precepts of public service, patriotism, duty, spartanism, and loyalty . . . was, in effect, training future idealists.'[44] In short, 'a faith in the influence of Christianity in the world . . . unified his work as an educator and an imperialist.'[45] Ethics, education and Empire formed a closed circle. Parkin was a compelling metaphysician, romantic and inspirationalist. His greatest quality was sincerity. It was spellbinding. As one of his masters at Upper Canada College wrote: 'He was the only man I have known who by the inspiration of an address, based on a real belief in human nature, could rouse boys to keep away from a neighbouring apple orchard.'[46] He was less successful as practitioner, innovator and administrator. It would appear that he had all the failings of a rhetorician. His period at Upper Canada College was not altogether successful. On the one hand, neither masters nor pupils could live easily with his high idealism and, on the other, he could not live happily with human imperfection. Disillusionment brought despondency compounded 'by the obvious discrepancy between the reality of a public school in Toronto and the English ideal which he was then describing in his biography of Thring'.[47] For all this he never lost sight of his ideal: character above commercialism. He placed a strong emphasis on 'manners, accent, comportment and conduct'. And he used the games field as he believed his hero Thring had, as a tool for character-training. He had less of an uphill task here than in other areas of school life. He was well in line with orthodoxy and with earlier diffusionist headmasters.

Upper Canada College had been founded in 1829. From its genesis it has been 'in the minds of a great many people, the pre-eminent independent school in Canada, [and] regarded as the cradle of the Canadian Establishment'.[48] Founded by Sir John Colbourne on his arrival as Lieutenant-Governor of Upper Canada, it was one of the earliest attempts on Canadian soil to transplant the English public school system.[49] Colbourne's desire was 'to foster in the new institution a love of the old, manly British field sports, a love which had always been a characteristic of English Public School men'. He requested from the Vice-Chancellor of Oxford University, a 'Cargo of Masters', men of scholarship, but more importantly men 'who would encourage and stimulate among the boys a love of "healthy and manly games" and good sportsmanship'.[50] Élitism, classical curriculum and 'birch rod' style of discipline at the school were not widely popular, but the 'indulged and privileged child' of the establishment nurtured by the powerful, as is not unusual, grew successfully to maturity.

Cricket was an early and important feature of school life and the suggestion has been made that it was played not simply because it was English but rather because it was considered to possess features which 'educators within a school of high prestige and notable moral training wished to engender'.[51] In fact association between origin and objective was strong. The 'features to be engendered' were desirable, as Parkin would have been quick to remark, because they were considered to be peculiarly English attributes – the property of 'the Anglo-Saxon race'. The philathletic passions of an early principal, F. W. Barron (1843–56), were seminal to the growth of athleticism at the college. Barron was an enthusiastic lover of all outdoor and athletic sports, who killed a sizeable number of birds with one stone. He was an accomplished skater, a skilful yachtsman, an aggressive boxer and a subtle fencer and, in addition, advocated cricket, hockey, running, leaping and jumping, as well as other sports and games. Cricket received his close attention. His tenacity 'nursed it to the status it attained and retained in the school'. This stress on cricket was far from being the product of mere recreational enthusiasm; the game was a profound political symbol, a means of differentiating between constitutional sense and nonsense. As the *Patriot*, a local journal, observed after an impressive victory by the college against the Toronto Cricket Club in July 1836: 'British feelings cannot flow into the breasts of our Canadian boys thro' a more delightful or untainted channel than that of British sports. A cricketer as a matter of course detests democracy and is staunch in allegiance to his king.'[52] At the same time Barron considered cricket a means of moral indoctrination. He was an absolute believer 'in games as moulders of manly character'. In short, hedonism, hegemony and morality were the early travelling companions of athleticism.

Influential as Barron was, it was not until logistics and fashion combined to enlarge facilities and stimulate orthodoxy that athleticism became a pronounced feature of school life. The union coincided with the principalship of George Cockburn (1861–81), a man deeply involved in the period persuasions of the English public school. He had been educated at Merchiston Castle and had taught at Fettes. He was, therefore, a product of that curious group of Scottish schools so out of harmony with Scottish tradition and certainly as zealous, if not more zealous, as any English public school in promoting the virtues of their adopted system. In the matter of games Cockburn was an expansionist: facilities, activities and organization received attention. At least one of his successors, George Dickson (1885–95), matched him in commitment. Precedent now well established, he was a conventional adherent to conventional values in the interests of both individual and institutional appropriateness of image. While Cockburn furnished an illustration of eager Scottish assimilation of an English ethic, Dickson provided an illustration of enthusiastic Canadian emulation. His background was wholly Canadian, but his predilection was for English practice. He exerted tight control over games and the games field. He was a latter-day Cotton, introducing a games fund as a means of providing adequate facilities to ensure effective control, while underpinning this practicality with desirable ideological idealism. Like Cotton, his pragmatism went further: 'his most important introduction was undoubtedly a new system of games management . . . which centralized control and direction under himself, the staff, and representing the boys, the stewards.'[53] With good reason, the most knowledgeable analyst of the games ethic at Upper Canada College has argued that Dickson was the influential figure in the formalization of athleticism in the school.[54]

Thus the machinery of games was well constructed and operating smoothly by the time Parkin took up his appointment. He continued in Dickson's 'promotional and expansionist vein' but characteristically, it would seem, with a strong imperialist emphasis, as in his attempt to make cricket, the college's oldest and most symbolic game, compulsory.[55] Cricket was the umbilical cord of Empire linking the mother country with her children. After Parkin's departure to become secretary-organizer of the Rhodes Scholarship, he was succeeded as principal by Henry William Auden (Shrewsbury and Cambridge). Auden, principal from 1902 to 1917, was also from the Celtic outpost of the English public school system – he too had been a master at Fettes. He was conventional in his theological subscription, and contributed to the liturgy of athleticism with a keen regard for cliché and a notable skill with facile simile. Colbourne, Barron, Dickson, Parkin and Auden were a willing and effective means of transmission and introduction. They embraced English convention wholeheartedly. They were potent instruments of diffusion. Their emphases were different, but their ambition was similar. Collectively they promulgated games for reasons of control, affiliation, idealism and élitism.

As in nineteenth-century Britain, the origins of athleticism in Canadian schools were at once attractively individualistic and tediously uniform. Charles Sanderson Fosbery, headmaster of St John's, Montreal, from 1900 to 1935, represented both facets of this curious manifestation. Fosbery inherited a school with a tarnished image. Mismanagement and misappropriation of funds had characterized the headship of his predecessor. On Fosbery's appointment morale was low, and he chose to inculcate a fresh sense of respectability and new feelings of loyalty by means of a technique well-known in British schools – 'emphasis was laid upon games and athletics'. He had considerable success. A pupil of the period recalled in later life 'the splendid school spirit [and] a healthy fighting pride . . . particularly the case in connection with sports', and added, 'All the boys were keenly proud of the school and realized that its prestige depended in large measure on them.'[56]

Fosbery's accord with the games ethic was the outcome of a variety of British experiences. He was educated at the Grammar School at Newark-on-Trent and at Trinity College, Dublin, and taught later at Cheltenham College and Howden Grammar School, Yorkshire, before becoming a schoolmaster in Canada. These experiences provided him 'with definite ideas on how a school should operate'.[57] He has much in common with Hely Hutchinson Almond of Loretto, not only in his stress on the character-training value of games but also in his Spencerian preoccupation with physical fitness. He had the health of each and every boy at heart. He peppered the college magazine with articles on sensible living. He urged that 'physical exercise must be practised with regularity'[58] and, with typical Almondian outspokenness, stated argumentatively that the general health of his pupils would be improved by less reliance on street cars. He was as much obsessed with ventilation as Almond was with tight collars and he was Almondian in philosophy *and* practice. His bedroom housed 'an iron cot, varnished dresser, chair and table, and a plain unshielded light hanging on a wire from its ceiling centre'. The floor was bare and the temperature always low.[59] Apparently ascetic, he was far from unworldly. He did not lack business acumen and social shrewdness. He quickly made sure that St John's possessed good playing-fields and, as the school historian has recorded, 'in less than five years he was to reap his reward in the fame and publicity that his successful athletes won for his School.'[60] Nor did he lack ambition. His desire for complete independence from old associations led to a change of location and a change of name. In 1889 he moved the school to Notre Dame de Grâce in the 'English' sector of Montreal and renamed it Lower Canada College.

At Bishop Ridley College in the late nineteenth century the Reverend John Ormsby Miller, the school's first headmaster, as we have seen already, devised a school motto of ringing conviction – 'May I be consumed by Service'; he intended his boys to be 'imbued with the character fashioned on the life of Christ, filled with a moral and physical steadfastness'.[61] As motto and motive suggest, Miller, the son of an English clergyman who had obtained a clerical position in Canada, was an unexceptional and thus wholly acceptable muscular Christian;

he loved God and cricket. He stood for a clear and clean ideal of boyhood which was outlined in his *The Young Canadian Citizen*.[62] This moral treatise mirrored closely the numerous books of public school sermons published by headmasters of the English public schools, which assisted their elevation within the ecclesiastical hierarchy.[63] The work contained the obligatory sections on duty, courage, purity, unselfishness, self-control and self-reliance. It was typical of its time in the close relationship it drew between physiological, psychological and moral soundness. Miller asserted that 'purity of body [and] self-reliance in the playground all had psychological benefits which in turn affected the moral side of a boy's nature.'[64] An early advertisement for the school read: 'Special attention is paid to moral training. The facilities for physical development are unrivalled in Canada. Cricket ground of eight acres, well equipped gymnasium, four tennis courts, boat house, bathing crib.' The juxtaposition of purpose and provision was not fortuitous!

Miller's writing reveals not merely rectitude but also a so far unexplored British influence – that of literature. Miller owed much to Ruskin, Bacon, Carlyle, Kingsley and, above all, Hughes, and demonstrates the potency of British literary imagery in shaping, sustaining and reinforcing an ideal of Canadian boyhood in the schools of the privileged. Thomas Hughes's *Tom Brown's Schooldays* was much admired throughout the Canadian upper-class educational system, and 'Tom's manly, muscular Christian character along with his heroic action provided one template for aspiring private schoolboys.'[65] Further fictional characters 'augmented Tom Brown's position as role model'. These had a distinctly Canadian identity – in its purest form that of the robust *coureur du bois* of the wilderness mythology; for example, Gerald Carr, the hero of John Morgan Gray's *One-eyed Trapper*. In a more diluted form, there is Larry Northcote, a curious amalgam of Tom Brown, Tom Sawyer and Robinson Crusoe in Gordon Hill Grahame's *Larry, or The Avenging Terrors*. And, in the person of Hughie Murray in Ralph Connor's *Glengarry School Days*, the euphoric idealism of Thomas Hughes himself was relocated in the vast open spaces of the Dominion. At a less exalted level of literary effort, stories of schoolboy heroes of great moral stature – lesser Tom Browns, in fact, who invariably 'played the game' – took up regular space in the magazines of the schools. As in Britain, such propaganda was rife.[66] Furthermore, real, as distinct from fictional, British exemplars and propagandists of the games ethic such as Hely Hutchinson Almond, J. E. C. Welldon and Cyril Norwood found an enthusiastic audience among Canadian masters and boys.

Westminster School is one of the most famous of English public schools. By the late nineteenth century it was wholly in harmony with upper-class educational fashion.[67] Unsurprisingly, some of its products, successfully indoctrinated and committed to schoolmastering, became zealous transmitters of ideological tradition both in Britain and its Empire. Christopher Lonsdale (Westminster and Cambridge), headmaster of Shawnigan School on Vancouver Island, British Columbia, from 1915 to 1951, was no exception. An early prospectus made it quite clear that the school was run on the lines of the British public school system. Lonsdale displayed the characteristic unease regarding intellectualism prevalent among British schoolmasters of the period: 'To be a success in life, a boy must have two things, character and personality. With these things there was no doubt about his being heard of in future life. With scholastic achievement alone he was more likely to be a failure.'[68] Yet Lonsdale was far from being an unreflective apostle of orthodoxy. He was bravely idiosyncratic, utilizing selectively and innovating judiciously. He evolved a 'Shawnigan mode of athleticism'. Uncontentiously it incorporated religion, robustness and regularity, but audaciously it utilized both the games field and the 'wilderness'. If character was the essence of education, hardship was the foundation of character and it was to be endured in forests as well as at football. The whole environment around the school was a training ground in physical hardiness indispensable for soldiers of Christ: 'Life at Shawnigan was Sparto-Christian, religious in tone . . . and bleak in the belief that it was good for the boys'[69] – unheated dormitories, icy dips in the lake and tree-clearing were the staple of an enduring existence.

Westminster was not merely responsible for shaping a 'Canadian' apostle; it also inspired at least one 'Canadian' proselyte – Robert Machray. Machray was reared in the dour Scottish educational tradition.[70] As a child he had a precocious predilection for scholarship. Gibbon's *Decline and Fall*, Buchanan's *History of Scotland*, D'Aubigné's *Reformation* and Hill's *Lectures on Divinity* all gave him premature pleasure.[71] Games meant little in his early years either as enjoyable activities or moralistic opportunities. He was given over to 'Godliness and Good Learning'. While Balliol rowing stimulated a strong-minded radicalism in fellow Scot, John Guthrie Kerr,[72] the physical activities of Sidney Sussex failed to shake Machray's placid indifference. He would refer equally and unenthusiastically to cricket, football, fives and tennis as 'playing ball'. He found it a useful expedient to plead poverty and eschew the delights of the sporting clubs despite the fact that 'numerous scholarships he won enabled him to pay all his college expenses'. After he was elected a Fellow he courteously joined the clubs, but never attended their meetings. The plain fact of the matter was that 'athletic sports had no charms for him'.[73]

In 1865 he was appointed Primate of Rupert's Land. There he 'sought to mobilize the resources of church and state for the formation of a new society that would be an outpost at the same time of Britain and of Christendom'.[74] He quickly 'fixed his attention on the state of education in Red River'. In his eyes Christianity and education went hand in hand and he declared it essential to his pastoral success to establish a college 'for those who wish a better education, in fear of God, in useful learning, and in conscientious attachment to [the] Church.' He named it St John's College School. He remained in charge from 1866 to 1903. If he knew anything of the reforms in the Scottish public school taking place under men like Almond, Wordsworth and Rogerson, he clearly cared little. The school was organized on the lines of a pre-Clarendon public school. He made no provision for playing-fields and paid much attention to prayer. However, eventually, like several of his fellow countrymen in far-off Scotland, he seemingly experienced a Pauline conversion in educational matters, although it is more probable that he demonstrated sensible Scottish pragmatism and fell in with the times. The catalyst, instrumental in achieving his extraordinary moral dissolution and recomposition, was a fellow clergyman and former Cambridge colleague, C. A. Jones, from 1865 to 1885 housemaster at Westminster School. In 1871 Machray visited England and spent a short but influential period with Jones in his house. Machray was apparently impressed by what he saw, and Westminster, noted for its character-training, provided a blueprint for his own school.[75] The outcome was systematic, continuous and dramatic. By the eighties a new ethos was dominant; the emphasis was not so much on Bible studies and book learning 'as on the development of character and "playing the game" '. Athletic machinery was enthusiastically constructed and systematically improved. Machray watched over the growth of his offspring with a calculating eye for the acceptable and desirable social values of the time and St John's grew and flourished 'until it became a great power in the land'. By the time of the Great War 'the standard of athletics in the school had become a metre stick by which its reputation was measured and compared with other private schools' and Machray's open and avowed ambition had become acceptance 'in the first flight in any games that are on the list'.[76]

Athleticism had a dual matrix: the public schools and the ancient universities. If Machray was unexcited by the passion for games displayed at Sidney Sussex, others, who also took their educational wares to Canada, proved less stoical in the possibly more inspirational atmosphere of St John's and Caius, and their university experiences and enthusiasms helped shape, in part, the educational institutions they ultimately created or contributed to in the Dominion of Canada. William Bolton became headmaster of St Paul's School in Victoria in 1885. As a Cambridge blue 'he saw to it that athletics . . . took their proper place in the school,'[77] and maintained and sustained a games programme until such sound orthodoxy helped ensure his elevation in 1906 to the first headmastership of University School where, for six years, he enunciated all the familiar and alleged virtues of adherence to the games ethic, espoused all the familiar activities allegedly promoting Christian 'manliness' and preached the soundness of the athletic gospel from the pulpit. Indisputably he was a typical late-Victorian public schoolmaster, who could have taken his place in any of the various categories of English public school and won the eventual, appreciative valetes for his conventionalism.

G. Exton Lloyd, headmaster of Rothesay Collegiate School, New Brunswick, from 1891 to 1896, was another conventional apostle of Sparto-Christian endeavour. Although a product of London University, hardly a haven of hearties, he would have been a particularly strong asset in the English public school system of the period with his concern for the sacred elements of the Victorian boarding school Trinity – militarism, athleticism and imperialism. Pronounced views on the value of military training were the consequence of his own service as Chaplain to the Queen's Own Regiment during the Red River Rebellion. In his opinion efficiency, obedience and hardiness were the certain products of that unrivalled instrument of education training, the cadet corps, which, when utilized in conjunction with a rigorous spiritual upbringing and systematic physical activity, assured the desired outcome: 'disciplined Christian education of spirit, mind and body'. He created a Christian Campus Martius at Rothesay. His boys were all soldiers in the making, following the flag of Jesus to spiritual conflicts as yet undiscernible and undeclared. Yet another Christian warrior, who carried the games tradition from Cambridge and established it in King's Collegiate School, Windsor, Nova Scotia, was Charles E. Willets, headmaster from 1876 to 1888. Before his arrival, games were desultory and disorganized; after it, every facility, it was claimed, was offered 'for the development of bodily activity, the Pupils being encouraged to take part in such games as Football, Cricket'.[78] In addition, a sergeant of the British Army drilled the boys four times every week. In stereotypic Victorian fashion, Willets 'saw clearly the physical and moral benefits of bodily activity as part of . . . the educational process' which allowed his pupils to 'fight life's battles in the world'.

Alick Mackenzie, headmaster of Lakefield School, Ontario, from 1895 to 1938 and the very personification of the school's rather unoriginal motto, 'Mens Sana in Corpore Sano', was given to reading *Tom Brown's Schooldays* to his pupils. It was so drummed into them that it served 'unconsciously . . . as their guidebook'.[79] He was also inclined to preach the value of 'the university of the forest'. In this combination of orthodoxy and unorthodoxy he was another who had much in common with Hely Hutchinson Almond.[80] However, his philosophical progress to educational idiosyncrasy was gradual. For many years he was conventional in both his Christianity and his muscularity. After graduation from Trinity College, Ontario, he became a master at Trinity College School, Port Hope. Here he pursued his religious physical duties with special zeal. He was an intense believer with none of the tepidity of an expedient faith. His involvement in athletic matters was considerable: drill, gymnastics, football and hockey coaching were a welcome part of his responsibilities.

Mackenzie was the epitome of 'vigorous Christian living'. Distrustful of the glittering intellect and the alleged lack of social balance which accompanied 'fostered brilliance or razor-edged efficiency', he was concerned 'to turn out men well adjusted mentally and physically'. He led by example: wood-splitting in spring, hockey in winter, football, alternating with gardening, in the autumn, and sailing in summer – taking trips in his yawl that would have daunted many younger men.[81] He would have delighted Charles Kingsley with his weather-beaten face, clear eye, great frame and big brown hands, oblivious to the niceties of theological controversy, devotee of 'practical reasoned Christianity', earnest in implanting Christian ideology, childlike in his exuberant good health.

A persistent theme in Canadian literature has been the effect of life in the wilderness on the collective national consciousness. Hence the fundamental logic of the identification of Canada with two wilderness symbols: the beaver and the maple leaf.[82] Throughout the *fin de siècle* years which witnessed the economic, social and political transformation of Canada 'beneath the buoyant optimism which accompanied this transition was a feeling of loss emanating from the realization that there was a price to be paid for the benefits accruing from a modern urban and industrial society . . . many Canadians became aware that the serenity, robustness and simplicity of country living was the price exacted for the comforts and accruments of city life.'[83] The apparent evils of urbanization, industrialization and materialism lay heavily on the Canadian mind during this era. Cities expanded or were created, urban populations grew rapidly. Disaffection with the monotony, isolation and artificiality of urban life resulted in a 'back to nature' movement symbolized by a spate of popular recreational journals: *Canadian Athletic*,

Pastoral, *Rod and Gun*, *Athletic Life*, *Canadian Outdoor Life*, *Outdoor Canada*, *Western Canada Sportsman*, *Sports and Canadian Alpine Journal*,[84] and simultaneously the therapeutic, remedial and ameliorative qualities of 'Old Dame Nature' were extolled by poet and novelist, preacher and pedagogue. The curative benefits ascribed to nature were not limited to adults, and for those with means boys' camps became popular. Camp Temagami, affectionately known as 'Cochrane's Camp', was probably the first of these in Canada.[85] Cochrane was a teacher at Upper Canada College, who saw his educational responsibilities extending beyond term time to vacations. His camp provided 'camping, canoeing, swimming, all manner of sport and plain wholesome food'.[86] Alick Mackenzie was of the same persuasion and, like Cochrane, sought through the habits of tracking, camping and exploring, the reincarnation of the physical hardiness of the backwoodsman. Mackenzie's pantheistic inclinations, developed in boyhood on the shores of Lake cu Shazawiga Mog, Lake Huron and on the wide waters of the Grand River, were given full rein at Lakefield. He 'gave the boys of his small school all possible freedom. He delighted in swimming and canoeing and they learnt both. He knew the woods and relished the camp-fire meals. So, in time, did they.'[87] In pursuit of self-sufficiency boys fished on Lake Katchewanooka for the school's breakfast on weekdays and in search of adventure filled the coves of the lake with canoes at weekends. Mackenzie's fervent ambition was to make his boys aware of the great unspoiled country which was their heritage.[88] In essence he revered a pantheistic Trinity – nature was God's temple, schoolroom and playground and, to a degree, he denied the validity of both private and state school systems. He disliked both excessive athletic and academic competition. One pupil, jaded by conventional Toronto schooling, wrote of his experiences: 'It was all a very long way from stiff and orderly Heath Mount . . . the outdoors, games, Lake Katchewanooka, gardening and the woods and fields had more of your time – and much more of your interest – than the schoolroom . . . it was wonderful beyond belief.'[89]

Cricket merited only a lowly place in Mackenzie's ranking of worthwhile Christian athletic activities – a timely arrangement of priorities. He represented evolving indigenous values. Confederation had accelerated maturation. Canada inexorably sought an identity independent from Britain. This attitude developed in much the same way as in the case of the individual child:

> at first there was hardly any sense of a different identity, then the irresponsibilities of the small boy manifested themselves. Next came the uncertainties and sudden antagonisms of adolescence, followed by the growing confidence of early manhood, not without over-sensitiveness at any display of the parental authority just ended. Lastly the separate establishment of married life entailed growing concern in one's own family affairs.[90]

Eventually, just as 'there were growing numbers who whether consciously or subconsciously, held that the traditional celebration of Empire Day was somewhat out of focus with a more up-to-date view of Canada's relationship with Great Britain',[91] so Canadians moved steadily towards a degree of cultural independence which manifested itself in part in the creation, cultivation and promotion of national games and sports. In time 'a distinctive Canadian sporting identity became apparent.'[92]

A popular and recurring theme of nationalism following Confederation was that of Canada's unique character, stemming largely from its location, severe winters, and the heritage of its 'hardy Northern races'.[93] The Englishman John Bain might sing thus of the athletic agonist:

> A King was he of high degree
> King of the boys who love,
> The lads they know can tackle low,
> And the lusty lads who shove[94];

but the Canadian Edward Sandys sang of the

> King of the winter in muscled prime
> Hither and thither with cadenced time,
> With iron nerve and fearless heart
> Glancing safe in his practised art

while speeding with easy skill over the ice 'in a long roll of manly pride'.[95]

There was much good, clean fantasy in Canadian moral assertion associated with winter sports. George Beers, nationalist and athlete, wrote pompously, with a firm glance in the direction of the Yankee, that 'the hardier character and habits of Canadians were displayed in their love of outdoor diversions' and added disingenuously that it was impossible to trace 'any taint of the vulgar or brutal' in these enjoyments, which were as pure as snow itself.[96] Beers, obsessed with creating a national identity through sport, referred disparagingly to cricket and Rugby as 'imported sports' and reserved his admiration for homegrown activities such as snowshoeing, 'the true national revel of robust Canucks'.[97] In other words, to Canadian moralists, 'manliness' of the Christian variety was as much a product of frozen lakes as elsewhere it was the product of muddy fields. So ice hockey, as part of an autocephalous impulse, became part and parcel of the games regime in the 'public schools' and was strenuously utilized and systematically codified by upright headmasters to promote a 'Canadian' interpretation of muscular Christianity.[98]

Notwithstanding the fact that the most significant factor in the history of sport in Canada in the nineteenth century was the paramountcy of British influence,[99] 'by the twentieth century ice hockey was becoming increasingly popular, cricket although still popular was being slowly modified to incorporate an essentially American influence.'[100] The truth of the matter was that, although Canada was at last a unified, political entity and communication was easier, its direction was 'usually from the North to South and vice-versa. It was faster and more economical . . . to travel from Toronto to Buffalo rather than to Winnipeg, from Winnipeg to St Paul rather than Vancouver, from New Westminster to Seattle rather than Montreal.'[101] The outcome was predictable: the influence of the United States increased while that of Britain declined. The Yankee helped fill the recreational vacuum left by the withdrawal of imperial garrisons with the result that Canada increasingly became North American in character.[102] There was a complication: 'Jealousy and fear of the American, that estranged and too successful elder brother, lies in the very origin of the English-speaking Canadian,'[103] wrote Arthur Lower, but to a considerable extent it was overcome. The rich and the powerful have an attraction all their own.

A new 'colonialism' replaced the old, and in association with this development it may well be true that the impediment which historically has most deterred Canada from developing a distinctive national identity has been its 'colonial' relationships.[104] It was a problem that equally affected its 'public schools'. The schools promoted both ancient British and modern American 'imperial' activities and attitudes on their playing-fields. This was exemplified during the early years of the twentieth century in the persons of Frank Shaughnessy, a coach at Lower Canada College, and Harry Griffiths, a master at Ridley College. At Lower Canada College, Shaughnessy's brutal 'American realism with regard to competitive athletics overshadowed . . . British moral theory'. His standards constituted an abrupt and total departure from expected school practice. To open a hole in the opposing line, players were told to thrust a hand under their opponent's thigh, lift him so that he was pivoted on one leg and hurl him aside. When pupils naively protested that this was not permitted under the rules, Shaughnessy retorted that the referee would never see it![105] His forceful, stimulating language, imitated by the boys, drove Fosbery from the playing-fields. Significantly, he was not 'recruited' by Fosbery but by the captain of football, yet Fosbery, lurking in the battered ruins of his once towering idealism, acquiesced in his appointment despite his much-repeated moral priorities and associated penal acts of chastisement. The truth of the matter was that the American brought success in his wake, and status through his success. He represented an American influence on Canadian sport, and revealed a commonplace, moral dilemma in nineteenth-century imperial 'public schools': whether to grow fat on the fruits of victory or stay thin in the interests of righteousness. In the person of Harry Griffiths, Miller at Ridley was mercifully excused ethical conundrums of the kind that embarrassed Fosbery. Griffiths, too, was an outstanding football coach as well as successful master in charge of cricket, but he won in the traditional manner, adhering rigorously to all the imperatives implicit in the phrase 'fair play'. His standards were distributed for all to digest in the pages of the school magazine in exhortatory articles with titles like 'A Good Sport', and bellowed over and over again as Ridleyites faced up to their opponents: 'Play hard, but play clean! Score first and keep on scoring! Tackle hard, tackle low and tackle often.'

Griffiths had equals all over Canada; Shaughnessy in several places was outnumbered and outflanked. To name but a handful of these committed strategists: F. B. Cumberland (Trinity College School 1864–73), who 'formulated the first code of rules for Rugby football ever put out in Canada';[106] F. Buckle (King's Collegiate School 1903–35), who was 'a vigorous sporting housemaster in the English public school mould'; F. A. B. Champain (University School 1908–13), of whom it was written 'his fielding [was] perfect, his bowling deadly and his batting striking and finished'; John Martland (Upper Canada College 1862–91), who 'would walk anywhere or any distance to see a college team perform'; and E. M. Watson (Rothesay Collegiate School 1899–1900), who 'rose early and retired late in order to keep the [cricket] club in the highest possible state of efficiency'.[107] All these men were Englishmen and represent many unsung and forgotten enthusiasts who transported the public school games and the games ethic across the Atlantic. Eventually, 'home-grown' masters were more numerous but equally zealous. By way of example, these included a coterie of Griffiths's colleagues at Ridley: A. F. Barr, E. G. Powell and G. M. Brock.

John Bull's imperialism, Canuck independence, Yankee hegemony were the three potent forces affecting the evolution of games in the Canadian 'public schools'. The loyalties, antagonisms and ambitions of the wider society during the year of political development were faithfully reflected in the evolving pattern of 'play' at Upper Canada, Bishop Ridley, St Johns and elsewhere. To change the metaphor but not the meaning, the pursuits on the playing-fields of the children of the 'Chosen' are one yardstick by which to measure the respective influences of diffusion and disassociation in Canada's search for a separate identity. In Canada's upper-class educational system English ethical values collided with and were pushed aside by American cultural imperatives, but both influences were resisted. Autonomy was prized and pursued, but the pressure of the powerful is not easily thwarted. The outcome was integration, compromise and adjustment.

By way of illustration appropriate to our theme, cricket, which declined seriously in health after Confederation, was not to die. In the 'public schools' it retained great stature by virtue of *its* virtue. In this regard, Ridley exemplified total conviction: 'Cricket was seriously encouraged . . . from the first day because both the traditions of the game and the purpose of the school sought to foster the fine boyhood attributes. Not the least of these was sportsmanlike conduct on and off the field. Cricket taught team spirit and unselfishness, an instinct to play hard and never let the side down, but it also instilled an instinctive refusal to win unfairly.'[108] At Trinity subscription was similarly unqualified:

> It is hard to conceive of a game which could be more useful in the training of our boys than cricket. What other game calls into use such a combination of mental and moral attributes or a greater degree of physical courage and skill? What other game so frowns upon the weaknesses and littleness of human nature, so elevates the better thoughts and instincts, so stimulates honourable rivalry, so cements friendships, so trains the qualities of mind and body that make a man worth being and life worth living?[109]

And it must be acknowledged that twentieth-century headmasters were no less zealous than their predecessors. W. R. Hibbard at Rothesay (1909–38), F. C. Orchard at Trinity (1913–33), W. W. Judd at King's (1914–27), W. Burman at St John's (1914–27) and W. L. Grant at Upper Canada College (1917–35) held fast to traditional views. Length of service in office helped greatly to sustain belief in the games ethic.[110]

The oriflamme of the Canadian 'public school' system remains emblazoned with wicket and willow. The imported English games ethic is still not wholly redundant even in the late twentieth century. Pre-Yankee ideals and their spokesmen are still extant. The idealism of the righteous is rarely casually abandoned, and the grip of the self-confident is usually firm. As late as the sixth decade of the twentieth century, it was observed with old-fashioned dignity by a censorious observer of Canadian modernity that 'an interesting survival at many of the independent boys' schools of Canada is cricket, the presence of which in spring and summer marks those schools off from the public school . . . in an age blighted by the cult of the sports hero and the disease of spectatoritis, it is important that the boys should be encouraged to play the game for the game's sake.'[111]

If news of the 'quick' reaches the ears of the dead and this assertion has carried to them, no doubt Sir John Colbourne and his nineteenth-century successors lie moderately content and tranquil in their final resting places, their evangelical effort ended. They were all strenuous muscular missionaries, but in no way did they overshadow the myriad missionaries who travelled east not west, and who, as we shall now see, gave the most serious attention to Norman Gale's cheery admonition:

> This will be a perfect planet
> Only when the Game shall enter
> Every country, teaching millions
> How to ask for Leg or Centre.
> Closely heed a level-headed
> Sportsman far too grave to banter:
> *When the cricket bags are opened*
> *Doves of Peace fly forth instanter!*[112]

7

CHRIST AND THE IMPERIAL GAMES FIELDS

Evangelical Athletes of the Empire

Christianity, Buddhism and Islam have in common the missionary imperative, yet only Christianity has become a universal religion,[1] largely as a consequence of a combination of nineteenth-century circumstances. The nineteenth century was 'pre-eminently the European century in world history, the period in which Europe was able to impose its will and its ideas on the whole of the inhabited world'.[2] With the European conquerors of Africa and Asia went the religion of Europe – Christianity. Earlier conquest had similarly carried it to the New World. By the twentieth century the universality of Christianity was an accomplished fact.

The imposition of the will of Europe on the rest of the world was the consequence of technology – maritime, military and industrial. European explorers, traders, soldiers and missionaries, not always in that order or in those exclusive categories, transported and sustained by the power of the industrial revolution, spread throughout the world. Even the penguins of Antarctica were not immune.

It was not inevitable, of course, that Christianity was the travelling companion of curiosity, commerce and aggrandisement. Again the force of circumstance played its part: 'the economic and imperial upsurge of Europe was accompanied by an unforeseen religious awakening which affected almost every Christian denomination in every country of the west.'[3] A revitalized Roman Catholic Papacy, a newly confident Orthodox Church freed from the Turkish yoke, and the reinvigorated Protestant Churches stimulated by the Evangelical Revival, celebrated their respective metamorphoses with a committed missionary zeal.

In Britain this zeal was in the hands of voluntary societies: the English Baptists (1792), the London Missionary Society (1795), the Church Missionary Society (1799), the British and Foreign Bible Society (1804), and ultimately many others. By the early twentieth century, in an article entitled 'Imperial Christianity', Sir Arthur Hirtzel[4] could remark wearily of a plethora of societies: 'Oxford Missions, Cambridge Missions, Dublin Missions, Universities Missions, even Archbishop of Canterbury's Missions'.[5] In Europe and America the same phenomenon was apparent: 'By the end of the century every nominally Christian country and almost every denomination, had begun to take its share in the support of the missionary cause,'[6] and only a handful of countries and isolated regions were untouched by the missionary effort. The Bible, in part or whole, had been translated into over 400 languages![7]

The Christian missionaries symbolized God in *action*. Their skills were practical as well as spiritual: medicine, agriculture, handicrafts and printing were typical accomplishments, but teaching was a special commitment linked closely, as it is, to preaching. This teaching often reflected a narrow ethnocentricity. Neill finds the words to express this particularly well: 'Missionaries in the nineteenth century had to some extent yielded to the colonial complex. Any western man was man in the full sense of the word; he was wise and good and members of other races, insofar as they became westernized, might share in the wisdom and goodness . . . western man was the leader, and could remain so for a very long time, perhaps for ever.'[8] Correspondingly, to the Anglican man in the street, the image of British evangelization became one of a world dotted with

> churches built in the suburban Gothic style, with romantic missionaries expounding the authorized version of the Bible, in the light of the Thirty-nine Articles, to congregations differing from ourselves only in the colour of their skins and the absence of their clothes, while clean little black choir-boys in clean little white surplices sing their various versions of *Hymns Ancient and Modern*, or, it may be, the *Hymnal Companion*.[9]

At first public reaction to the missionary enterprise was one of indifference, but as the nineteenth century progressed 'the acceptability of the missionary in the secular mind' became more firmly established.[10] The curious paradox is that acceptability grew as secular doubt increased. Missionary support was at its strongest in the post-Darwinian era. One explanation of this state of affairs suggests the causes were fivefold: the missionary was the bearer of civilization, the promoter of trade, the advocate of a disciplined imperialism, the creator of imperial boundaries and a philanthropist who won admiration irrespective of his doctrinal affiliations.[11] The increasing popularity of missionary work was reflected in the growing annual income of the Church Missionary Society: 1814 – £13,000, 1823 – £34,000, 1825 – £40,000, 1843 – £115,000, 1872 – £150,000, 1882 – £190,000 and 1899 (Centenary Year) – £212,000.[12] Acceptability was further revealed in the spread of African missions. Between 1800 and 1860 there were no more than nine in any decade; 'between 1860 and 1870 the figure rose to twelve, from 1870 to 1880 there were twenty-three, from 1880 and 1890 there were thirty-two, between 1890 and 1900 the figure had climbed to fifty-four and from the turn of the century until 1914 there would be another sixty-two.'[13]

In the early twentieth century, certainty in the righteousness of the missionary effort grew in leaps and bounds. In tracts such as *The Call of Empire*, published in 1917, and *Church and Empire*, published in 1907, bishops, professors, priests and administrators paraded all the easy clichés of ethnocentric conceit. In his chapter in Holland's *The Call of Empire*, Sir Arthur Hirtzel chanted this complacent paean: 'there is a high idealism in the conception of Empire. For what really motivates the imperialist is the firm belief that the race to which he belongs is the noblest and the civilization and ideals for which it stands are the highest, are in fact, so high that all the world accept them.'[14] Evangelization, in his view, was inseparable from the central doctrines of Christianity; a duty laid upon Christians by the direct command of God. If this was not considered a sufficient mandate, he further argued that if the Christian West failed to establish an empire of Christ in the East, then the non-Christian East would create an anti-Christian empire in the West. Others, while full of certainty of the need for the task, were less threatened by the vision of a

Buddhist Britain and found an argument for the spread of Christianity in the child-like nature of the native races.[15] One contributor to *Church and Empire* wrote that the role of Christianity was to meet the need of the savage in some Kaffir kraal possessed of the 'embryo of the religious instinct inherent in every man'. For although he is 'but a child, with a child's vision, he has a child's innate demand to fill his world with being'.[16] 'Christianity,' the writer continued, 'is imperial because it is Catholic and is imperative because it is universal. This is its essential character, this is its final sanction, and this, after all, is its complete and attractive, and entirely satisfying verification.'[17]

For much of the nineteenth century the upper classes of Victorian Britain were scarcely noted for their missionary fervour. However, the campaigning of bodies like the Church Missionary Society, which had an opportunist talent for self-publicity,[18] eventually drew the upper-class members of the public schools and ancient universities into missionary work,[19] many of whom by virtue of upbringing and aptitude faithfully and fully fitted the image of the muscular Christian. This fact gave rise, in some instances, to a particular kind of missionary endeavour which reflected the style and purpose of English education of the Victorian and Edwardian eras. In consequence, many of its proponents were imbued with the quality of 'missionary muscularity'.

There are two images of these gentlemen, as Patrick Scott has so acutely observed; an image in reality and an image in language.[20] Both have significant religious dimensions.

The image in language is closely linked to the Evangelical of late-Victorian England. The Evangelical Movement had certain attributes which distinguished it from Liberal and Catholic Anglicanism. It was greatly concerned with conversion and with status, and consequently made a special effort to attract philistine public schoolboys and hearty 'Oxbridge' undergraduates. This dual obsession served several purposes. Men who personified good social standing, linked magically to saleable concepts of Christian chivalry, could be used as exemplars both to recruit still more of their ilk and at the same time raise the tone of the movement. For:

Evangelicalism had a suspect social image: it tended to be lower middle class, to have ties with the dissenters, to have clergy who were not quite gentlemen preaching sermons in proprietary chapels which were not quite parish churches, or making speeches for missionary societies which were not quite officially recognized by the Church of England. Cricket, and cricketers, had a plus social value to give to Evangelicalism.[21]

As a result, in the late nineteenth century hand in hand with the growth of the games cult in the public schools and universities went the exploitation of athletic ability for religious purposes within the Evangelical Movement. The outstanding example, of course, was the exposure given by the religious press of the period to the Cambridge Seven,[22] the group of upper-class Englishmen who became China missionaries in the 1880s. According to the journalists of the religious newspapers and weeklies, who incidentally illustrated as bland a disregard for accuracy then as some do today,[23] these men were 'a striking testimony to the power of the uplifted Christ to draw to himself, not the weak, the emotional, the illiterate only, but all that is noblest in strength and finest in culture'.[24] As Scott remarks, their hold on the religious public came essentially from their gentlemanly sporting credentials. In this regard they were comforting status symbols for evangelicalism. And they had a further significance. They symbolized not merely social respectability but also reassuring masculinity – a point Scott fails to emphasize sufficiently. Puseyism, with its suspect preoccupation with dressing up, incense and ornamentation, had to be denied as the image of religion.[25] Stalwarts of the cricket, football and polo fields played their part in this. In the exploitation of men like the Cambridge Seven, 'Sport was not part of the ethos of religion . . . but a desirable additive, something that seemed like a superior exercise in public relations.'[26]

Scott warns us not to mistake the caricature of the propagandist for the reality of the man and urges us to turn to the 'believing batsmen' if the muscular missionaries of a past empire 'are to be more than caricatures in the progressive imagination'.[27] More to the point, these men were frequently caricatures of the romantic imagination.

Women propagandists in particular wrote in undisguised sexual terms of the attractive 'physicality' of the athletic clergyman in Empire. No finer example is available than that by Jessie Page in her biography of John Coleridge Patteson, Bishop of Melanesia, who died a martyr's death in the South Seas. Page's portrait of Patteson was not her own. In the belief that she could scarcely improve upon it, she chose to quote from the definitive study of Patteson by another female writer, Miss Charlotte Yonge:

> He was tall and of a large powerful frame, broad of the chest and shoulders and with small neat hands and feet, with more of sheer muscular strength and power of endurance than of healthiness, so that though seldom breaking down, and capable of undergoing a great deal of fatigue and exertion, he was often slightly ailing; and was very sensitive to cold . . . The most striking feature was his eyes, which were of a very dark clear blue, full of an unusually deep, earnest . . . inward expression. His smile was remarkably bright, sweet and affectionate, like a gleam of sunshine and was one element of his great attractiveness, so was his voice which had the rich full sweetness inherited from his mother's family, and which always excited a winning influence over the hearers.[28]

Patteson, and indeed his predecessor, George Augustus Selwyn,[29] exemplify perfectly the exercise in public relations that Scott has drawn to our attention. In these Christian heroes robust normality invariably prefaced an attitude of extraordinary morality verging on priggishness. Page was at pains to stress to her readers that Patteson was 'a regular boy' who went in for vigorous games: 'Full of pluck, he was always on the spot in the field where the greatest danger lay, and should he at any time get a knock or suffer a blow, he silently and bravely stood it like a man.'[30] An illustration of physical courage – the endurance of an untreated broken collarbone for three weeks without complaint, was carefully juxtaposed with one of moral rectitude – his departure from the annual dinner of the Eton Eleven at the customary singing of bawdy songs, in order to lay emphasis on his essential masculinity.

Of course, men as well as women were anxious to emphasize whenever possible the manliness of the missionary. In his *Patteson of Melanesia: A Brief Life of John Coleridge Patteson*, Paton provides a typical example of the evangelical publicist in action[31] in his description of Patteson's hero, Selwyn, courageous and competent sportsman, who,

> like the knights in olden days . . . believed that wrongs were meant to be righted, and that the strong were given their strength for the protection of the weak. He had the courage of a lion and the gentleness of a lamb. His duty took him one day into an unsavoury part of Windsor, known as Beer's Lane. A notorious bully stood across his way and ordered him back. Selwyn attempted to pass him, but the bully attacked him fiercely; suddenly Selwyn's fist shot out from his shoulder, and the denizen of Beer's Lane found himself sprawling in the middle of the road. After that the young curate was granted the freedom of the city.[32]

Charles Harford-Battersby reported of G. L. Pilkington, killed in the upheavals in Uganda in 1897:

> It was his utter manliness that first struck me: here was a thorough man ringing true from top to bottom. Then that he was a man of God: one who knew God and believed in God. So he was a man of power. How well I remember my first glimpse of him, eleven years ago, as he came swinging round the corner – the great, tall, strapping figure; the beaming face – almost as red as his scarlet tie – his hat far enough back to show his broad forehead; a huge, calf-skin Bible under his arm and a club of a walking stick in his hand.[33]

Similarly it was reported of T. L. Pennell, the Afghan missionary: 'The nine years at Eastbourne had worked a revolution in the personal appearance of young Pennell. He arrived a small and delicate boy of nine, too frail to swing a cricket bat or kick a goal. He arrived in London an athletic giant, standing six feet two in his stockinged feet, well-proportioned, carrying no superfluous flesh . . . as hard as nails.'[34]

The encomiums of genteel lady writers and others lend themselves easily to the ridicule of the twentieth-century parodist, yet in the men themselves there was a 'genuine unity of vocation' – a subscription to Christian manliness revealed by preaching *and* playing. Missionaries took cricket to the Melanesians, football to the Bantu, rowing to the Hindu, athletics to the Iranians, with a firm purpose. In the dissemination of British sports and games, the social historian should not overlook religious enthusiasts and diffusionists like Patteson, Pilkington, Pennell, Clifford Harris,[35] A. C. Clarke,[36] Carey Francis,[37] Chester Macnaghten and C. W. Waddington,[38] Cecil Wilson[39] and many others who took both the gospel of Christ and the gospel of games to the most distant corners of the Empire and even beyond.[40]

Athletic evangelists went to every part of the Empire, sometimes blazing exotic new trails. Patteson created Valis-we-poa (the Big Grass) on Norfolk Island for his Melanesian Christian cricketers, a spacious cricket field edged on one side by cliffs over 200 feet high.[41] Sometimes these evangelists followed energetically in others' footsteps, consolidating the imaginative efforts of past agents of cultural diffusion. A. G. Fraser[42] (1873–1962) took God and games sequentially to King's School in Uganda, Trinity College in Ceylon and Achimota College in the Gold Coast. He was followed along parts of the same route by H. M. Grace[43] (King's to Achimota) and Grace was followed in turn by R. W. Stoppard[44] (Trinity to Achimota). Others also travelled the same ideological imperial highway.[45]

The Indian subcontinent in the early part of the twentieth century supplied three outstanding exemplars of the muscular missionary movement: T. L. Pennell,[46] A. G. Fraser and C. E. Tyndale-Biscoe.

Theodore Leighton Pennell (1867–1912) was a late nineteenth-century medical missionary who spent much of his adult life among the tribes of Afghanistan. To win the largest number of souls to Christ, in addition to his medical work, he opened a school at Bannu for Pathans, Hindus, Muslims and Sikhs. Pennell himself had been educated at Eastbourne College and his Bannu school was a faithful imitation of an English public school down to and including cold baths. Shortly after Pennell's death in 1912, Brigadier-General G. K. Scott-Moncrieff, who had met him on the North West Frontier, wrote in *Blackwood's Magazine*: 'every morning, even in the sharp, cold winter, the boys all had to swim, the doctor himself leading them.' Scott-Moncrieff thought highly of the school at Bannu and remarked that 'the older boys had quite imbibed the spirit of public school *esprit de corps* and were of the greatest value in enforcing a code of good form and honour. They all adored the doctor and his greatest pleasure in life was in his association with them, playing football and cricket with the utmost keenness.'[47]

For his part, Pennell wrote proudly in his autobiography, *Among the Wild Tribes of the Afghan Frontier*, published three years before his death, of the general transition that he had helped bring about on the Frontier, from the indigenous sports of tent-pegging and wrestling to the missionary school games of cricket and football. 'The old order changes and gives place to the new,' he observed. 'The simpler native games are gradually giving place to the superior attractions of cricket and football, and the tournaments – between schools of the provinces are doing much . . . to develop among these frontier people a fascination for these sports which have done so much to make England what she is.'[48] The wider purpose of Western games merely hinted at in the passage is made quite explicit in this extract from a biography of Pennell by Ernest Hayes: 'Pennell combined work and education by playing with the boys at both cricket and football, showing them how "to play the game" in a bigger and nobler sense.'[49] In view of the combative, ill-tempered and excitable Pathan nature he had his work cut out, but the moral significance of the enterprise ensured that he stuck firmly to his task. Others were equally committed but less sure of their success. On a visit to England in the 1890s, Cecil Wilson, then Bishop of Melanesia, confided to an undergraduate audience of Jesus College, Cambridge, that he was delighted that the natives of Melanesia were making such good progress at cricket but disappointed that they still showed such a predilection for cannibalism![50]

At precisely the same time as Pennell was transforming young Afghans into white-flannelled, if barefooted, imitations of young English gentlemen, A. G. Fraser (1873–1962) was effecting the same cultural metamorphosis among the Tamils and Sinhalese at Trinity College, Ceylon, with the same profound moral purpose. Fraser showed 'an exaggerated zeal in encouraging games at Trinity'.[51] His biographer, W. E. F. Ward, has recalled how

> he used to conduct a post-mortem on the previous day's match at morning assembly . . . and would describe with pitiless accuracy every moment when a player held on to the ball when he ought to have passed, or committed a slovenly piece of fielding at cricket. It was not

lack of skill or an error in judgement that he castigated thus publicly: it was a mistake which seemed to him to result from a player thinking too much of himself and too little of the team.[52]

A little before he had accepted the principalship of Trinity, it was Fraser's initiative which had brought about the establishment of the King's School, Budo, in 1904 for the sons of Ugandan chiefs, complete with a 'beautiful playing field'.[53] In 1900, along with the Christian message, he had taken a football to Uganda, playing at first with his Christian servants.[54] Many years later, when he was invited to become the first principal of Achimota College in the Gold Coast, he saw to it that the institution was suitably endowed with those affluent instruments of upper-class Christian character-training[55] – expensive playing-fields. On its formal opening in 1927 A. H. R. Joseph, the games master brought by Fraser to Achimota from Trinity, wrote:

> . . . the College had two large cricket ovals and four football fields . . . On the School side one hockey field was ready and two were under construction. During the last ten years we have gone on adding to or improving these playing fields. First, the cricket ovals had to be re-levelled and surfaced at considerable cost. Then the scrub and bush between the football fields were cleared and the surface levelled, so as to make one continuous stretch of playing fields. As hockey began to grow in popularity, two new laterite and 'swish' fields were prepared . . . We have also made two more fields on the School side, and have encroached on several lawns to provide for the many games of rounders and netball that go on during the year. As the playing fields are so far away from the houses, cricket nets were made close to houses; there are nine of them now, and Guggisberg and Cadbury (then named Park) House made a fair-sized hockey field near their own houses.[56]

However committed Pennell, Fraser and others were to a peculiarly British concept of education, the *preux chevalier* of imperial Christian knights was certainly Cecil Earle Tyndale-Biscoe (1863–1949), in charge of the Church Missionary School, Srinagar, Kashmir, from 1890 to 1947. Tyndale-Biscoe was an imperial standard-bearer of Victorian moral righteousness. He was a late nineteenth-century embodiment of Western ethnocentricity and a symbol of forceful cultural hegemony, but he was much more: he was a man of astounding tenacity, courage and compassion who subscribed with simple directness to the holistic creed of the Victorian upper-class knight errant:

> Christianity is a life that has to be lived. Christ Jesus was a perfect man as well as God, and to be a Christian one has to strive after perfect manliness – strength of body, strength of intellect, strength of soul – and to show that strength by practical sympathy for the weak. It is only those who are true men who can appreciate the Ideal Man. Some one has to create desire for the ideal, and this cannot be done by talk, but by putting before the boys our great example, Christ Jesus, and asking them to join us in trying to follow that life, the life of service.[57]

Tyndale-Biscoe is a cultural diffusionist of great interest and not a little importance. He took the physical activities of the English public school and ancient university, wrapped them in a packaging of moral certitude and introduced them successfully to a culture whose religious, social and sexual mores ran directly contrary to much of what he represented and advocated. In this act of proselytization hostility was simply a spur, local custom merely an irritant and righteousness an indispensable prerequisite.

Cecil Earle Tyndale-Biscoe came from the gentry. His father, William Earle Tyndale,[58] inherited Holton Park in Oxfordshire from his uncle and in 1850 he married Eliza Carey Sandeman of the Sandeman's port family. There were eight children of the marriage – seven sons and one daughter. Cecil, born in 1863, was the fourth son. He had a deeply religious upbringing and as early as six years of age had pledged himself to go to Africa 'to set the nigger free'[59] – a pledge renewed at Bradfield, his public school, to which he went in 1875, and at Cambridge eight years later. In childhood meningitis affected his memory and his concentration. He became a backward pupil and, in consequence, he later argued, eventually a sympathetic schoolmaster. At Bradfield he suffered the horrors characteristic of public school education of the period[60] and subsequently he was grateful to his education by ordeal for the training in fortitude, endurance and determination it afforded. At school he gave early notice of his resolution. His determined action resulted in the dismissal of a particularly sadistic schoolmaster. Typically, his most affectionate memory of Bradfield was the steeplechase which, he remarked in his autobiography, 'taught me to love obstacles. There is always some way of conquering them. Little did I imagine that these Bradfield steeplechases were preparing me for one lasting fifty years in a country of which I had then never heard.'[61]

At Cambridge he managed to be both pious and hearty.[62] He coxed the University crew to victory in the boat race of 1884 and in the same summer, in the service of the Children's Special Mission Service and in his light blue blazer, attracted public schoolboys to religious services on Llandudno beach. In 1887 he was ordained. The immediate impetus to missionary work came from the results of his clerical examinations. His influential meeting with the Bishop of London to review his performance went as follows:

> 'Shocking! Shocking! You don't know anything, Biscoe!'
>
> 'I know I do not,' I replied.
>
> BISHOP: 'Then how do you think you can teach anybody if you don't know anything yourself?'
>
> BISCOE (scratching his head): 'Well, sir, perhaps there may be *some* people in the world almost as ignorant as I am.'
>
> BISHOP: 'I doubt it! I doubt it! You are only fit to teach the blacks, there now!'[63]

On the strength of this innocently offensive advice Tyndale-Biscoe applied to the Church Missionary Society[64] for service in Central Africa, and was refused on grounds of health. With an illogicality akin to that of the military postings in Waugh's *Put Out More Flags*, he was told instead 'to proceed to Kashmir to help Rev. J. H. Knowles at his school'.[65] The irony of the decision was not lost on his family, and the news of his appointment was greeted with hilarity. The journey to the Indian sub-continent with three C.M.S. missionaries bound for the Punjab was almost uneventful; fractious porters at Marseilles forced the four British padres to stand resolutely back to back with fists raised in self-defence, but the remainder of the trip was peaceful.

Tyndale-Biscoe's own destination was Srinagar, the capital of Kashmir – 'a huge rabbit-warren sort of place of 125,000 inhabitants. All streets crooked, all streets narrow, all streets filthy.'[66] It was smelt before it was seen, and his early experience of the school was similarly unappetizing:

> As I entered, the stench almost knocked me backwards. It was winter, therefore all the lattice windows covered with paper were closed. Every boy was covered up in a dirty blanket and under the blanket a fire-pot [live charcoal in an earthenware pot encased in a basket called a 'Kangri'], so the hot air passed through the filthy blanket, damp from snow or rain. In the winter, bathing is at a discount, so you can probably realize something of the atmosphere which greeted us. As Mr Knowles introduced me to the bundles I was able to study their faces. In the front row I saw many beards and whiskers, for practically all were married and some of them fathers.[67]

They were mostly from the Hindu ruling class. This fact did not impress him. He fancied himself as an expert semiographist and he read in their features an unwholesome sensuality combined with a supercilious religiosity. This was a common enough reaction of the insular Anglo-Saxon missionary and exactly mirrored that of another imperialist in distant Africa about the same time, who, on viewing the early products of the mission school, wrote that it was 'hard to suppress a repugnance for the hulking youths who instead of being – as they ought to be – engaged in hard, wholesome, manual labour, are dawdling and yawning over slate and primer, and in whose faces sensual desires struggle for expression with hypocritical sanctimoniousness.'[68] These words could easily have been Tyndale-Biscoe's. He had come to precisely the same conclusion and quickly decided that his pupils required above all else a schooling in knight-errantry. It became his deliberate policy to send them out 'to the fires in the city . . . to rescue animals in distress and later to save women and girls.'[69] His conception of a school was a 'bulwark against Satan', comprising a social system and a moral atmosphere in which 'Christian' chivalry could grow.

But first he had a more pressing problem to overcome. Srinagar, he soon discovered, was a city of Sodom. Bradfield had acquainted him with the conditions and the cure. Pain was the medicine for lust, and so boxing became part of the C.M.S. school curriculum. He had always thanked God for his knuckles, so valuable in dissuading pederasts at his public school. Of necessity, therefore, a skilful boxer, he endorsed without qualification the biblical passage: 'Blessed be the Lord my strength, who teacheth my hands to war and my fingers to fight.'[70] Young Kashmir was taught the noble art. The molested could now defend themselves. He did not stop there. He harassed the 'Srinagar Sodomy Club' until English law was adopted and its leaders were imprisoned. Long-standing social mores were thus proscribed, the Brahmin priests were incensed, the local community was irritated, but Tyndale-Biscoe's first attempt at Western moral imperialism was successful. It was to be the first of many victories.

Next his boys became involuntary and then voluntary fire-fighters. On the first outbreak of fire close to the school, he ordered his pupils to provide help. As high-caste members of society they preferred to continue their lessons rather than indulge in demeaning manual activities. It was a point of view which failed to win his sympathy. In his own words, 'I then took action and drove them out of the classroom . . . At the double I herded them with my stick to the fire. Arrived there, we found that scores of citizens had already taken their seats at every available place in order to enjoy themselves at an entertainment for which they would have nothing to pay. As the flames spread from one house to another they seemed highly delighted, shouting out "Hurrah!" '[71] Tyndale-Biscoe was appalled. He commandeered pots from reluctant boatmen, armed the larger boys with sticks to prevent the police from stealing valuables from the burning houses – their customary privilege – and organized the rest of his pupils as a fire-fighting force. The school fire-service which later fought many fires in Srinagar had been created.

Kashmiri indifference to the suffering of animals was an attitude Tyndale-Biscoe worked hard to overcome. Eventually he developed in many of his boys a new compassion sometimes carried to enthusiastic excess. One example gave him special delight: 'I was standing in the school compound and happened to look at the entrance gate which was under an arch, when lo and behold! a pair of donkey's ears appeared, so high up that they could hardly pass under the arch. Then gradually, as this apparition came into fuller view I perceived that a donkey was riding on a man's back, its forelegs sticking out over the man's chest.' A C.M.S. pupil following behind explained eagerly that as he came to school he saw a small donkey doing its best to carry a large man. He thought it better that the man should carry the donkey, and he had made the two change places.[72]

In the first days of the school all the efforts of J. H. Knowles to promote exercise on the British model had been to no avail: 'No Brahmin boy,' he informed his new master, 'will move faster than the pace of an ox. He never runs, boats or plays games for fear of growing muscle and losing caste.'[73] Tyndale-Biscoe had no patience with this indigenous snobbery. With a cunning the Renaissance popes would have admired, he extended his autocratic methods to swimming, an exceedingly low-caste occupation in Kashmir, and well beneath the dignity of his asinine pupils. Boys were persuaded to swim by the age of thirteen by the simple expedient of increasing the school fees by one quarter every twelve months for non-swimmers beyond that age. Eventually swims across the local Dal and Wular lakes (four miles and five miles respectively) became a regular annual event for the stronger school swimmers, and one of the proudest achievements of his years in Kashmir was to establish a life-saving corps which over the years rescued more than 400 people from drowning.[74]

As an ex-rowing blue nothing was dearer to Tyndale-Biscoe's heart and few things were more appropriate to Kashmir, a country of lakes, than rowing. When, in a moment of nostalgia with thoughts 'natural to a sporting English gentleman . . . trained from his youth in an atmosphere of manliness and fair-play',[75] Lord Lansdown, Viceroy of India, on a prize-giving visit in the early nineties, gazed out the window of the school on to the broad, smooth waters of the Jhelum beneath and observed how pleasant it would be to see a headship of Jhelum to rival the headship of the Thames, it was a challenge Tyndale-Biscoe accepted. The obstacle was straightforward and considerable. Oarsmen developed low-caste muscular arms and 'No Brahmin had so vulgar an appendage as muscle on the arm.'[76] Nothing daunted, Tyndale-Biscoe built a boat. It proved impossible to get pupils into it. And he had false hopes for an equally reluctant Brahmin staff. However, he forcibly persuaded two young teachers at least to inspect the craft, and in no time at all with a firm push from behind they were sprawled in it, floating swiftly downstream to a four-spanned bridge. The incentive to row was self-evident. In Tyndale-Biscoe's jaunty words, 'minus the moral article . . . they bent their material backbones and . . . made a beginning in making that low-caste stuff commonly called muscle.'[77] Rowing became an integral part of school life, boat outings for families, the sick and the elderly became commonplace school activities on free afternoons. The school emblem of crossed paddles with heart-shaped blades was a fitting symbol of this transformation – exemplifying the virtues of the products of the muscular Christian in Empire – strength, kindness and service.[78] Enthusiasm for the new activities gradually spread and in 1909 the first inter-school regatta was held with state, Hindu, Islamic and Christian schools in friendly competition. The Church Missionary Society School won by thirty lengths!

It would be naive to attribute to Tyndale-Biscoe simple subscription to the maxim: *animo non astutia*. In his self-appointed task of 'grinding grit into Kashmir' when the occasion warranted it, in contrast to his more common peremptory style of action, he could adopt an amusing subtlety of approach. In attempting the functional westernization of his high-caste Brahmins in the interests of hygiene, fitness and morality, he carefully introduced physical practices which ensured a revolution in ornamentation and dress. The nose-ring with its golden pendant hanging over the lip, which prevented any opportunity for wiping the nose and caused unpleasant concretions and sores, was gradually abandoned when on the introduction of boxing it was discovered to be 'a painful appendage'; and the huge golden rings, which tore the boys' ear-lobes, causing infection, and which were held in place with string over the top of the head, proved a distinct disadvantage when high cock-alorum (a glorified form of leap frog) became part of the physical fitness programme: 'the ear-rings went and "high cock-alorum" remained.'[79] The 'pheron', the seldom-washed long gown worn by his pupils, was an early target of his ambitious reforms. It allowed the boys to play cricket, but scarcely the cricket of his experience: 'by keeping their hands up their sleeves they had the cloth of their garment between their hands and the untouchable cricket ball. When they had to stop or catch a ball they spread out their garment over their knees, or between their legs and thus stopped or caught the ball. So a game of cricket as played by the C.M.S. schoolboys was a well-conducted comic opera from start to finish.'[80] He foresaw accurately that the garment would prove unpleasantly impractical during *compulsory* exercises on the horizontal bar: 'a holy Brahmin hanging . . . by his hocks – his only apparel being a very filthy nightgown telescoped over his head, and a very dirty rag tied fore and aft to a string which encircled his waist . . . was certainly not a pretty sight and even the Brahmins themselves agreed with me in this matter.'[81] The gown was replaced voluntarily by trousers. And 'by virtue of such practical imperatives the pupils emancipated themselves from tradition and gradually dress reformed itself, not by orders of the brutal westerner, but like the flowers of the field; the old ones just faded away . . .'[82]

Today association football is the most popular game in the world, played in every quarter of the globe and for the most part disseminated in the recent past by British imperialist soldiers, teachers, traders and missionaries. Srinagar furnishes a delightful illustration of the introduction of soccer to a distant outpost of Empire through the medium of a self-righteous autocratic muscular missionary. The effort comprises a vignette of imperial self-confidence, incorporating ethnocentricity, arrogance and determination in the face of indigenous religious customs and social habits. In 1891 Tyndale-Biscoe took a wife and a football to Kashmir. The football aroused no interest. Its reception by the assembled school was scarcely heartening:

TB This is a football.

BOYS What is the use of it?

TB For playing a game.

BOYS Shall we receive any money if we play that game?

TB No!

BOYS Then we shall not play that game.

BOYS What is it made of?

TB Leather.

BOYS Take it away! Take it away!

TB Why should I take it away?

BOYS Because it is *jutha* [unholy] we may not touch it, it is leather.

TB I do not wish you to handle it. I want you to kick it . . . and today you are going to learn how to kick it, boys.

BOYS We will not play that *jutha* game.[83]

Despite his pupils' obduracy, instruction about the pitch, positions and rules followed. The response was less than enthusiastic. As Tyndale-Biscoe has recorded:

> Before the end of school I perceived that there would be trouble, so I called the teachers together and explained to them my plans for the afternoon. They were to arm themselves with single-sticks, picket the streets leading from the school to the playground, and prevent any of the boys escaping en route. Everything was ready, so at 3 o'clock the porter had orders to open the school gate. The boys poured forth, and I brought up the rear with a hunting-crop. Then came the trouble; for once outside the school compound they thought they were going to escape; but they were mistaken. We shooed them down the streets like sheep on their way to the butchers. Such a dirty, smelling, cowardly crew you never saw. All were clothed in the long nightgown sort of garment I have described before, each boy carrying a fire-pot under his garment and so next to his body. This heating apparatus has from time immemorial taken the place of healthy exercise. We dared not drive them too fast for fear of their tripping up (as several of them were wearing clogs) and falling with their fire-pots, which would have prevented their playing football for many days to come.[84]

The ground was reached, the sides were picked, the ball put in position, the whistle blown, and blown again. The boys were adamant. They had absolutely no intention of kicking 'an unholy ball'. Tyndale-Biscoe, for his part, had every intention that they should. The teachers were lined up with their sticks menacingly along each goal line; the boys were given five minutes to reflect on their decision. Five minutes passed. The masters charged, sticks and voices raised. The game began: 'all was confusion . . . as [pupils] tried to kick the ball but generally missed it, their clogs flew in the air and their pugaris were knocked off while their nightgowns flapped in one another's faces; a real grand mix-up of clothes and humanity.'[85] There was worse to come: suddenly there were squeals of agony and horror and the game came to a halt. One unfortunate had stopped the ball with his face. He was polluted. His horror-stricken friends took him sobbing to Tyndale-Biscoe. A wash in the canal was brusquely prescribed. The game, or rather the rough and tumble, proceeded until time was called and the first game of football in Kashmir played by Brahmins was over.

The repercussions were to continue for some years. The bearded centre forward who first kicked the ball was forbidden to return to, and thus defile, his home. He went to live with relatives. Later the boys resorted to carrying pins up their sleeves during matches – some fifty balls were deflated before culprits were informed they would pay the price of each deflated bladder and the practice stopped. After ten years, when football was respectable, the Hindu and Muslim schools took up the game and witchcraft was utilized in the eager pursuit of victory. Opponents would frequently bring a Brahmin priest to cast a spell of incapability over the missionary school goalkeeper and, to Tyndale-Biscoe's disgust, his boys 'often succumbed to this nonsense and lost the match as they deserved'.[86]

Different cultural interpretations of the games ethic caused further problems. He felt considerable irritation when a local master was apparently unable to count beyond eleven when fielding a football side of twelve or more and the tendency to recruit professional boatmen to strengthen a rowing eight in a lean year took time and patience to overcome. At cricket matches the local habit of moving the boundary flags out when the missionary school was batting produced in him a special alertness. The facility with which the Kashmiri misinterpreted the true nature of competition is beautifully exemplified by an incident during one Kashmir inter-college athletic championship meeting which took place before the British President, the Maharaja and a large crowd. The Church Missionary Society School and the state school had reached the final of the tug-of-war. On the order to pull both teams strained and heaved without effect. As Tyndale-Biscoe later recounted:

> then one of my staff pointed out to me that the end of the state school rope was anchored round a raised flower-bed. I at once pointed this out to the shouting official. He answered, 'No matter!' and went on shouting to the state school team to pull harder. I then spoke to him peremptorily, ordering him to release the anchorage which he did, but almost immediately the end of the rope was anchored again. This time I went up to the official in anger, and ready for action, and forced him to release the rope. No sooner had the rope been released than the state school team were pulled over the line. Then when the teams changed sides they were pulled over again . . . there was no anchorage at that end of the ground.[87]

Despite disparate views on ethical matters, athletics, rowing, cricket and football prospered and the Christian gentleman's code of behaviour was partially if not wholly assimilated. At the time he wrote *Kashmir in Light and Shade*, which was published in 1922, Tyndale-Biscoe could observe that he had recently watched 'an inter-class match, most keenly contested, the referee being not a teacher but a schoolboy. His decision was not once disputed, nor was there any altercation between any of the players; it was a truly sporting game.'[88]

As with so many others the length and breadth of the Empire, Tyndale-Biscoe had the most serious of motives in his determination to take the games ethic to Kashmir. Athletic activities were the precursor of social service.[89] It was his profound desire as a Christian 'to introduce his pupils to HIM who taught all men to love one another and show it by practice . . . talking would not accomplish this . . . bundles could not do this, therefore bundles must be turned into boys by athletic exercises and athletic boys turned into manly citizens by continued acts of kindness.'[90] In his certain view, athletics created the muscle and skill to fight evil and to promote good; sinew was strengthened 'not in sports for sports' sake but for the benefit of the city'.[91] These were not idle words. There was no lack of opportunity for knight-errantry in Srinagar: during cholera epidemics staff and pupils filled up cesspools and cleaned streets and compounds of filth; in summer hospital patients of all denominations were given outings on the local lake; in winter the pupils chopped wood for the poor; throughout the year they saved lives from fire and water, rescued animals from torture and death, fought the vicious and sadistic. He could assert with some justification that his objective in sport was to make muscle and increase strength for the sake of the weak and the oppressed. His aim was 'head of the river' not 'top of the form' in the interests of Christian compassion.

In his celebration of Cecil Earle Tyndale-Biscoe's efforts in Kashmir, entitled *Fifty Years Against the Stream*, Eric Tyndale-Biscoe, his third son,[92] made much of the fact that his father swam against the strongly flowing current of Hindu religion.[93] It is also a fact that his ideals ran contrary to the materialistic ambitions of his pupils' parents. They were wholly indifferent to the activities of the river, lake and playing-field.[94] They wished simply to reinforce their traditional dominance by acquiring powerful 'manifestations of modernity'.[95] In this they were no different to other peoples under British imperial subjection. English was the priority 'to help their sons become traders profitable to the family, or salary-earning Government servants'.[96] As C. P. Groves has written of the African chiefs, they sought not a new culture but a new weapon in order to share the white man's power.[97] It was the same for the Hindu parent in Srinagar. Tyndale-Biscoe's concern with exercise was, to their way of thinking, a time-consuming indulgence they tolerated in order to obtain the valuable prize of the English tongue. Furthermore, 'in his delicate operation of strengthening the moral backbone of large numbers of boys in Kashmir'[98] he received little support from fellow imperialists on the sub-continent. Emilia Dilke, later to regret her adolescent insensitivity, caught the hostility of Anglo-India to the missionary in this comment written in 1889: 'Naturally as one of an Anglo-Indian family, I had to begin with something like an antipathy to the missionary in the East. Allusions were constantly made in my hearing to the impertinence of his pretensions, his want of birth, or wit, or learning . . . till it seemed to me in the pertness of sixteen that if a missionary could not be induced to stay at home, the sooner he fell in with cannibals the better.'[99] In contrast to Central Africa, missionary education failed to win the approval of British administration. In Central Africa it was considered that it promoted social order: in India and Kashmir it was feared that it would stimulate social upheaval.[100] Despite his games-playing orthodoxy Tyndale-Biscoe, with his extraordinary ideas, was seen as an eccentric radical who too often caused embarrassment. In plain truth he was viewed as a Christian simpleton who induced raised eyebrows by virtue of his odd actions. Like Welldon, when he was Metropolitan Archbishop of India, Tyndale-Biscoe took his religion a little too seriously for some.[101] His Christian intensity was less than truly British. And to further the unease of the orthodox he frequently revealed more of a resemblance to Kipling's unconventional hero in *Stalky and Co.* than to Vachell's more acceptable hero in *The Hill*. During service with the Punjab volunteers, for example, he once successfully dressed up as an old woman and discovered the disposition of the enemy, only to be reprimanded by his commanding officer for not really playing the game.[102] Then, to add insult to injury, he was not obsessively addicted to conversion. He was conscious of the fact that this would produce deracinated outcasts. He was fully aware of the penalties and agonies of the converted Muslim, Buddhist and Hindu.[103] He was far less troubled, of course, about changing Brahmin customs within the framework of Brahmin society. That could only improve it. He wanted simply Brahmins with clean bodies, clothes and minds, strong limbs and chivalrous spirits. There was a Kingsleian simplicity in his ambition. He was a Victorian Valiant-in-Truth. His aims were uncomplicated – hygiene, hardiness and heart. The dilemmas of imperialism passed him by.

There can be no denying Tyndale-Biscoe's bigotry, ruthlessness and occasional insensitivity in striving to achieve these ambitions. He was often contemptuous, peremptory, self-righteous and self-opinionated. In matters of morality he was a monologist. And he broke the rules of others with complete assurance, while insisting on full subscription to his own. With his 'vision of knights issuing forth from the school to battle with wrong and put it right' he encouraged physical violence,[104] had his own staff publicly beaten for immorality[105] and flogged others for lack of compassion. He could adapt the old jingle of a wife, a dog and a walnut tree with perfect equanimity, and rephrase it:

> A wife, a dog and a walnut tree,
> The more you beat them, the better they be,
> But truer still of the Kashmiri[106]

and express a short-sighted and absolute self-confidence in the efficiency of his own educational methods. In 1922, for example, he wrote complacently that in Srinagar Hindu and Muhammadan were hard at it, punching one another's heads and thoroughly enjoying themselves. 'Communal tomfoolery' characteristic of Calcutta and other places where they were crying out for 'home rule' was unknown.[107] He was later to learn better. He could remark, grandiloquently and chauvinistically, that the spirit of chivalry came from Christ, 'and Christ alone, whatever else men may say'.[108] With his sanguine self-assurance, he is the perfect whipping boy for a latter-day anti-imperialist Lytton Strachey.

However, to those who feel an obligation to consider the man in his full complexity, to his weaknesses must be added his strengths – courage, compassion, idealism and tenacity. Above all, he was tenacious. He was far too much of a realist to believe in ameliorative abiogenesis, at least in human affairs. In his book *Character Building in Kashmir* he used simple simile and metaphor in a clumsy yet profound attempt to find words to define both the nature and the means of achieving his life's work. He wrote that to carry out the great purpose set by Christ, and to make Kashmiri fellows into manly, Christian gentlemen, was like rowing upstream, but the effort had to be made. He prefaced this observation with a trite little allegorical verse, the last two couplets of which read:

> . . . it isn't discussion or staring or fussing
> will coax us a crop from the clay;
>
> It's draining, manuring, persisting, enduring,
> It's patiently PEGGING AWAY.[109]

It has the literary merit of a homily on a Woolworth's calendar, but to judge it simply at this level is to do considerable injustice to the action it inspired.

In his obituary, entitled 'The Making of Men in Kashmir', in *The Times* of 11 August 1949, it was recorded that his 'passion for social righteousness and the overthrow of inequitable custom' had stimulated in Kashmir 'ameliorative legislation and administration reform' and that, in addition, his pupils 'came gradually to see why bodily improvement and games ranked equally with mental progress'.[110] Possibly, in the full context of the history of Kashmir he scarcely breached the social order of things. Yet his gifts were permanent. He stimulated a review of attitudes to the weak, women and animals. He was the Christian warrior incarnate. He delighted in conflict; he had marvellous victories; he did some good. He tempered a Darwinist social system with Christian moderation. He certainly gave the Kashmiri Western games to play. He had more than a transitory cultural significance. Perhaps the most fitting evaluation of his robust philosophy of education came from a fellow oarsman from his Cambridge days, the famous Australian rowing coach, Steve Fairbairn: 'I have often said of rowing "as you meet your stretcher so you will meet your God". That cox Tyndale-Biscoe met his stretcher perfectly.'[111]

In his concluding remarks in *A History of Christian Missions*, Stephen Neill warns against slapdash assertions regarding the constructive and destructive impact of the Western missionary effort. Caution and restraint, he advises, are required in any assessment of its influence. After duly exercising these qualities himself, he felt able to make a number of legitimate observations. Certainly, some missionaries saw themselves as agents of diffusion making available to all 'that culture which has been accepted unquestioningly as culture *par excellence*'.[112] In this self-appointed role, objectivity was blurred by patronizing – even contemptuous – attitudes towards the subjugated peoples. Such frailties stemmed directly from assumptions regarding the nature and source of cultural superiority and such fallibility was to be expected. The treasure of the Gospel was contained in earthen vessels, and the doctrine of Jesus Christ could not easily be separated from 'cultural adulteration'.[113] Consequently, overestimation of Western tradition resulted in underestimation of indigenous custom. All this is certainly true. This chapter provides at least one outstanding exemplar of ethnocentric self-assurance. Neill, however, bravely asserts that in conjunction with much certain harm some good resulted from the missionary impulse, but admits that the assertion will be strenuously debated for a long while yet. Fortunately, we are less concerned here with such issues. Our foremost purpose, of course, has been to plot the early dissemination of public school games and the associated ethic to a selection of nations during the heyday of the British Empire, while at one and the same time attempting to uncover and understand the motives of the disseminators. In this process of cultural diffusion the nineteenth-century knights errant of Christian chivalry played a large part, taking physical equipment, playing rules and a behavioural code to all races of the Empire with serious purpose.[114] This seriousness of endeavour should not be overlooked. To most, if not all of them, games were much more than mere entertainment for leisure hours. They were a significant instrument of moral training. A point made perfectly, if facetiously, by a post-imperialist iconoclast in these amiable and amusing lines already encountered:

. . . this is the game for gentlemen
Till on our race the sun shall set.
The greatest glory of our land
Whose crimson covers half the maps
Is in the field where the wickets stand
And the game is played by DECENT CHAPS.[115]

SELECT BIBLIOGRAPHY

Suggestions for further reading:

GENERAL: *Empire*

John Bowle, *The Imperial Achievement*, Secker & Warburg, 1974.
Charles Dilke, *Greater Britain*, 3rd edn, Macmillan, 1869.
Richard Faber, *The Vision and the Need: Late Victorian Imperialist Aims*, Faber, 1966.
R. Hyam, *Britain's Imperial Century: A Study of Empire and Expansion*, Batsford, 1976.
James Morris, *Pax Britannica: The Climax of Empire*, Penguin, 1968.
Heaven's Command: An Imperial Progress, Penguin, 1973.
Farewell the Trumpets: An Imperial Retreat, Penguin, 1978.
Alan Sandison, *The Wheel of Empire*, Macmillan, 1967.
L. C. B. Seaman, *Victorian England: Aspects of English and Imperial History 1873–1901*, Methuen, 1973.
John Seeley, *The Expansion of England*, Macmillan, 1883.
Robin Winks, *A Historiography of the British Empire, and Commonwealth*, Duke University Press, Durham, N.C., 1966.

GENERAL: *The Public Schools*

T. W. Bamford, *The Rise of the Public Schools*, Nelson, 1967.
J. Gathorne-Hardy, *The Public School Phenomenon 1897–1971*, Penguin, 1979.
John Honey, *Tom Brown's Universe*, Millington, 1979.
J. A. Mangan, *Athleticism in the Victorian and Edwardian Public School: The Emergence and Consolidation of an Educational Ideology*, Cambridge University Press, 1981.
Rupert Wilkinson, *The Prefects*, Oxford University Press, 1964.

CHAPTER ONE

J. D'E. Firth, *Rendall of Winchester*, Oxford University Press, 1954.
C. R. C. Fletcher, *Edmond Warre*, Chatto & Windus, 1922.
R. J. Mackenzie, *Almond of Loretto*, Constable, 1905.
J. E. C. Welldon, *Forty Years On*, Nicholson and Watson, 1935.

CHAPTER TWO

Sir Theodore Cook, *Character and Sportsmanship*, Williams and Norgate, 1927.
Maude Diver, *Captain Desmond, V.C.*, Blackwood, 1907.
Geoffrey Drage, *Eton and Empire*, Drake, 1890.
J. G. Cotton Minchin, *Our Public Schools. Their Influence on English History*, Swan Sonnenschein, 1901.
Henry Newbolt, *Poems, New and Old*, Murray, 1929.
T. C. Worsley, *Barbarians and Philistines*, Robert Hale, 1940.

CHAPTER THREE

Abd Al-Rahim, *Imperialism and Nationalism in the Sudan*, Clarendon Press, 1969.
Oliver Albino, *The Sudan: A Southern Viewpoint*, Oxford University Press, 1970.
K. D. D. Henderson, *The Making of the Modern Sudan*, Faber, 1955.
H. C. Jackson, *Sudan Days and Ways*, Macmillan, 1954.
Sir Harold MacMichael, *The Anglo-Egyptian Sudan*, Faber, 1934.

CHAPTER FOUR

Christine Bolt, *Victorian Attitudes to Race*, Routledge & Kegan Paul, 1971.
Michael Crowden, *The Story of Nigeria*, Cass, 1970.
F. H. Hilliard, *A Short History of Education in British West Africa*, Nelson, 1945.
Sir Frederick Lugard, *The Dual Mandate in British Tropical Africa*, Blackwood, 1922.
Ontonti Nduka, *Western Education and the Nigerian Cultural Background*, Oxford University Press, Ibadan, 1964.
I. F. Nicolson, *The Administration of Nigeria 1900–1960: Men, Methods and Myths*, Clarendon Press, 1969.
Margery Perham, *Lugard: The Life of Frederick Dealty Lugard* (Vol. I: *The Years of Adventure*, Collins, 1956; Vol. II: *The Years of Authority*, Collins, 1960).

CHAPTER FIVE

Ian Malcolm, *India Pictures and Problems*, Grant Richards, 1907.
Thomas R. Metcalf, *The Aftermath of Revolt: India 1857–1870*, Princeton University Press, Princeton (N.J.), 1965.
Syed Nurullah and J. P. Nayaka, *A History of Education in India during the British Period*, 1951.
Herbert Sherring, *Mayo College, Ajmere, 'The Eton of India': A Record of Twenty Years 1875–1895*, 1897.

CHAPTER SIX

Carl Berger, *The Sense of Power: Studies in the Areas of Canadian Imperialism, 1867–1914*, University of Toronto Press, Toronto, 1970.
Carolyn Gossage, *A Question of Privilege, Canada's Independent Schools*, Peter Mentin, Toronto, 1977.
Nancy and Maxwell L. Howell, *Sports and Games in Canadian Life – 1700 to the Present*, Macmillan Canada, Toronto, 1969.
Arthur Lower, *From Colony to Nation*, Longmans, Green & Co., Toronto, 1946.
J. O. Miller, *The Young Canadian Citizen*, Dent, Toronto, 1919.
P. S. Penton, *Non Nobis Solum*, Corporation of Lower Canada College, Montreal, 1972.

CHAPTER SEVEN

Ernest H. Hayes, *Doctor Pennell, Afghan Pioneer*, n.d.
Henry Scott Holland, *The Call of Empire*, 1917.
Stephen Neill, *A History of Christian Missions*, Penguin, 1964.
Jessie Page, *Bishop Patteson. The Martyr of Melanesia*, 2nd edn, Partridge, 1891.
T. L. Pennell, *Among the Wild Tribes of the Afghan Frontier*, Seeley, 1909.
J. C. Pollock, *The Cambridge Seven. A Call to Christian Service*, Varsity Fellowship, 1955.
Cecil Earle Tyndale-Biscoe, *Character Building in Kashmir*, Church Missionary Society, 1920.
Tyndale-Biscoe of Kashmir: An Autobiography, Seeley Service & Co., 1951.
Grinding Grit into Kashmir, Church Missionary Society, 1922.
E. D. Tyndale-Biscoe, *Fifty Years Against the Stream*, Wesleyan Mission Press, Mysore, 1930.
W. F. Ward, *Fraser of Trinity and Achimota*, Ghana Universities Press, Accra, 1965.

NOTES

CHAPTER ONE

1. Quoted in T. W. Bamford, *The Rise of the Public Schools*, Nelson, 1967, p. 241.

2. Rupert Wilkinson, *The Prefects*, Oxford University Press, 1964, p. 102.

3. J. Gathorne-Hardy, *The Public School Phenomenon 1897–1971*, Penguin, 1979, p. 213.

4. ibid., p. 212.

5. The public schools produced harsh critics of imperialism, notably, of course, Arthur Scawen Blunt, Leonard Woolf and George Orwell.

6. See Michael Apple, *Education and Power*, Routledge & Kegan Paul, 1982, *passim*.

7. See C. S. Gillett, *John Millington Sing, Some Memories*, Mowbray, n.d.

8. Cyril Norwood (1875–1956) was one of the most distinguished public school headmasters of the first half of the twentieth century. He held, successively, the headmasterships of Bristol Grammar School, Marlborough and Harrow.

9. Cyril Norwood, *The English Tradition of Education*, Murray, 1929, p. 103.

10. See C. R. C. Fletcher, *Edmond Warre*, Murray, 1922, *passim*.

11. Shane Leslie, *The Oppidan*, Chatto & Windus, 1922, p. 43.

12. H. B. Tristram, *Loretto School, Past and Present*, Fisher Unwin, 1911, p. 99.

13. R. J. Mackenzie, *Almond of Loretto*, Constable, 1905, p. 326.

14. *Loretto's Hundred Years 1827–1927: Special Supplement to the 'Lorettonian'*, 1927, p. 17.

15. Mackenzie, *Almond of Loretto*, p. 338.

16. Hely Hutchinson Almond, 'The Conservation of the Body' in *Christ the Protestant and Other Sermons*, Blackwood, 1899, pp. 150–51.

17. ibid., p. 155.

18. Mackenzie, *Almond of Loretto*, p. 127.

19. Almond, *Christ the Protestant*, p. 151.

20. John Percival (1834–1918) was educated at Appleby Grammar School and Queen's College, Oxford. After a short period as a schoolmaster at Rugby, in 1862 he was appointed the first headmaster of Clifton College where he remained until 1879. From 1886 to 1895 he was headmaster of Rugby and, from 1895 to 1917, Bishop of Hereford.

21. *Harrovian*, Vol. VII, No. 4. Tuesday 5 June 1984, p. 46.

22. Almond, *Christ the Protestant*, p. 283.

23. Quoted in Tristram, *Loretto School*, p. 267.

24. H. H. Almond, 'The Breed of Man' in *Nineteenth Century*, Vol. XLVIII, 1900, pp. 663–4.

25. Hely Hutchinson Almond, 'The Public School Product' in *New Review*, Vol. XVI, 1897, p. 96.

26. Almond, 'Breed of Man', p. 656.

27. H. H. Almond, 'Athletics and Education' in *Macmillans Magazine*, Vol. XLIII, 1881, p. 293.

28. ibid., p. 293.

29. J. M. Rendall, 'Youth and the Empire' in *United Empire*, Vol. XIX, 1928, p. 684.

30. 'The Spirit of a Lion and the Appetite of a Robin: Margaret Best and the School Empire Tours' in *Royal Commonwealth Society Library Notes*, No. 226, April/June.

31. ibid., p. 3.

32. J. D'E. Firth, *Rendall of Winchester*, Oxford University Press, 1954, p. 196.

33. Letter to Phillip Kerr dated August 1926 (File 2611 on Dr Rendall, Rhodes Trust, Rhodes House, Oxford).

34. Letter from Rendall dated 25 March 1925 from 'Extracts from Correspondence between Sir Edward Grigg and Rendall' (Rhodes Trust).

35. Letter from Rendall dated 25 March 1925.

36. Letter from Mr W. A. Way, headmaster of Grey Institute, Port Elizabeth, South Africa (Rhodes Trust).

37. Firth, *Rendall*, pp. 203–4.

38. Rendall, 'Youth and the Empire', p. 685.

39. *Australian and New Zealand Report*, 8 July 1925, p. 5 (Rhodes Trust).

40. Firth, *Rendall*, p. 216.

41. ibid., p. 216.

42. ibid., p. 216.

43. ibid., p. 218.

44. Rendall, 'Youth and the Empire', p. 284.

45. From the introduction by J. E. C. Welldon to Arthur Stanley, *Patriotic Song*, Pearson, 1891, p. viii.

46. Seventh Ordinary General Meeting of the Royal Colonial Institute, 14 May 1985, in *Proceedings of the Royal Colonial Institute*, Vol. CCVI, 1894–5, p. 822.

47. J. E. C. Welldon, 'The Imperial Purpose of Education' in *Proceedings of the Royal Colonial Institute*, Vol. XXVI, 1894–5, p. 823.

48. ibid., pp. 827–8.
49. ibid., p. 829.
50. ibid., p. 832.
51. ibid., p. 839.
52. J. E. C. Welldon, *Forty Years On*, Nicholson & Watson, 1935, p. 140.
53. J. E. C. Welldon, *Recollections and Reflections*, Cassell, 1915, p. 180.
54. Welldon, *Forty Years On*, p. 262.
55. Kenneth Rose, *Superior Person*, Weidenfeld and Nicolson, 1963, pp. 345–6.
56. J. E. C. Welldon, 'The Early Training of Boys in Citizenship' in *Essays on Duty and Discipline*, Cassell, 1910, p. 12.
57. Welldon, *Recollections*, p. 180.
58. ibid., p. 307.
59. From the introduction by Welldon to Pelham Warner's *How We Recovered the Ashes*, Chapman and Hall, 1904, p. xxvii.
60. Welldon, *Forty Years On*, pp. 116–17.
61. *The Times*, 20 April 1916, p. 9.
62. J. E. C. Welldon, 'The Training of a Gentleman' in *Nineteenth Century*, Vol. LIX, 1906, p. 406.
63. Welldon, *Forty Years On*, pp. 332–3.
64. Leo Amery, *My Political Life*, Vol. I, Hutchinson, 1953, pp. 37–8.
65. Welldon, *Forty Years On*, p. 110.
66. ibid., p. 254.
67. P. B. Bryant, *Harrow*, Blackie, 1936, p. 152.
68. Henry Erskine Cowper, 'British Education, Public and Private and the British Empire, 1880–1930', Ph.D. Dissertation, University of Edinburgh, 1979, p. 37.
69. It must be said that Rendall was both more reticent and more balanced in his claims than Almond or Welldon.
70. See J. A. Mangan, *Athleticism in the Victorian and Edwardian Public School: The Emergence and Consolidation of an Educational Ideology*, Cambridge University Press, 1981, *passim*.

CHAPTER TWO

1. Arnold Lunn, *The Harrovians*, 6th edn, Methuen, 1926, p. 66.
2. E. C. Mack, *Public Schools and British Opinion since 1860* (1941), p. 108; Rupert Wilkinson, *The Prefects: British Leadership and the Public School Tradition* (1964), pp. 100–109; see also T. W. Bamford, *The Rise of the Public Schools* (1967), pp. 237–47, and J. Honey, *Tom Brown's Universe* (1979), p. 155.
3. Henry Newbolt, *Poems, New and Old*, Murray, 1929, p. 89.
4. ibid., p. 77.
5. *Radleian*, No. 3, April 1865, p. 9.
6. *Cheltonian*, No. 20, October 1895, p. 11.

7. W. E. Bowen, *Edward Bowen. A Memoir*, Longmans, Green & Co., 1902, pp. 404–5.

8. Letter dated 22.7.1900 (Charterhouse Archives).

9. J. G. Cotton Minchin, *Our Public Schools. Their Influence on English History*, Swan Sonnenschein, 1901.

10. ibid., p. 52.

11. ibid., p. 44.

12. ibid., p. 201.

13. ibid., p. 161.

14. ibid., p. 142.

15. J. A. Cramb, *Reflections on the Origins and Destiny of Imperial Britain*, Macmillan, 1900, p. 36.

16. William Ernest Henley, 'England, My England' in Arthur Stanley (ed.), *Patriotic England. A Book of English Verse*, Pearson, 1901, p. 138.

17. For an interesting discussion of the novelist Maude Diver, see Benita Parry, *Delusions and Discoveries: Studies on India in the British Imagination*, Penguin, 1972, pp. 78–93.

18. Maude Diver, *Captain Desmond, V.C.*, Blackwood, 1907, p. 8.

19. ibid., p. 44.

20. Maude Diver, *The Great Amulet*, Blackwood, 1908, p. 216.

21. T. C. Worsley, *Barbarians and Philistines*, Hale, 1940, p. 85.

22. *Haileyburian*, No. 149, March 1886, p. 16.

23. Sir Theodore Cook, *Character and Sportsmanship*, Williams and Norgate, 1927, p. 321.

24. Dr J. R. P. Sclater, 'The Imperial Significance of Games' in *Empire Club of Canada: Addresses Delivered to the Members During the Year 1929*, Best, Toronto, 1979, p. 138. I am indebted to Katharine Moore for this reference.

25. ibid., p. 138.

26. John Astley Cooper, 'Many Lands – One People' in *Greater Britain*, 15 July 1891, pp. 458–62. Cooper developed his ideas in a wide range of newspapers, periodicals and journals. See, for example, 'An Anglo-Saxon Olympiad' in *Nineteenth Century*, No. 187, September 1892, pp. 380–88; July 1893, pp. 81–93; and No. 223, September 1895, pp. 426–41.

27. Cooper, 'Many Lands', p. 461.

28. W. P. Cullen, 'The Proposed Periodic English-speaking Contest and Festival' in *Greater Britain*, 15 October 1892, pp. 291–2.

29. R. P. P. Rowe, 'The Proposed Pan-Anglican Festival' in *Greater Britain*, 15 October 1892, pp. 294–7.

30. Quoted in John Astley Cooper, 'The Proposed Periodic Britannic Contest and All-English Speaking Festival' in *Greater Britain*, 15 November 1891, p. 597.

31. Quoted in John Astley Cooper, 'The Reception Given to the Idea by the Press of the English-Speaking World' in *Greater Britain*, 15 October 1892, p. 299.

32. ibid., p. 303.

33. ibid., p. 303.

34. ibid., p. 304.

35. ibid., p. 308.

36. Quoted in *Greater Britain*, 15 November 1891, p. 598.

37. See Katharine Moore, 'The Origin and Evolution of the British Empire Games from 1891 to 1950', paper presented at the Commonwealth Games Conference, Brisbane, Australia, September 1982.

38. John Astley Cooper, 'The British Imperial Spirit of Sport and War' in *United Empire*, Vol. VII, 1916, pp. 581–96.

39. ibid., p. 581.

40. ibid., p. 582.

41. ibid., p. 582.

42. ibid., p. 582.

43. James Morris, *Pax Britannica: The Climax of Empire*, Penguin, 1968, p. 21.

44. *Lorettonian*, No. 5, March 1900, p. 24.

45. Every public school has its official magazine. Most date from between 1860 and 1880 and have been in continuous existence since their inception. For a discussion of the institutional role of the school magazine, see Mangan, *Athleticism in the Victorian and Edwardian Public School*, Appendix III, p. 243.

46. The *Eton Chronicle* was established in 1863, the *Haileyburian* in 1868 and the *Cheltonian* in 1874.

47. *Haileyburian*, No. 44, February 1874, pp. 292–3.

48. *Haileyburian*, No. 86, May 1879, p. 256.

49. *Cheltonian*, February 1885, p. 80. The dead, who gave their lives in the creation, preservation and expansion of Empire, were frequently given a more permanent and public recognition than their obituaries in the school magazine. For example, a memorial screen was erected in Lipton's Chapel at Eton in memory of those who fell in the various African and Afghan campaigns prior to 1881, and unveiled by the Prince of Wales in June 1882. Those celebrated were not always soldiers. At Haileybury there is a tablet outside the chapel which reads:

> On this tablet are recorded the names of forty members of the Indian Civil Service sometime students of Old Haileybury College who lost their lives in the active discharge of their duty, during the outbreak of mutiny and insurrection throughout India in the years 1857 and 1859.

50. *Eton Chronicle*, No. 246, June 1879, p. 1186.

51. *Haileyburian*, No. 89, October 1879, pp. 303–4.

52. *Haileyburian*, No. 140, April 1885, p. 438.

53. N. J. A. Coghill (1852–79) was at Haileybury from 1865 to 1869. The school chapel contains a brass tablet recording that there was once a painting under the dome in his memory and that of G. F. Hodson, also killed at Isandhlwana. The painting was covered over in 1936 when the chapel was rearranged.

54. *Eton Chronicle*, No. 346, June 1881, p. 1382.

55. *Cheltonian*, October 1897, p. 475.

56. *Cheltonian*, March 1889, p. 36.

57. Mack, *Public Schools and British Opinion since 1860*, p. 8. The accuracy of Mack's assertion can be seen from this poetic fragment in honour of the Eton Memorial to the memory of the dead of the South African War:

> So, in some sacred moment, when the dream
> Of deeds that wait the doing, rises high,
> Haply some generous heart may whisper then:
> 'If these could fight and fall, Wherefore not I?
> I will be true as these, whose memories gleam,
> The jewels of a Mother of mighty men'.

(*Eton Chronicle*, No. 1053, June 1904, p. 493.)

58. *Eton Chronicle*, No. 852, August 1900, p. 526.

59. *Eton Chronicle*, No. 907, January 1901, p. 957.

60. *Haileyburian*, No. 299, July 1900, p. 174. The scrapbook of E. F. Ledward in the Haileybury archives contains newspaper cuttings providing details of the extent of Lyttelton's commitment to imperialism during the Boer War – he is reputed to have beaten pro-Boer rebels as a gesture in support of authority, given talks on the progress of the war and declared a whole holiday on the relief of Mafeking.

61. The same note was struck but even more explicitly by Lord Sydenham on speech-day, 28 July 1914, when speaking of Haileybury's links with India. 'There was,' he declared, 'no nobler service than that which lay open in front of the present boys in India.' Many years earlier, the *Eton Chronicle* had recorded that 'the possession of India affords us a large field for doing good, and so we admire the possession of the Indian Empire' (March 1878).

62. Speech-day lecture, 1899 (Haileybury College Archives).

63. Sermon delivered at the opening of new form rooms, 1908, p. 2 (Haileybury College Archives).

64. Sir Walter Lawrence (1851–1940), Old Cheltonian, distinguished member of the Indian Civil Service and author of *The India We Served*.

65. *Cheltonian*, August 1912, pp. 193–4.

66. 'The Haileybury Jubilee', supplement to the *Haileyburian*, No. 421, July 1912, *passim*.

67. *Standard*, 31 May 1911, p. 8.

68. A particularly good example of the former is to be found in the *Eton Chronicle* of July 1907, which contains a lecture by General Neville Lyttelton on his experiences of the war in the Transvaal, and a fine example of the latter is to be found in the *Eton Chronicle* of May 1879, which contains a long letter from an Old Etonian, filled with details of the exciting action at Ginginlovo during the Zulu Campaign.

69. The *Eton Chronicle* in May 1895, for example, provided details of a lecture by Captain Younghusband on his explorations in Asia. Imperial explorers, irrespective of sex and background, were always welcome visitors in the public schools of the period. Stanley visited Eton in May 1896, and later in

the same year Mary Kingsley lectured there on 'Elephant Hunting by the West African Tribes'.

70. *Eton Chronicle*, No. 317, July 1880, p. 1270.
71. *Eton Chronicle*, No. 481, October 1888, p. 346.
72. *Haileyburian*, No. 164, October 1887, pp. 461–2.
73. Morris, *Pax Britannica*, p. 21.
74. George Drage, *Eton and the Empire*, Drake, 1890, p. 40.
75. *Cheltonian*, December 1885, p. 146.
76. *Haileyburian*, No. 410, November 1910, p. 134.
77. Details from the *Haileybury Register 1862–1946*.
78. Morris, *Pax Britannica*, p. 405.
79. Patrick Dunae, *Gentlemen Emigrants*, Duncan and McIntyre, Vancouver, 1981.
80. *Punch*, 6 September 1873, p. 99.
81. *Eton Chronicle*, No. 379, March 1884, p. 1574.
82. *Haileyburian*, No. 107, November 1910, p. 134.
83. *Cheltonian*, December 1885, p. 146.
84. *Cheltonian*, December 1885, p. 160.

CHAPTER THREE

1. This chapter draws substantially on hitherto unpublished correspondence and interviews with some sixty former members of the Sudan Political Service, many of whom generously wrote at length to the author. Their comments provide most valuable insights into the social background of later members of the Service, their various motives for joining and, perhaps most important of all in the light of their own belief in its value and the divergent opinion of at least one earlier commentator, the significance of the public school system of education in developing gubernatorial attitudes and skills. In addition to the material provided by former members of the Service, information regarding school and university careers and social backgrounds was provided by the archivists and librarians of some forty public schools and the universities of Oxford, Cambridge, Wales, Glasgow, Edinburgh, St Andrews and Aberdeen. I am especially grateful to Mr Edward Craven of Sutton Valence School, Mr P. Yeats-Edwards of Winchester College, Mr Peter King of Hurstpierpoint College, Mr J. B. Lawson of Shrewsbury School, Mr Mark Baker of Wellington College, Mrs Jennifer Macrory of Rugby School and Mr B. T. W. Handford of Lancing College, who each provided especially valuable information.
2. Letter to the author from J. P. S. Daniell (Sudan Political Service 1938–55) dated 22.1.80. Several former members who have written to the author were selected for both the Indian Civil Service and the Sudan Political Service and chose the latter!
3. The Sudan Political Service, of course, came under the Foreign Office, not the Colonial Office, but clearly those who served in the Sudan were part of a

world-wide imperial service. Perham has put this point succinctly in her comments on Sir Douglas Newbold, a distinguished member of the Sudan Political Service, in the introduction to K. D. D. Henderson's *The Making of the Modern Sudan*, Faber, 1953: 'As an administrator, it is possible to see Newbold in widening concentric circles of relevance. The widest of them is that of the whole setting of modern imperialism . . . he was an officer in a service, that, whatever its name, was essentially colonial' (p. x).

4. Abd Al-Rahim, *Imperialism and Nationalism in the Sudan*, Clarendon Press, 1969, p. 40.

5. Sir Harold MacMichael, *The Anglo-Egyptian Sudan*, Faber, 1934, p. 65.

6. While most of the officers (some became permanent members) from the Egyptian Army were gradually replaced in the Service by civilian staff, for many years a number of army officers were recruited on short-term contracts for service in the more troublesome areas.

7. Al-Rahim, *Imperialism and Nationalism*, p. 40.

8. Earl of Cromer, *Modern Egypt*, Vol. II, Macmillan, 1908, p. 548. Sir Evelyn Baring (later Lord Cromer) arrived in Egypt in September 1883 to represent the British Government as Agent and Consul-General. He served in this capacity until 1907. A succinct outline of his imperial career in Egypt is to be found in Richard Hill's *A Biographical Dictionary of the Anglo-Egyptian Sudan*, Clarendon Press, 1951, pp. 72–3.

9. Some idea of the extent of public school representation at the ancient universities at this time may be obtained from A. Gray and F. Brittain, *A History of Jesus College*, Cambridge University Press, 1900, pp. 176–7. Gray and Brittain reveal that of 1,290 entrants to Jesus between 1849 and 1898, 850 were from English public schools.

10. As Robert O. Collins points out in his *Land Beyond the Rivers: the Southern Sudan 1898–1918*, Yale University Press, New Haven & London, 1971, the term 'Sudan Political Service' was never official but gradually came into use in the 1920s to distinguish the administrative from the departmental and technical staff of the Sudan Civil Service. The latter numbered several thousand during its imperial existence.

11. Percy C. Martin, *The Sudan in Evolution*, Constable, 1921, pp. 45–6.

12. Several former members of the Service have provided the author with details of the competition for places in the period immediately before the Second World War. J. A. A. Blaikie (Sudan Political Service 1936–55) has written 'in June [of 1935] I heard that I was one of twelve applicants out of over 100 who were invited to attend the final selection meeting' (letter dated 29.1.80). Dr P. P. Howell (Sudan Political Service 1938–55) is of the opinion that some 400 candidates were interviewed at their universities in 1938. For further information on competition for places, see Martin, *Sudan in Evolution*, p. 44, and S. Bell and B. D. Dee, *The Sudan Political Service*, 1956. This latter book, known affectionately and familiarly by cognoscenti as 'The Book of Snobs', contains the educational and career records of members of the Service.

13. Letter to the author from Dr Hugh Malet (Sudan Political Service 1951–4) dated 10.4.80.

14. Sir Harold MacMichael, G.C.M.G., D.S.O. (1882–1969), obtained a First at Cambridge, was in the Cambridge University Boxing and Fencing Team from 1901 to 1904, served with distinction in the Sudan, reaching the rank of Civil Secretary, held high official posts in Tanganyika, Palestine and elsewhere, and was the author of a number of books on Sudanese history.

15. Sir Harold MacMichael in his introduction to Bell and Dee, *Sudan Political Service*, p. 4.

16. Letter to the author from G. R. F. Bredin (Sudan Political Service 1921–48) dated 14.3.81.

17. A. H. M. Kirk-Greene, 'The Sudan Political Service: A Profile in the Sociology of Imperialism' in *International Journal of African Historical Studies*, Vol. 15, No. 1, 1982, p. 22.

18. Robert O. Collins, 'The Sudan Political Service: A Portrait of the Imperialists' in *African Affairs*, Vol. 71, No. 284, July 1972, pp. 300–301.

19. Collie Knox, *It Might Have Been You*, Chapman & Hall, 1938, p. 205, quoted in Kirk-Greene, 'Sudan Political Service', p. 27.

20. See, for example, Bamford, *The Rise of the Public Schools*, pp. 237–47; Mack, *Public Schools and British Opinion since 1860*, p. 108; and Wilkinson, *The Prefects: British Leadership and the Public School Tradition*, pp. 100–109. Recent useful papers taking us beyond this generalization include that of I. F. Nicolson and C. A. Hughes, 'A Provenance of Proconsuls: British Colonial Governors 1900–1960' in *Journal of Imperial and Commonwealth History*, 1975, and A. H. M. Kirk-Greene's 'Scholastic Attainment and Scholarly Achievement in Britain's Imperial Services: the Case of the African Governors', paper delivered to the Canadian Association of African Studies Conference, Summer 1980.

21. See Mangan, *Athleticism in the Victorian and Edwardian Public School*, p. 212.

22. John Honey, *Tom Brown's Universe*, Millington, 1979, pp. 238 ff.

23. ibid., p. 243.

24. Mangan, *Athleticism*, *passim*.

25. Honey, *Tom Brown's Universe*, p. 252.

26. Letter to the author from Dr S. S. Richardson (Sudan Political Service 1949–55) dated 4.3.80.

27. Nicolson and Hughes, 'A Provenance of Proconsuls', p. 81.

28. It is interesting to compare this state of affairs in the Sudan Political Service with that in the Indian Civil Service during the same period and described in R. Hunt and J. Harrison, *The District Officer in India 1930–1947*, Scolar Press, 1980, pp. 2–4. The authors refer to the reduced attraction of the I.C.S. to English public schoolboys and the consequent shortage of suitable recruits, due *inter alia* to the counter attractions of the Colonial Service with its improved conditions of service and no competitive examination, the expansion of the Home Civil Service and the increasing 'Indianization' of the I.C.S., making a career in India 'less secure'.

29. Several members of the Service in correspondence with the author have hinted modestly at this state of affairs at the time of their simultaneous selection to the Sudan Political Service, the Colonial Service and the Indian Civil Service.

30. See G. Bernbaum, *Social Change and the Schools*, Routledge & Kegan Paul, 1967, pp. 4–5.

31. See especially the memorandum by the Private Secretary for Appointments (Sir R. Furse) entitled 'Recruitment and Training of Colonial Servants', Colonial Office Conference, 1927, Appendices to the Summary of Proceedings, Cmd. 2884, June 1927, p. 14.

32. A typical example is L. W. A. Raven (Sudan Political Service 1934–55), the son of an army sergeant who attended a grammar school but won a blue for soccer at Oxford.

33. R. O. Collins recounts how early in the life of the Service the Provost of Trinity College, Dublin, complained to Sir Reginald Wingate, the then Governor-General of the Sudan, about the insufficient number of Trinity men in the Sudan administration (at this time it contained five Trinity graduates). The complaint had little effect. In the remaining forty years of the Service only one Trinity applicant was accepted. The Provost's ungentlemanly accusations of discrimination, notes Collins, 'only confirmed Wingate and his successors in the wisdom of preferring Oxford and Cambridge' (Collins, 'Sudan Political Service', p. 296).

34. It is the view of J. F. S. Phillips (Sudan Political Service 1945–55) that Scots had gained a considerable reputation in all branches of imperial service in the nineteenth century, and consequently they were *persona grata* in the Sudan Political Service even when they lacked the usual Oxbridge credentials. His view is certainly supported by the fact that Scotland supplied more boys from state schools and indigenous universities than Ireland, Wales or the Dominions (letter to the author dated 17.3.81). Perhaps the career of the Scot, John Campbell, provides a little insight into how ordinary Scots achieved this reputation. From a humble Lanarkshire background he won a scholarship to Allan Glen's, a Glasgow fee-paying secondary school, in 1887, joined a local factory in his teens and, at the age of twenty-two, after 'eighteen months' hard self-directed study', came second in the India Civil Service List. He then won a bursary at Christ College, Oxford, where he 'took premier place in the final examinations' of the I.C.S., and subsequently held many important posts in the Service. Details from *Allan Glen's Monthly*, January 1909, p. 8.

35. H. C. Jackson, *Sudan Days and Ways*, Macmillan, 1954, p. 15.

36. Daniell, letter to the author dated 22.1.80.

37. Letter to the author from C. B. Kendall (Sudan Political Service 1943–56) dated 28.3.81.

38. Kirk-Greene, 'Sudan Political Service', p. 44.

39. *Marlborough College Register 1843–1952*; *Rugby School Registers 1858–1891, 1892–1921 and 1911–1946* and *Rugby School Who's Who (1975)*; *Winchester College Registers 1901–1946 and 1915–1960*. Details from Monkton Coombe, St Bees and Sutton Valence were provided by Mr R. A. C. Meredith, Mr W. Fox and Mr Edward Craven respectively.

40. *Uppingham School Magazine*, July 1880, p. 162.

41. See J. A. Mangan, 'Athleticism: A Case Study of the Evolution of an Educational Ideology' in B. Simon and I. Bradley (eds.), *The Victorian Public School*, Gill & Macmillan, Dublin, 1975, pp. 147–67.

42. Sir Harold MacMichael in his introduction to Bell and Dee, *Sudan Political Service*, p. 4.

43. Letter to the author from R. J. S. Thomson (Sudan Political Service 1943–55) dated 2.3.80.

44. Daniell, letter to the author dated 22.1.80.

45. Jackson, *Sudan Days and Ways*, pp. 56–7.

46. Collins, 'Sudan Political Service', p. 297, quoted in Kirk-Greene, 'Sudan Political Service', p. 28.

47. Kirk-Greene, 'Sudan Political Service', p. 21.

48. Letter to the author from Sir James Robertson (Sudan Political Service 1923–53) dated 15.4.81. For a description of the status and power of the public school 'blood' see Mangan, *Athleticism*, Chapter 6: 'Fez, "blood" and hunting crop: symbols and rituals of a Spartan culture'.

49. Odette Keun, *A Foreigner Looks at the British Sudan*, Faber, 1930, p. 49, quoted in Kirk-Greene, 'Sudan Political Service', p. 29.

50. Kirk-Greene, 'Sudan Political Service', p. 36.

51. From Kirk-Greene, 'Sudan Political Service', p. 7. The presence of so many 'scholars' or their equivalents in the Service suggests that a substantial number of the members of the Sudan Political Service were from upper-middle-class families of quite moderate means, and the sons had to work hard to obtain a privileged education at Oxford or Cambridge. In fact, many of these 'scholars' were the sons of clerics from quite small livings.

52. For an interesting discussion of how post-war students viewed colonial service, see David C. Potter, 'Manpower Shortage and the End of Colonization: The Case of the Indian Civil Service' in *Modern Asian Studies*, Vol. 7, Part I, 1973, pp. 47–74. It is also interesting to note that of the eighty-five members of the Sudan Political Service recruited in the period 1945 to 1952 only twenty-five were offered pensionable posts; the remainder were on short-term contracts.

53. Curiously there were no recruits from Durham University, a collegiate university founded in 1832 and modelled on the classical universities. The Sudan Political Service developed simultaneously with the provincial universities and university colleges. For all the notice it appears to have taken of them (or they of it) they might not have existed!

54. Daniell, letter to the author dated 22.1.80.

55. Letter to the author from W. N. Monteith (Sudan Political Service 1938–54) dated 18.1.80.

56. See, for example, Pierre Crabites, *The Winning of the Sudan*, Routledge & Kegan Paul, 1934; Keun, *A Foreigner Looks at the Sudan*; Dame Margery Perham in Henderson, *Modern Sudan*, XIII–XV; and Abd Al-Rahim, *Imperialism and Nationalism*, p. 45. For a critical view of the Service, see Oliver Albino, *The Sudan. A Southern Viewpoint*, Oxford University Press, 1970.

57. Nicolson and Hughes, 'A Provenance of Proconsuls', pp. 104–5.

58. Joseph A. Schumpeter, *Imperialism and Social Change* (trans. H. Norden), Kelly, New York, 1951, pp. 31 ff.

59. Possible exceptions were the so-called 'Bog Barons'. These were experienced, short-contract army officers who were first used to pacify, then to

administer the Southern Sudan populated by war-like pagan tribes. The role of these 'Barons' was aristocratic, autocratic and benevolent, hence their sobriquet. For a sympathetic discussion of these men, see Collins, 'Sudan Political Service', pp. 298–9.

60. William Langer, 'A Critique of Imperialism' in *Foreign Affairs*, Vol. XIV, 1935, pp. 102–14, quoted in Louis L. Snyder, *The Imperialism Reader*, Van Nostrand, New York, 1962, p. 97.

61. Witness the ceaseless effort and ultimate exhaustion and death of Sir Douglas Newbold, chronicled movingly in Henderson, *Modern Sudan*, 1955.

62. A. P. Thornton, *Doctrines of Imperialism*, Wiley, 1965, p. 27.

63. W. J. M. Mackenzie, *Politics and Social Science*, Penguin, 1967, pp. 351–2.

64. Nicolson & Hughes, 'A Provenance of Proconsuls', pp. 80–82.

65. Collins, 'Sudan Political Service', pp. 300–301.

66. Mackenzie, *Politics*, pp. 351–2.

67. See, for example, W. B. Baillie, *An English School*, Methuen, 1949, pp. 24–5.

68. Collins, 'Sudan Political Service', p. 300. This myth is further perpetuated in L. H. Gann and Peter Duignan, *The Rulers of British Africa 1870–1914*, Croom Helm, 1978, p. 5.

69. Letter to the author from J. S. R. Duncan (Sudan Political Service 1942–56) dated 20.2.81.

70. Letter to the author from D. A. Penn (Sudan Political Service 1949–55) dated 5.3.81.

71. Collins, 'Sudan Political Service', pp. 300–301.

72. It is the opinion of a number of my correspondents that Collins writes loosely of 'English' members of the Service when he means 'British'; certainly it is not wholy clear on occasion whether Collins is using the term 'English' when he actually means 'British'. However, it seems unlikely as he uses both terms in his paper and, of course, to use English and British interchangeably in the context of a careful analysis of the social backgrounds of British members of the Sudan Political Service would be inexcusably casual. However, Collins makes no attempt to define what he means by 'gentry' or 'squirearchy' and uses both terms indiscriminately. In the interest of clarity he might usefully have consulted Bateman's classification of land-holders contained in F. M. L. Thompson's *English Landed Society in the Nineteenth Century* (1963). If Bateman's classification is followed then it is probable that very few members of the Sudan Political Service from the shires were gentry, and that some were not the sons of squires but of 'Greater Yeomen' (see Thompson, pp. 116–17). Sir Donald Hawley, who believes that Collins's views on the social composition of the Service are incorrect, writes in this context: 'My paternal grandfather, who was a schoolmaster, was the first to leave that part of Buckinghamshire and Northamptonshire, from which the Hawley family came. They were yeomen stock. My paternal grandfather came from a family of teachers and medium rank officials. My maternal grandfather was a business man.' Sir Donald Hawley's father was a chartered accountant, and the family lived in London (letter to the author dated 27.4.1981).

73. These include A. E. D. Penn (Sudan Political Service 1926–51), A. C. Beaton (Sudan Political Service 1927–54), C. W. Beer (Sudan Political Service 1929–54), L. W. A. Raven (Sudan Political Service 1934–55), James McCargow (Sudan Political Service 1942–9), and C. W. North has written interestingly in this context:

> I was recruited following a career in the Burma Civil Service as a Political Officer (1935–1947) and was therefore an experienced District Officer when I joined in 1950. I had also had two years (1948–1950) as a District Officer in Tanganyika.
>
> It is true, I think, that my social background and (lack of) athletic prowess would have debarred me from appointment to the Sudan Service had I competed in 1938 when I was successful in gaining appointment to the Burma Frontier Service.
>
> My father was very much of (lower) working class origin but qualified as a fishing trawler Master and had a distinguished career as a Chief Skipper R.N.V.S. in the Minesweeping Dover Patrol 1914–1918.
>
> We were very humble and very poor when I went up to Oxford in 1938 – my father having died in 1928 [letter to the author dated 19.2.81].

74. Letter to the author from J. S. F. Phillips (Sudan Political Service 1945–55) dated 17.2.81.

75. Letter to the author from A. K. Markland (Sudan Political Service 1946–55) dated 17.1.1981.

76. Details provided by Mr James McCargow in an interview in December 1980.

77. Letter to the author from W. G. McDowall (Sudan Political Service 1940–55) dated 15.2.1981.

78. Details provided by Mr Edward Craven, archivist of Sutton Valence School.

79. Letter to the author from J. P. S. Daniell dated 11.3.1981.

80. See, for example, J. P. D. Dunbabin, *Rural Discontent in Nineteenth-Century Britain*, Faber, 1974, pp. 173–86. See also R. S. Neale, *Class in English History 1850–1860*, Blackwell, 1981, pp. 154–92.

81. Thompson, *English Landed Society*, p. 210.

82. ibid., p. 210.

83. Letter to the author from Allan Arthur (Sudan Political Service 1948–54) dated 14.1.1981.

84. The vicar of the Durham pit village was the Reverend Oates Sagar, father of J. W. Sagar (Sudan Political Service 1903–24), who went to Durham School. Sagar was a King's Scholar at Durham, awarded after competitive examination. The present librarian of Durham School, Mr Barry Phillips, writes of the Reverend O. Sagar that he was probably the first vicar of the uninspiring-sounding parish of Deaf Hill near the mining village of Trimson Colliery and 'very much a poor country parson rather than landed gentry' (letter to the author dated 13.1.1981). Canon G. D. Oakley, father of A. S. Oakley (Sudan Political Service 1924–48), was posted in turn to Birkenhead, Liverpool and Bristol, and served for much of his church career in these industrial posts. The Reverend H. F. T. Barter, father of G. H. Barter (Sudan Political Service 1925–49), served in sequence in Pimlico (1892–4), Oakham (1895–8), West

Kirby (1898–1904), a Cheshire suburb of Liverpool and Wakefield (1904–15). Others found themselves at various stages in their careers in such diverse urban or suburban localities as Chatham, Sevenoaks, Notting Hill, Harrogate, Bristol, Belfast, Reading, Huddersfield, Carlisle and New Brighton.

85. Details are to be found in various editions of *Crockford's Clerical Directory* between 1880 and 1950.

86. Letter to the author from D. C. Carden (Sudan Political Service 1942–54) dated 19.2.1981.

87. Quoted in Mangan, *Athleticism*, p. 208.

88. See Chapter 2, *passim*.

89. Meynell, Henry, 'A Sermon preached at the Dedication of the School at St Saviours, Ardingly, Sussex, August 1 1883', Parker & Co., London, 1883, p. 7. Most, if not all, public school pulpits were the location of similar earnest assertions. For typical examples spanning the decades, see H. Montagu Butler, *Sermons Preached in the Chapel of Harrow School*, Macmillan, 1869; G. G. Bradley, *Freedom and Bondage: A Sermon Preached in the Chapel of St Peter's College, Radley, on St Peter's Day 1882*, Parker & Co., 1882; and J. F. C. Welldon, *Youth and Duty: Sermons to Harrow Schoolboys*, Religious Tract Society, 1903.

90. Letter to the author from P. S. Young (Sudan Political Service 1936–44) dated 15.1.81.

91. McDowall, letter to the author dated 15.2.81.

92. Letter to author from D. Vidler (Sudan Political Service 1937–55) dated 5.2.81.

93. Further comments include those of D. H. A. Wilson (Sudan Political Service 1929–55). Wilson writes: 'I am sceptical of the assertion that "the Service ethos" of the Sudan Political Service came from the English rural squirearchy. Public School and University certainly, but these cannot be identified with the squirearchy' (letter to the author dated 14.2.1981); and Paul writes:

> As regards the first of Collins' quotations, I do not think it has much relevance, and if it ever had it had ceased to have it by the time I joined the service in 1929. At no time were we the exclusive preserve of a huntin', fishin' and shootin' squirearchy. It is to be remembered also that prior to 1914 a great many posts in the service were filled by secondment from the Egyptian Army, and that when recruitment began again after the War the intake was more than ever middle class . . .
>
> As regards the second [it] . . . is not true that none of us came from business and professional backgrounds: in fact the vast majority of us did.
>
> I was myself born and bred in Helensburgh and was educated at Glenalmond and Cambridge. My father was a partner in the small shipbuilding firm of Matthew Paul & Co. of Dumbarton which had been founded by his grandfather . . . Of the three other members of the service who joined at the same time as I did, one was the son of an Edinburgh businessman, one of a London solicitor, and the third of a retired Indian Army Officer.
>
> Our esprit-de-corps was derived very largely, I think, from our public school and university background, but more especially I believe from the influence of one man, Reginald Wingate . . . above all he imbued the service, and the service imbued all who

served in it, with the ideal that we were not to rule but to serve, and a dedication to the people whom we administered which served us well right to the very end [letter to the author dated 14.3.81].

94. Bredin, letter to the author dated 14.3.81.

95. Letter to the author from Edward Pearson (Sudan Political Service 1946–54) dated 13.1.81.

96. Daniell, letter to the author dated 22.1.80.

97. Monteith, letter to the author dated 18.1.80.

98. Duncan, letter to the author dated 20.2.81.

99. Vidler, letter to the author dated 5.2.81.

CHAPTER FOUR

1. Lugard's achievements are celebrated in two volumes by his distinguished biographer, Dame Margery Perham: *Lugard: The Years of Adventure*, 1956, and *Lugard: The Years of Authority*, Collins, 1960. A more superficial account of Lugard's life is to be found in A. Thompson and Dorothy Middleton, *Lugard in Africa*, Hale, 1959. By way of contrast, a particularly critical view of Lugard as colonial administrator is contained in I. F. Nicolson, *The Administration of Nigeria 1900–1960: Men, Methods and Myths*, Clarendon Press, 1969, pp. 180–215.

2. An incongruity interestingly discussed by a Nigerian educationist, Ontonti Nduka in his *Western Education and the Nigerian Cultural Background*, Oxford University Press, Ibadan, 1964, pp. 84–112. Among other things he pointed out that it was not Western science, philosophy or religion that impressed the natives: 'it was the material wealth, together with the power, which was associated with it, which caught the imagination.'

3. Perham, *Lugard*, Vol. II, p. 292.

4. From Sir Frederick Lugard, *The Dual Mandate in British Tropical Africa*, quoted in M. Carnoy, *Education as Cultural Imperialism*, McKay, New York, 1974, frontispiece.

5. For a discussion of this point, see Mangan, *Athleticism in the Victorian and Edwardian Public School, passim.*

6. W. Furness, *The Centenary History of Rossall School*, Aldershot, 1945, p. 26.

7. Letter from Lugard to Sir Frank Fletcher dated 27.11.43 (MSS. Brit. Emp. s.30, *Lugard Papers*, Rhodes House Library, Oxford).

8. James (1844–1931) had a distinguished career in English education – assistant master at Marlborough (1872–5), headmaster of Rossall School (1875–86), principal of Cheltenham College (1889–95), headmaster of Rugby (1895–1909), president of St John's College, Oxford (1909–31). He was proud of his former pupil and kept in touch with Lugard all his life, writing him congratulatory letters at appropriate moments in his imperial career.

9. For a discussion of the contribution of G. E. L. Cotton, headmaster of Marlborough from 1852 to 1858, to the development of the public school

system, see J. A. Mangan, 'Athleticism: A Case Study of the Evolution of an Educational Ideology' in B. Simon and I. Bradley, *The Victorian Public School*, Gill & Macmillan, Dublin, 1975, pp. 147–57.

10. Lugard to Fletcher (1953): 'The absorption in classics demanded all our time.'

11. It is interesting to note that Lugard wrote two editions of *Political Memoranda* (instructions to his Nigerian administrative officers) in 1906–19. The first edition, written before his Hong Kong experiences, omits Education as a section heading. See A. H. M. Kirk-Greene (ed.), *Political Memoranda*, IX, 1970.

12. Perham, *Lugard*, Vol. II, p. 338.

13. In 1900, the uprising by the Boxers against Europeans in China led to the capture of Peking by the Great Powers involved. The defeated Chinese eventually signed a penal treaty weighted with huge indemnities. America used her indemnities to endow scholarships for Chinese students at her universities.

14. Sir Frederick Lugard, *Education in the Colony and Southern Province of Nigeria*, Appendix II, 11, MSS. Brit. Emp. s.76, *Lugard Papers*. The preoccupation is given particular emphasis in his famous *The Dual Mandate in British Tropical Africa*, 1922, pp. 425–30. And his preoccupation with this issue is seen clearly from this statement from his pen: 'if moral discipline and standards of duty do not keep pace with material development, society will drift towards the rocks like a ship without ballast or rudder' ('Education in Tropical Africa' in *Edinburgh Review*, Vol. 242, 1925, p. 3).

15. Perham, *Lugard*, Vol. II, p. 341.

16. Consider also his tense comment on the European traders in West Africa: 'they are a class I most distrust', quoted in Perham, *Lugard*, Vol. II, p. 170.

17. R. H. Tawney, *Equality*, Allen & Unwin, 1931, p. 31. This is a much-discussed attitude in the English public schools. For an early outspoken comment, see Sir John Lubbock, *Addresses Political and Educational*, 1879, pp. 252–8.

18. Letter from Lugard to his sister Emma dated 15.6.1875, MSS. Brit. Emp. s.30, *Lugard Papers*. A recent interesting analysis of public school anti-materialism is that of David Ward, 'The Public Schools and Industry after 1870' in *Journal of Contemporary History*, Vol. 2, No. 3, 1967, pp. 37–52.

19. Corelli Barnett, *The Collapse of British Power*, Eyre Methuen, 1972, pp. 27–38.

20. Perham, *Lugard*, Vol. II, pp. 337–54.

21. Sir F. D. Lugard, 'The Hong Kong University' in *Nineteenth Century*, Vol. LXVIII, 1910, p. 652.

22. A wholly typical example is the following from G. G. Coulton, *Public Schools and Public Needs*, Simpkin, Marshall, Hamilton, Kent & Co., 1901: 'The moral part of a boy's education is in this country considered of the first importance, and the wisdom of this view – that the training of character must first of all be looked to – is now recognized by the great bulk of foreign expert

opinion, though the means to such an end are not developed and systematized abroad as they are here.'

23. Lugard, *Dual Mandate*, pp. 652–3.

24. This is particularly evident in his Nigerian 'Memorandum Number 4; Education': 'Polo, cricket, football, and other suitable games, in which the staff will participate, will be encouraged alike for their effects on health and manliness, and for the opportunities they afford of bringing masters and pupils together on friendly terms' (p. 139).

25. Lugard, *Dual Mandate*, p. 652.

26. For succinct description of the background to amalgamation, see A. H. M. Kirk-Greene, *Lugard and the Amalgamation of Nigeria*, Cass, pp. 5–9. For a fuller description, see Michael Crowden, *The Story of Nigeria*, 4th edn, Cass, 1978, pp. 188–206.

27. *The Dictionary of National Biography* (1941–50), p. 535.

28. *Report by Sir F. D. Lugard on the Amalgamation of Northern and Southern Nigeria and Administration 1911–1912*, 1940, Cmd. 468, p. 59.

29. Perham, *Lugard*, Vol. II, p. 489.

30. Farewell letter from Lugard to Alexander Boyle (later Sir) dated 23.12.1918, MSS. Brit. Emp. s.75, *Lugard Papers*. Sir Alexander Boyle was a loyal colleague in Nigeria.

31. Lugard, *Dual Mandate*, p. 425.

32. It was obligatory for public school headmasters, ambitious for themselves and their schools, to publish their sermons. Many did so. It was a valuable form of public relations. For a consideration of the contents of such sermons and their role in public school life, see Mangan, *Athleticism*, p. 163.

33. Lugard, *Dual Mandate*, p. 429.

34. Some idea of the contribution of the missions to Nigerian education may be obtained from the fact that as late as 1964 it was estimated that over 80 per cent of education was still in the hands of missionary bodies and voluntary agencies (Nduka, *Western Education*, p. 131).

35. Memorandum from the Church Missionary Society Archives, quoted in Sonia F. Grahams, *Government and Mission Education in Northern Nigeria 1908–1919*, Ibadan University Press, Ibadan, 1966, p. 132.

36. Perham, *Lugard*, Vol. II, p. 5.

37. ibid., p. 20.

38. ibid., p. 340.

39. Sir F. D. Lugard, *The Hong Kong University Scheme and the Scheme of the China Emergency Committee*, 7 May 1909, p. 3, quoted in Perham, *Lugard*, Vol. II, p. 342.

40. Perham, *Lugard*, Vol. II, p. 495.

41. For a fuller discussion of this point, see J. A. Mangan, 'Social Darwinism, Sport and English Upper-Class Education' in *Stadion*, Vol. II, Autumn 1982, pp. 95–116.

42. Sir Frederick Lugard, 'British Policy in Nigeria' in *Africa*, Vol. 9, No. 4, 1937, p. 389.

43. Lugard, *Dual Mandate*, p. 431.

44. Mangan, 'Athleticism: A Case Study of the Evolution of an Educational Ideology', pp. 117–18.

45. Lugard, *Dual Mandate*, p. 433.

46. Lugard to Fletcher (1943).

47. Lugard, 'Education in Tropical Africa', p. 9.

48. Cricket was a critical instrument of moral improvement in colonial administration. For a discussion of this point, see R. Hyam, *Britain's Imperial Century: 1815–1914: A Study of Empire and Expansion*, Batsford, 1976, pp. 131–2.

49. ibid., p. 9.

50. Perham, *Lugard*, p. 493.

51. ibid., p. 491.

52. Sir F. D. Lugard, 'Education and Race Relations' in *Journal of the African Society*, Vol. 37, 1933, p. 5.

53. Lugard, *Dual Mandate*, p. 432.

54. Lugard (1925). Further examples of this ethnocentricity include: 'I am impressed with the belief that the African boy requires every force which can be brought to bear if his natural proclivities are to be overcome and he is to learn self-control and discipline' (MSS. Brit. Emp. s.76, 'Education in the Colony and Southern Protectorate of Nigeria', Appendix II, *Lugard Papers*); and: 'I entirely agree with you and Kitchener that they [natives of India] are not fit for self-government' (letter to J. Chamberlain dated 23.11.1909, MSS. Brit. Emp. s.66, *Lugard Papers*).

55. R. A. Huttenback, *Racism and Empire*, Cornell University Press, Ithaca, 1976, p. 15.

56. Charles Lyons, *To Wash an Ethiop White: British Ideas about African Educability*, Columbia University Teachers College Press, New York, 1975, p. 89.

57. See Christine Bolt, *Victorian Attitudes to Race*, Routledge & Kegan Paul, 1971, p. 137. In the specific context of Nigerian administrators other than Lugard, see Robert Heussler, *The British in Northern Nigeria*, Oxford University Press, 1968, p. 43.

58. Lugard, *Dual Mandate*, pp. 68–73.

59. Heussler, *British in Northern Nigeria*, p. 182.

60. Syed Hussein Alatas, *The Myth of the Lazy Native*, Cass, 1977, pp. 212–13.

61. ibid., p. 216.

62. Frederick William Farrar, 'Aptitudes of Races' in *Transactions of the Ethnological Society*, Vol. V, 1867, quoted in M. D. Biddiss, *Images of Race*, Leicester H. R., 1979, pp. 150–51. For similar 'scientific' pronouncements, see Bolt, *Victorian Attitudes*, pp. 133ff.

63. Biddiss, *Images of Race*, p. 152.

64. J. A. Cramb, *Reflections on the Origins and Destiny of Imperial Britain*, Macmillan, 1900, pp. 112–13.

65. Quoted in Huttenback, *Racism*, pp. 15–16.

66. J. E. C. Welldon, *Recollections and Reflections*, p. 239.

67. Lugard, *Dual Mandate*, p. 435.

68. James Morris, *Heaven's Command*, Penguin, 1973, p. 389.

69. Lugard, *Dual Mandate*, p. 452. See also p. 445.

70. Nduka suggests with considerable accuracy that the primary aim of the colonial government was to produce 'serviceable subordinates' (*Western Education and the Nigerian Cultural Background*, p. 35).

71. F. Lugard, Morris Ginsberg, H. A. Wyndam, 'The Problem of Colour in Relation to Inequality' in *Supplement to Journal of Philosophical Studies*, 1926, p. 7.

72. Mangan, *Athleticism, passim.*

73. Nicolson, *Administration of Nigeria*, p. 208.

74. Bolt, *Victorian Attitudes*, p. 118.

75. Lugard, *Dual Mandate*, p. 88.

76. These widespread imperial assumptions are interestingly discussed in Carnoy, *Education as Cultural Imperialism, passim.*

77. Lugard was distinctly cool towards the idea of a university for Nigeria in his *Dual Mandate* (p. 455). The first institute of higher education in Nigeria was opened in 1938.

78. Nduka, *Western Education*, p. 51.

79. Lugard, *Dual Mandate*, p. 455.

80. The subsequent development of West African education is outlined in F. H. Hilliard, *A Short History of Education in British West Africa*, Nelson, 1957, pp. 127–66.

81. Nduka, *Western Education*, p. 105.

82. ibid., p. 35.

83. Perham, *Lugard*, Vol. II, p. 463.

84. By way of contrast, for a description of present-day alleged corruption, bribery and nepotism in Nigeria see the *Daily Telegraph*, Thursday, 18 October 1979, p. 6. Nduka in 1964 was savagely critical of events in Nigeria. He spoke of a morally bankrupt nation, and continued, 'A nation built on the foundation of bribery and corruption in high and low places, nepotism, political jobbery, and the baser elements in human nature is heading for trouble, despite all appearances to the contrary. It is only wishful thinking to believe that our young people, let alone the apparently indifferent intelligentsia, are blissfully ignorant of some of the goings-on during elections to local government councils, and the Regional and Federal losses of legislature' (*Western Education*, p. 159).

85. For a discussion of this point, see J. A. Mangan, 'Ethics and Ethnocentricity: Imperial Education in British Tropical Africa' in William J. Baker and J. A. Mangan, *Sport in Africa: Essays in Social History*, Holmes & Meier, New York, forthcoming.

CHAPTER FIVE

1. Sir James Andrew Brown (1812–60); educated at Harrow and Oxford; tenth Earl and first Marquis of Dalhousie; Governor-General of India 1847–56. Annexations during his period as Governor-General included an addition to Oudh, Lower Burma, Nagpur and Jhansi.

2. E. Thompson and G. T. Garratt, *Rise and Fulfilment of British Rule in India*, Macmillan, 1934, p. 468.

3. Thomas R. Metcalf, *The Aftermath of Revolt: India 1857–1870*, Princeton University Press, Princeton (N.J.), 1964, pp. 219–26.

4. Thompson and Garratt, *Rise and Fulfilment*, p. 468.

5. Sir Alfred Comyn Lyall, *Rise and Expansion of the British Dominion in India*, 3rd edn, 1893, pp. 328–9.

6. Sir Alfred Comyn Lyall (1835–1911), educated at Eton and Haileybury, held various posts in the Indian civil service.

7. The title Governor-General was changed to Viceroy after the Mutiny.

8. Quoted in R. C. Majumdar and A. D. Pusalker (eds.), *The History and Culture of the Indian People*, IX, Paragon, New York, 1963, p. 966.

9. Sayid Ghulam Mustafa, 'English Influences on Indian Society', unpublished M.Ed. Thesis, University of Durham. This is a massive (522 pages), elegant and erudite work written by a Muslim Indian educated at an Indian public school. It provides one Indian's view of the Westernization of the Indian upper classes.

10. Metcalf, *Aftermath of Revolt*, p. 226.

11. Mustafa, 'English Influences', p. 208.

12. Metcalf, *Aftermath of Revolt*, pp. 136–7.

13. The term is usefully employed in Francis G. Hutchins, *The Illusion of Permanence: British Imperialism in India*, Princeton University Press, Princeton, 1967, p. 154.

14. B. Parry, *Delusions and Discoveries: Studies on India in the British Imagination 1880–1930*, Allen Lane, 1972, p. 26. For a typical twentieth-century example of such attitudes, see James Halliday, *A Special India*, Chatto & Windus, 1968, pp. 231–3. Halliday is the *nom de plume* of David Symington, Oxford and I.C.S. (1926–41).

15. Reverend J. Johnston, *Abstract and Analysis of the Report of the 'Indian Education Commission', with Notes and Recommendations in Full*, Hamilton Adams & Co., 1884, p. 92.

16. Michael Edwardes, *High Noon of Empire: India under Curzon*, Eyre and Spottiswoode, 1965, p. 141.

17. Quoted in Surendra Mohan Mehta, 'Public Schools in India', unpublished M.A. Thesis, London University, 1961, pp. 79–80.

18. Sir Thomas Raleigh, *Lord Curzon in India: Being a Selection from his Speeches as Viceroy and Governor General 1898–1905*, Macmillan, 1906, p. 245.

19. *Progress of Education in India, Fourth Quinquennial Review 1897–98 to 1901–02*, 1904, p. 182.

20. Richard Harte Keatinge (1825–1904) was educated at private schools in

Dublin. He joined the Bombay Artillery in 1842. After a distinguished military career, during which he won the V.C. in the Mutiny, he held a number of civil posts, including Political Agent at Kathiawar and, later, Chief Commissioner, Central Provinces. He was one of the early advocates of the Chiefs Colleges.

21. *Forty Years of the Rajkumar College 1870–1910*, compiled by H. H. Sir Bhavasinhji, K.C.S.I., Maharaja of Bhavnazar, prepared and abridged from the papers of the late Chester Macnaghten, M.A., Vol. I, p. 326.

22. See, for example, Herbert Sherring, *Mayo College, Ajmere, 'The Eton of India': A Record of Twenty Years 1875–1895*, I, 1897, p. 181ff.

23. In 1898 Nowgong College amalgamated with Daly College, Indore.

24. Mayo, Daly and Aitchison Colleges were named after distinguished British administrators in India. The sixth Earl of Mayo (1822–72) became Viceroy in 1869 and it is recorded in *The Dictionary of National Biography* (1886, VI, 23), 'he encouraged the establishment of colleges for the education of the sons and chiefs in the native states. The Mayo College at Ajmere and the Rajkumar College at Kathiawar were the result of his efforts.' Sir Henry Dermot Daly (1821–95), after a distinguished military career in India, became Agent to the Governor-General for Central India at Indore in 1861 and worked for the establishment of the college there. Sir Charles Umpherston Aitchison (1832–96) entered the Indian Civil Service in 1855; by 1882 he was Lieutenant-Governor of the Punjab and was largely responsible for the development of the Chiefs College at Lahore.

25. Raipur would appear to be the closest of the second-grade colleges to the Chiefs Colleges. It was created for the sons of the Chhattisgarch Feudatory States and in 1896 had thirteen pupils. By 1902 numbers had risen to twenty-two. It had a European headmaster – a mark of superior status. In 1921, in fact, it was recognized as a Chiefs College.

26. For reasons which are not wholly clear Nowgong received little attention in the literature about the schools at this time.

27. *Fourth Quinquennial Review*, p. 186.

28. For a minutely detailed description of the origins of the College at Rajkot and the role of the British in its inception, see *Forty Years of the Rajkumar College 1870–1910*, Vol. II, *passim*.

29. *Fourth Quinquennial Review*, p. 186.

30. ibid., p. 186.

31. ibid., p. 163.

32. Ian Malcolm, *Indian Pictures and Problems*, Grant Richards, 1907, p. 65.

33. *Fourth Quinquennial Review*, p. 187.

34. ibid., p. 187.

35. Sherring, *Mayo College*, pp. 77ff.

36. ibid., p. 86.

37. See Mangan, *Athleticism in the Victorian and Edwardian Public School*, *passim*.

38. H. H. Dodwell (ed.), *Cambridge History of India*, VI, pp. 34–6.

39. *Report of the Commission of Indian Education* (1883), p. 482.

40. Bhavasinhji, *Rajkumar College*, Vol. I, p. 158.

41. ibid., p. 159.

42. Three of these Indian public school headmasters were assistant masters at Marlborough at one time or other. F. A. Leslie-Jones was a Marlborough master from 1897 to 1904. V. A. Stow was at Marlborough from 1905 to 1906 and was first principal of Rajkumar College, Rajpur, and then for several years principal of Mayo College. E. C. Marchant was at Marlborough from 1931 to 1938. In 1939 he became principal of Daly College, Indore.

43. *The Times*, 11 May 1895, p. 5. Macnaghten taught cricket to the famous Indian batsman Ranjitsinji, as the *Second Quinquennial Review* was quick to note as a point in the college's favour.

44. See the introduction by Robert Whitelaw to Macnaghten's *Common Thoughts on Serious Subjects: Addresses delivered between the years 1887–9 to the elder boys of Rajkumar College in Kathiawar*, revised edition, 1912. These 'Addresses' were translated into native languages for use in state schools!

45. Sir James Peile (1833–1906) was a distinguished Indian administrator. He held a variety of posts in India, including that of Director of Public Instruction, Bombay (1869–73), in which role he made his speech at the Rajkumar College and that of Political Agent of Kathiawar (1874–8). He eventually became a member of the Indian Council in London (1887–1902).

46. *The Times*, 11 May 1895, p. 5.

47. Bhavasinhji, *Rajkumar College*, Vol. I, p. 334.

48. ibid., p. 334.

49. Macnaghten, *Common Thoughts*, XXII.

50. *The Times*, 11 May 1895, p. 5.

51. Narullah Khan, *The Ruling Chiefs of Western India and the Rajkumar College*, Thacker, Bombay, 1898, p. 33.

52. Sherring, *Mayo College*, p. 46.

53. Bhavasinhji, *Rajkumar College*, Vol. I, p. 410. Charles Willoughby Waddington (1865–1946) was educated at Charterhouse and Oxford. He became vice-principal of Jajkot in 1892 and principal in 1896. In 1903 he was appointed principal of Mayo College, Ajmere, a post he held until 1917.

54. ibid., pp. 409–10.

55. ibid., p. 412. J. C. Mayne was educated at Tonbridge and Oxford. He taught at Brighton College from 1891 to 1898, then in several Indian schools before becoming principal of Rajkot in 1903.

56. *Radleian*, 3 March 1906, p. 314.

57. ibid., p. 314.

58. Malcolm, *Indian Pictures*, facing p. 64.

59. *Fifth Quinquennial Review 1902–1907*, pp. 250–51.

60. Malcolm, *Indian Pictures*, p. 65.

61. ibid., p. 67.

62. *Report of the Commission on Indian Education*, p. 457.

63. Johnston, *Abstract and Analysis*, pp. 21–2. There is some controversy as to the extensiveness of the indigenous system, however; see Sir Philip Hartog, *Some Aspects of Indian Education, Past and Present*, Oxford University Press, 1939, p. 3.

64. Syed Nurullah and J. P. Nayaka, *A History of Education in India during the British Period*, 2nd edn, Macmillan, Bombay, 1951, pp. 38ff.

65. Majumdar, *History and Culture of the Indian People*, pp. 20–21.

66. Wilfred Scawen Blunt, *India under Ripon: A Private Diary*, Fisher Unwin, 1909, p. 156.

67. Mustafa, 'English Influences on Indian Society', p. 224.

68. Johnston, *Abstract and Analysis*, p. 83. Bhavsinhji, with first-hand knowledge, stated that large numbers were uneducated: *Rajkumar College*, Vol. II, p. 3.

69. Khan, *Ruling Chiefs*, p. 8.

70. See note 20, pp. 215–16.

71. *Cambridge History of India*, VI, p. 346.

72. There are numerous instances of individual support by Indian royalty, but perhaps the most exotic is the visits to his palace, some distance from the school, arranged by the Maharaja of Bhavnagar for the whole of Rajkumar College. He supplied his own trains for the journey! He was, incidentally, the first and, for some time, the only pupil at the college and arrived by elephant on the opening day.

73. *Fifth Quinquennial Review*, p. 181.

74. Raleigh, *Lord Curzon in India*, p. 251.

75. ibid., p. 257.

76. Sherring, *Mayo College*, p. 161.

77. ibid., p. 161.

78. Raleigh, *Lord Curzon in India*, p. 244.

79. ibid., pp. 234ff.

80. *Sixth Quinquennial Review 1907–1912*, 1914, p. 227.

81. *Aitchison Chiefs College: Old Boys Register*, 1928, p. i.

82. *Report of the Mayo College, Ajmere, for 1932–33*, Appendix F.

83. By 1970 there were some twenty-seven public schools in India.

84. For a statement of the ideals of the Indian public school in the second half of the twentieth century, see *The Indian Public School. Essays outlining the aims of members of the Indian Public Schools Conference*, 1942. See also J. S. Malikael, 'The Public School System in India' in *Canadian and International Education*, Vol. 4, No. 1, June 1975, pp. 69–88.

CHAPTER SIX

1. Pierre Berton, *Why We Act Like Canadians*, McClelland & Stewart, Toronto, 1982, p. 47.

2. Welf H. Heick (ed.), *History and Myth: Arthur Lower and the Making of Canadian Nationalism*, University of British Columbia Press, Vancouver, 1975, p. 285.

3. Carl Berger, *The Sense of Power: Studies in the Areas of Canadian Imperialism 1867–1914*, University of Toronto Press, Toronto, 1970, p. 4.

4. Heick, *History and Myth*, p. 286.

5. Morris Mott, 'The British Protestant Pioneers and the Establishment of Manly Sports in Manitoba, 1870–1886' in *Journal of Sports History*, Vol. 7, No. 3, Winter 1980, p. 104.

6. ibid., p. 105.

7. J. B. Purdy, 'The English Public School Tradition in Nineteenth-Century Ontario' in F. H. Armstrong, H. A. Stevenson, J. D. Wilson (eds.), *Aspects of Nineteenth-Century Ontario*, University of Toronto Press, Toronto, 1974, p. 239.

8. ibid., p. 240.

9. ibid., p. 248.

10. Arthur Lower, *From Colony to Nation*, Longmans, Green & Co., Toronto, 1946, p. 432.

11. See Mangan, 'Social Darwinism, Sport and English Upper-Class Education', pp. 93–116.

12. Purdy, 'English Public School Tradition', pp. 248–9.

13. Carolyn Gossage, *A Question of Privilege. Canada's Independent Schools*, Peter Martin, Toronto, 1977, p. 19.

14. Lower, *From Colony to Nation*, p. 229.

15. Ralph C. Wilcox, 'Games and Good Learning: the Contribution of the English Public School to Canadian Amateur Sport', unpublished paper, University of Alberta, Edmonton, Canada.

16. Jack Haas and William Shaffer, *Shaping Identity in Canadian Society*, Prentice-Hall, Scarborough, 1978, p. 285.

17. Wilcox, 'Games and Good Learning', p. 16.

18. T. Chandler, 'From "Play Up and Play the Game" to "Winning Is the Only Thing" ', paper presented to the I.S.C.P.E.S. Third International Congress, Minneapolis, July 1982, p. 3.

19. C. Podmore, 'Private Schools – An International Comparison' in *Canadian and International Education*, Vol. 6, No. 2, 1977, pp. 8–33.

20. M. Ormsby, *British Columbia: A History*, Macmillan, Toronto, 1958, p. 257.

21. *Montreal Gazette*, 1 May 1861, quoted in Peter L. Lindsay, 'A History of Sport in Canada, 1807–1868', unpublished Doctoral Dissertation, University of Alberta, 1969, p. 20.

22. David Brown, 'Athleticism in Canada's Private Schools for Boys', unpublished Ph.D. Thesis, University of Alberta, 1984, Chapter II, p. 7.

23. See Thomas C. Cochrane, *Railroad Leaders 1845–1890. The Business Mind in Action*, Russell & Russell, New York, 1965, pp. 12–15.

24. Charles Kingsley, *Yeast*, Nelson, 1906.

25. David Newsome, *Godliness and Good Learning*, Murray, 1961.

26. Reverend N. Burwash, 'Imperialism in Education' in W. Clark (ed.), *Empire Club Speeches*, Toronto, 1904, p. 37. I am grateful to Katharine Moore for this reference.

27. J. O. Miller, *The Young Canadian Citizen*, Dent, Toronto, 1919, p. 59.

28. Berger, *Sense of Power, passim.*

29. Robert M. Stamp, 'Empire Day in the Schools of Ontario: The Training

of Young Imperialists' in Alf Chaiton and Neil McDonald, *Canadian Schools and Canadian Identity*, Gage Educational Publishing, Toronto, 1977, pp. 100–115.

30. Sir George William Ross was born in 1841 near Jain, Ontario. A teacher in his earlier years, he later became a barrister and politician. He took a great interest in Canadian education within the wider context of the British Empire and was founder and president of the Dominion Educational Association.

31. Stamp, 'Empire Day in the Schools of Ontario', p. 102.

32. ibid., p. 108.

33. ibid., p. 109.

34. Sir George Parkin (1846–1922) was born in New Brunswick, Canada. After teaching in Canadian primary and secondary schools, in 1889 he became the representative of the Imperial Federation League. From 1895 to 1902 he was principal of Upper Canada College and in 1902 he became the first organizing secretary of the Rhodes Scholarship Trust.

35. The phrase is John S. Ewart's and is to be found in his *The Kingdom of Canada*, Morang, Toronto, 1908, p. 53.

36. Terry Cook, 'George R. Parkin and the Concept of Britannic Idealism' in *Journal of Canadian Studies*, Vol. X, No. 3, 1975, p. 19.

37. ibid., p. 19.

38. ibid., p. 22.

39. ibid., p. 23.

40. ibid., p. 24.

41. ibid., p. 24.

42. Lower, *From Colony to Nation*, p. 441.

43. Berger, *Sense of Power*, p. 34.

44. Cook, 'Parkin and the Concept of Britannic Idealism', p. 252.

45. Berger, *Sense of Power*, p. 37.

46. Parkin Papers, Vol. 107, W. L. Grant, 'Private Memo for Sir John Willison (re) Sir George Parkin', circa 1924–6, quoted in Berger, *Sense of Power*, pp. 37–8.

47. Berger, *Sense of Power*, pp. 37–8.

48. Gossage, *A Question of Privilege*, p. 39.

49. Letter to the author from David Brown dated 10.9.83.

50. Gossage, *A Question of Privilege*, p. 41.

51. G. G. Watson, 'Sports and Games in Ontario Private Schools: 1830–1930', unpublished Master's Thesis, University of Alberta, 1970, p. 56.

52. From the *Patriot*, 15 July 1936, quoted in Brown, 'Athleticism', Chapter 3, p. 41.

53. *College Times*, Vol. XI, No. 6, 8 February 1893, pp. 63–4.

54. Brown, 'Athleticism', Chapter 4, p. 66.

55. Brown ('Athleticism', Chapter 5, p. 94) puts this reason forward as the motive but, in addition, offers the utilitarian reason that Parkin wished to get the day boys to play games. The one does not exclude the other.

56. C. G. Heward, 'Pre-L.C.C. Days. Genealogical Notes. Memories of St John the Evangelist School' in *Lower Canada College Magazine*, June 1939, p. 12.

57. Brown, 'Athleticism', Chapter 4, p. 69.

58. C. S. Fosbery, 'Health' in *The Eagle*, 1, 6 June 1907, p. 56.
59. Brown, 'Athleticism', Chapter 4, p. 70.
60. P. S. Penton, *Non Nobis Solum*, Corporation of Lower Canada College, Montreal, 1972, p. 65.
61. Brown, 'Athleticism', Chapter 4, pp. 76–7.
62. For the full reference, see n. 27, p. 219.
63. See Mangan, *Athleticism*, p. 24.
64. Brown, 'Athleticism', Chapter 4, p. 19.
65. ibid., Chapter 6, p. 110.
66. ibid., Chapter 8, p. 182.
67. See J. Carleton, *Westminster School*, Rupert Hart-Davis, 1965.
68. Report of an address entitled 'The Ideal Boy' given by C. W. Lonsdale to the Rotary Club of Duncan, British Columbia, in the *High River Times*, 30 October 1930, included in the 'Scrapbook of C. W. Lonsdale, Miscellaneous Clippings, Re-education and the School, 1926–1931', p. 99, Shawnigan Lake School Archives, quoted in Brown, 'Athleticism', Chapter 3.
69. Brown, 'Athleticism', Chapter 4, pp. 72–3.
70. James Scotland, *The History of Scottish Education*, University of London Press, 1969.
71. Robert Machray, *Life of Robert Machray, D.D., LL.D., D.C.L., Archbishop of Rupert's Land and Primate of all Canada*, Macmillan, 1909.
72. See J. A. Mangan, 'Imitating their Betters and Disassociating From their Inferiors: Grammar Schools and the Games Ethic', paper delivered at the History of Education Society Annual Conference, December 1982, pp. 21–2.
73. Machray, *Life*, p. 54.
74. R. T. Handy, *A History of the Church in the United States and Canada*, Clarendon Press, 1976, p. 348. I owe this quotation to Dr D. Brown.
75. Brown, 'Athleticism', Chapter 3, p. 43.
76. *St John's College Magazine*, Vol. XXIV, No. 1, November 1911, p. 42.
77. Brown, 'Athleticism', Chapter 3, p. 44.
78. Advertisement from King's College Record, October 1886.
79. John Morgan Gray, *A. W. MacKenzie, M.A., D.D., The Grove, Lakefield, A Memoir*, The Grove Old Boys' Association, Toronto, 1938, p. 12.
80. J. A. Mangan, 'Almond of Loretto: Scottish Educational Visionary and Reformer' in *Scottish Educational Review*, Vol. II, No. 2, November 1979, pp. 97–106.
81. Gray, *A. W. MacKenzie*, p. 15.
82. George Altmeyer, 'Three Ideas of Nature in Canada 1893–1914' in *Journal of Canadian Studies*, Vol. XI, No. 3, August 1976, p. 21.
83. ibid., p. 34.
84. ibid., p. 23.
85. ibid., p. 27.
86. ibid., p. 25.
87. Gossage, *A Question of Privilege*, p. 129.
88. ibid., p. 131.
89. Gray, *A. W. MacKenzie*, p. 62.

90. Lower, *From Colony to Nation*, p. 441.

91. Stamp, 'Empire Day in the Schools of Ontario', p. 111.

92. G. Redmond, 'Some Aspects of Organized Sport and Leisure in Nineteenth-Century Canada' in *Society and Leisure*, Vol. II, No. 1, April 1979, p. 75.

93. G. Redmond, 'Diffusion in the Dominion: "Muscular Christianity" in Canada, to 1914', paper presented at the History of Education Society Annual Conference, December 1982, p. 17.

94. J. A. Mangan, 'Athleticism: A Case Study of the Evolution of an Educational Ideology' in B. Simon and I. Bradley (eds.), *The Victorian Public School*, Gill and Macmillan, Dublin, 1975, p. 165.

95. Redmond, 'Diffusion in the Dominion', p. 18.

96. Peter L. Lindsay, 'George Beers and the National Game Concept – a Behavioural Approach' in *Second Canadian Symposium on the History of Physical Education and Sport*, October 1972, p. 9.

97. ibid., p. 10.

98. Watson, 'Sports and Games in Ontario Public Schools', p. 26.

99. Redmond, 'Organized Sport and Leisure', p. 75.

100. G. Watson, 'The Founding and Major Features of the Sport and Games in the Little Big Four Canadian Private Schools' in *Canadian Association for Health, Physical Education and Recreation Journal*, Vol. 40, No. 1, Fall 1973, pp. 28–37.

101. Nancy and Maxwell L. Howell, *Sports and Games in Canadian Life – 1700 to the Present*, Macmillan, Toronto, 1969, p. 290.

102. ibid., pp. 134–5.

103. Lower, *From Colony to Nation*, p. 441.

104. Hass and Shaffer, *Shaping Identity*, p. 331.

105. Brown, 'Athleticism', Chapter 5, pp. 122–3.

106. ibid., p. 123.

107. For the various descriptions of these men, see Brown, 'Athleticism', Chapter 5, pp. 128–31.

108. Kim Beattie, *Ridley – The Story of a School*, St Catharines, Ontario, 1963, Vol. II, p. 137.

109. H. Roxborough, *One Hundred Not Out: The Story of Nineteenth Century Canadian Sport*, Ryerson Press, Toronto, 1966, p. 156.

110. Letter to the author from David Brown, dated 28.9.83.

111. Trevor Wigney, *The Independent Boys' Schools of Canada*, Institute of Higher Learning, University of Toronto, 1966, p. 9.

112. Norman Gale, 'Pax Britannica' in *Messis Bat and Ball*, Norman Gale, Rugby, 1930, p. 40.

CHAPTER SEVEN

1. Stephen Neill, *A History of Christian Missions*, Penguin, 1964, p. 14.
2. ibid., p. 243.
3. ibid., p. 250.

4. Sir Arthur Hirtzel (1870–1937) was educated at Dulwich and Oxford. He entered the India Office in 1894 and rose in due course to Permanent Under-Secretary (*Who Was Who 1929–1940*, p. 645). His views on Christian imperialism are set out with particular force in his book *The Church, the Empire and the World*, published in 1919.

5. Sir Arthur Hirtzel, 'Imperial Christianity' in Henry Scott Holland, *The Call of Empire*, S.P.G. Westminster, 1917, p. 10.

6. Neill, *Christian Missions*, p. 252.

7. ibid., p. 254.

8. ibid., p. 259.

9. Hirtzel, 'Imperial Christianity', p. 26.

10. Cecil Peter Williams, 'The Recruitment and Training of Overseas Missionaries in England between 1850 and 1900', unpublished M. Litt. Thesis, Bristol University, 1976, p. 237.

11. ibid., p. 237.

12. Geoffrey Moorhouse, *The Missionaries*, Eyre Methuen, 1973, p. 156.

13. ibid., p. 273.

14. Hirtzel, 'Imperial Christianity', p. 7.

15. For a discussion of the concept of the child-like native, see J. A. Mangan, ' "Gentlemen Galore" – Imperial Education for Tropical Africa: Lugard the Ideologist' in *Immigrants and Minorities*, Vol. I, No. 2, July 1982, pp. 148–68.

16. W. T. Gaul, 'South Africa: The Anglican Church and Imperial Needs' in J. Ellison and G. H. S. Walpole (eds.), *Church and Empire*, Longmans, 1907, p. 216.

17. ibid., p. 216.

18. Williams, 'Overseas Missionaries', p. 145.

19. Eugene Stack, 'The Church Missionary Society' in *Fortnightly Review*, Vol. XLIV, November 1888, p. 787.

20. Patrick Scott, 'Cricket and the Religious World in the Victorian Period' in *Church Quarterly*, Vol. 2, No. 3, October 1970, pp. 134–44.

21. ibid., p. 137.

22. See J. C. Pollock, *The Cambridge Seven. A Call to Christian Service*, Inter-Varsity Fellowship, 1955.

23. Scott, 'Cricket and the Religious World', p. 139.

24. ibid., p. 134.

25. For some indication of the impact of Puseyism and the consequent reaction to it in the English public school system, see Mangan, *Athleticism*, pp. 40–41.

26. Scott, 'Cricket and the Religious World', p. 139.

27. ibid., p. 134.

28. Jessie Page, *Bishop Patteson. The Martyr of Melanesia*, Partridge, 1891, p. 45. Patteson (1827–71) was educated at Eton and Oxford and served in Melanesia and New Zealand between 1855 and 1871. He was appointed first Bishop of Melanesia in 1861.

29. George Augustus Selwyn (1809–78) was educated at Eton and

Cambridge. He served in Melanesia from 1842 to 1867. John Richardson Selwyn, his son (1844–98), also served in Melanesia from 1873 to 1890.

30. Page, *Bishop Patteson*, p. 20.

31. Frank H. L. Paton, *Patteson of Melanesia: A Brief Life of John Coleridge Patteson, Missionary Bishop*, S.P.C.K., 1930, p. 23.

32. Melanesian missionary bishops, it would seem, were an especially manly breed. The *New Zealand Herald* welcomed Cecil Wilson to the Bishopric of Melanesia with these words: 'Looking at the well-knit athletic figure, his finely moulded head, his broad brow and his serious yet kindly expression, one is reminded of his first predecessor as "the Christian, yet the man of the world, the scholar, yet the athlete, first and foremost in all the contest of English courage" ', quoted in *Chanticlere* (magazine of Jesus College, Cambridge), No. 28, 1894, pp. 129–30.

33. Charles F. Harford-Battersby, *Pilkington of Uganda*, Marshall, 1898, p. 44.

34. Ernest H. Hayes, *Doctor Pennell, Afghan Pioneer*, Seeley Service, n.d., p. 11.

35. Clifford Harris, a gentle and saintly 'giant', taught at the Stuart Memorial College, Isfahan, Persia – a Christian public school established in the late 1920s. He led a strenuous life at the school – playing games, running and climbing. His last active effort before he tragically died of typhus 'was a piece of practical work for the games of his boys', clearing the football field of twenty inches of snow. See R. W. Howard, *A Merry Mountaineer. The Story of Clifford Harris of Persia*, Church Missionary Society, 1931.

36. A. C. Clarke, a member of the Church Missionary Society, served in India from 1895 to 1929. He was principal of Baring High School, Batala, from 1912 to 1914, of Edwarde's College, Peshawar, from 1919 to 1921, and warden of St John's College, Lahore, from 1921 to 1922. Cecil Earle Tyndale-Biscoe thought highly of his educational efforts in India, considering that in the interests of character-building he was 'turning out boys like himself, keen sportsmen and gentlemen' (C. E. Tyndale-Biscoe, *Tyndale-Biscoe of Kashmir: An Autobiography*, Seeley Service, n.d., p. 80).

37. For details of the educational work of Carey Francis, see L. B. Greaves, *Carey Francis of Kenya*, Rex Collings, 1969.

38. The imperial careers of both Macnaghten and Waddington are outlined, of course, in Chapter 5.

39. Cecil Wilson was Bishop of Melanesia from 1894 to 1917 after parish work in Southern England and Australia. He wrote of his missionary experiences in his autobiography, *The Wake of the Southern Cross: Work and Adventures in the South Seas*, Murray, 1932, p. 17.

40. An outstanding example is J. T. Stevenson, headmaster of St George's College, Quilmes, Argentina, from 1898 to 1935, and author of *The History of St Georges College, Quilmes, Argentina 1895–1935*, S.P.C.K., 1936. For an interesting appraisal of Stevenson's work, see D. Brown, 'Variations on a Victorian Educational Ethic Theme. The Public School Abroad', unpublished paper, University of Alberta, 1981.

41. Wilson, *Southern Cross*, p. 17. In 1866, largely for climatic reasons, Patteson moved his college for Melanesian students from New Zealand to Norfolk Island and 'in a year or two the College was like a good Public School . . . Service was held in Chapel every day . . . [and] most of the afternoon was spent on the playing fields' (E. Grierson, *Bishop Patteson of the Cannibal Islands*, Seeley Service, 1927, pp. 156–60).

42. A. G. Fraser (1873–1962) was educated at Merchiston, and Edinburgh and Oxford Universities. After three years in Uganda from 1900 to 1903, he was first principal of Trinity College, Ceylon (1904–24), and then principal of Achimota College, Gold Coast (1924–35).

43. H. M. Grace was educated at Trent College and Cambridge University. He went to Uganda in 1914 as a member of the Church Missionary Society. He was headmaster of the High School, Kampala (1921–6), King's School, Budo (1926–34), and principal of Achimota (1935–40).

44. R. W. Stoppard was assistant chaplain at Oundle from 1932 to 1934. He was principal of Trinity College, Ceylon (1935–41), and then principal of Achimota College, Gold Coast.

45. Grace was succeeded at King's by L. J. Gaster from Trinity, and Gaster was in turn succeeded by Dennis Herbert from Achimota.

46. Theodore Leighton Pennell (1867–1912) was educated at Eastbourne College and University College, London. He was an outstanding medical student, and became a Fellow of the Royal College of Surgeons at the early age of twenty-five. He joined the Church Missionary Society in 1892 and spent his adult life in the North West Frontier. See obituaries in the *British Medical Journal*, Vol. 1, 1912, p. 761, and the *Lancet*, 6 April 1912, p. 961; and also Alice M. Pennell, *Pennell of the Afghan Frontier. The Life of Theodore Leighton Pennell, M.D., B.Sc., F.R.C.S.*, Dutton, New York, 1914.

47. G. K. Scott-Moncrieff, 'Dr Pennell of Bannu' in *Blackwood's Magazine*, Vol. CXCII, No. MCLXI, July 1912, p. 10.

48. T. L. Pennell, *Among the Wild Tribes of the Afghan Frontier*, Seeley Service, 1909, p. 157.

49. Hayes, *Afghan Pioneer*, p. 74.

50. *Chanticlere*, Vol. IV, No. 38, Easter 1898, p. 227.

51. W. E. F. Ward, *Fraser of Trinity and Achimota*, Ghana Universities Press, Accra, 1965, p. 5.

52. ibid., p. 5.

53. ibid., p. 17.

54. ibid., p. 32.

55. In his first annual report in 1924 Fraser wrote: 'Character training is much the most important thing. It must come in the religious teaching . . . but still more in the spirit of the daily round, the thoroughness in work, the team play, the training in love of country, and in practical service' (C. Kingsley Williams, *Achimota: The Early Years, 1924–1948*, Accra, 1952, p. 11).

56. ibid., p. 74.

57. C. E. Tyndale-Biscoe, *Character Building in Kashmir*, Church Missionary Society, 1920, p. 13.

58. William Earle Tyndale, Cecil's father, on inheriting Holton Park from his uncle Elisha Biscoe, added Biscoe to his surname.

59. Tyndale-Biscoe, *Autobiography*, p. 21.

60. ibid., pp. 23–31.

61. ibid., p. 30.

62. For a description of the religious atmosphere of Cambridge at the time, see J. C. Pollock, *A Cambridge Movement*, Murray, 1953, p. 45.

63. Tyndale-Biscoe, *Autobiography*, p. 45.

64. The Church Missionary Society was founded in 1799. It was the product of the Church of England Evangelical movement. It pioneered missions in many parts of the world, including Africa, Ceylon and India. It is still flourishing today with some 40,000 members throughout the world, and its missionaries are spread throughout sixty-nine Anglican dioceses 'from West Africa to Japan'. See S. Neill *et al.*, *The Concise Dictionary of the Christian World Mission*, United Society for Christian Literature, 1970, p. 111, and F. L. Cross and E. A. Livingstone, *The Oxford Dictionary of the Christian Church*, Oxford University Press, 1974, p. 308.

65. Tyndale-Biscoe, *Autobiography*, p. 45.

66. Tyndale-Biscoe, *Character Building in Kashmir*, p. 10.

67. Tyndale-Biscoe, *Autobiography*, p. 52.

68. H. H. Johnston, 'British Missions and British Missionaries in Africa' in *Nineteenth Century*, November 1887, p. 715.

69. Tyndale-Biscoe, *Autobiography*, p. 52.

70. Tyndale-Biscoe, *Grinding Grit into Kashmir*, London, 1922, p. 8.

71. Tyndale-Biscoe, *Autobiography*, pp. 57–9.

72. ibid., p. 93. There were many instances of more appropriate actions recounted in the various books and booklets written about the school. In *A Mission School and Social Service* (S.M.S., 1910), for example, Tyndale-Biscoe recorded that in the harsh winter of 1888–9 'the boys rescued and fed over 100 starving donkeys' (p. 14).

73. Pat Yates, *Coolie Sahib, Tyndale-Biscoe of India*, Edinburgh House Press, 1938, p. 9.

74. In one year alone 278 boys were taught to swim. 'No slight task . . . it means hard dogged perseverance, and it has been done in the teeth of the wishes of the parents, so it has been both a moral and physical conflict' (*A Mission School and Social Service*, p. 12). Among the C.M.S. school 'firsts' in the annals of Kashmir was the achievement of Phyllis Tyndale-Biscoe, the wife of his son Eric, who in 1933 became the first woman to swim the Wular Lake (*Autobiography*, p. 237).

75. Tyndale-Biscoe, *Character Building*, p. 4.

76. ibid., p. 6.

77. ibid., p. 8.

78. ibid., pp. 16–17.

79. Tyndale-Biscoe, *Grinding Grit*, p. 11.

80. Tyndale-Biscoe, *Autobiography*, p. 128.

81. Tyndale-Biscoe, *Grinding Grit*, p. 11.

82. ibid., p. 11.
83. Tyndale-Biscoe, *Kashmir in Light and Shade*, Seeley Service, 1922, p. 277.
84. Tyndale-Biscoe, *Autobiography*, p. 130.
85. ibid., p. 131.
86. ibid., p. 132.
87. ibid., p. 134.
88. Tyndale-Biscoe, *Kashmir in Light and Shade*, p. 280.
89. ibid., p. 275.
90. ibid., p. 268.
91. Tyndale-Biscoe, *Character Building*, p. 20.
92. Tyndale-Biscoe had three sons: Harold, born in 1892, Cecil Julian, born in 1895, and Eric Dallas, born in 1907. Eric taught at the C.M.S., Srinagar, for many years, Julian became an educational administrator in Tanganyika and Harold, after a varied career which included the R.A.F. and the Burma Forestry Commission, went to live in the Seychelles after the Second World War. He changed his name to L'Estrange (his maternal grandmother's name), married a Seychelloise and, taking on his father's mantle, 'became involved in the corruption and injustice rampant in the Islands and practised by police officialdom against poorer people'. See *Jesus College Register 1901–75*, p. 330, Jesus College Archives, University of Cambridge.
93. E. D. Tyndale-Biscoe, *Fifty Years Against the Stream*, Wesleyan Mission Press, Mysore, 1930.
94. Tyndale-Biscoe, *Autobiography*, pp. 102 and 196.
95. E. H. Berman, *African Reactions to Missionary Education*, Teachers College Press, New York, 1975, p. 25.
96. C. P. Groves, *The Planting of Christianity in Africa, 1874–1914*, Vol. III, Lutterworth Press, 1955, p. 238.
97. ibid., p. 239.
98. The words are those of Baden-Powell in his introduction to Tyndale-Biscoe's *Character Building in Kashmir*.
99. Emilia F. S. Dilke, 'The Great Missionary Success' in *Fortnightly Review*, Vol. XLV, 1889, p. 677.
100. For the situation in East Africa see Roland Oliver, *The Missionary Factor in East Africa*, Longmans Green, 1952, p. 277. For attitudes to India, see Tyndale-Biscoe, *Autobiography*, p. 79.
101. Kenneth Rose, *Superior Person*, p. 346.
102. Tyndale-Biscoe, *Autobiography*, p. 157.
103. See, for example, his sympathetic consideration of the convert Mama in his *A Valiant Man of Kashmir*, Church Missionary Society, 1930.
104. 'The boys were ordered to watch carefully as they walked the streets, and to make way for every woman or child, old man or coolie with a load, to stand in the snow and give them the path; but if they saw any man push a weaker person into the snow they were to drop their shoulder as they came abreast him and let him have it in the ribs, with the natural result. This we kept up as long as the snow lasted, and they have done it every winter' (*A Mission School and Social Service*, p. 3).

105. Tyndale-Biscoe, *Autobiography*, p. 75.
106. Tyndale-Biscoe, *Character Building*, p. 87.
107. Tyndale-Biscoe, *Grinding Grit*, p. 10.
108. Tyndale-Biscoe, *Kashmir in Light and Shade*, p. 287.
109. Tyndale-Biscoe, *Character Building*, p. 95.
110. *The Times*, 11 August 1949, p. 7.
111. Steve Fairbairn, letter to *The Times*, 30 July 1932, p. 15.
112. Neill, *Christian Missions*, p. 412.
113. ibid., p. 415.
114. A purpose that becomes markedly apparent when the educational priorities of other missionaries are examined. See, for example, Richard Heyman, 'The Initial Years of the Jeanes School in Kenya 1924–31' in V. M. Battle and C. H. Lyons, *Essays in the History of African Education*, Teachers College Press, Columbia University, New York, 1970. The Jeanes School was based on an American educational idea and represented a quite different ethic to that which characterized the work of public school missionaries. It concentrated on developing agricultural skills and encouraged indigenous folk-lore, songs and games to promote African culture and reduce cultural alienation and destruction. It is also interesting to note that the importance of, and emphasis on, character-training through games in imperial education is completely lost on observers with a different cultural tradition. See, for example, the rather prosaic discussion of the evolution of education in Kenya by the American James Sheffield in his *Education in Kenya: An Historical Study*, Teachers College Press, Columbia University, New York, 1973. For an outline of the significance of the games ethic in Kenyan 'public school' education, see L. B. Greaves, *Carey Francis of Kenya*.
115. Donald Hughes, 'The Short Cut' in Leslie Ronald Frewin, *The Poetry of Cricket: An Anthology*, Macdonald, 1964, p. 109.

INDEX

Illustration numbers are printed in *italic*.

INDEX

INDEX

INDEX